# The Impracticality of Practical Research

There is an alluring, daunting, and haunting desire in contemporary social science for research to find the practical knowledge that enables a good life in a just and equitable society. This desire haunts the 19th-century emergence of the social sciences, became more pronounced in the postwar mobilizations of research, and today is captured in the international assessments of national school systems and professional education that identify the pathways for governments to modernize school systems and provide for people's well-being. This is expressed by the link between American policy and research in which reforms are verified by "scientific, empirical evidences" about "what works."

The book explores the idea of practical and useful knowledge as historically changing over time, and their (re)visioning in contemporary research concerned with educational reform, instructional improvement, and professionalization. The study of science draws on a range of social and cultural theories and historical studies to understand the politics of science and scientific knowledge concerned with social and educational change. The hope is that research can change social conditions to make a better life and making of people whose conduct embodies the qualities and characteristics of that "better life"—the good citizen, parent, or worker. Yet this hope continually articulates the dangers and dangerous populations that threaten the future envisioned. Thomas Popkewitz explores how the research to correct social wrongs paradoxically is entangled with the inscription of differences that excludes and abjects in the efforts to include.

**Thomas S. Popkewitz** is Professor of Curriculum and Instruction in the School of Education at the University of Wisconsin–Madison.

# The Impracticality of Practical Research
A History of Contemporary Sciences of Change That Conserve

**THOMAS S. POPKEWITZ**

*University of Michigan Press* ♦ *Ann Arbor*

Copyright © 2020 by Thomas S. Popkewitz
All rights reserved

For questions or permissions, please contact um.press.perms@umich.edu

Published in the United States of America by the
University of Michigan Press
Manufactured in the United States of America
Printed on acid-free paper
First published April 2020

A CIP catalog record for this book is available from the British Library.

*Library of Congress Cataloging-in-Publication data has been applied for.*

ISBN 978-0-472-13173-0 (hardcover : alk. paper)
ISBN 978-0-472-03774-2 (paper : alk. paper)
ISBN 978-0-472-12642-2 (e-book)

Cover photograph: West Lake, Hangzhou, by Thomas Popkewitz.

*In Memory and in What the Future Holds*

*In finishing this book, there were losses of two people who, in different ways, are important to me and to whom I want to dedicate this book.*

*Thea Aschkenase, my mother-in-law, who endured unfathomable horrors and losses at the hands of the Nazis in Auschwitz, yet maintained her humanity and caring during her life.*

*And,*

*Rita Foss Lindblad, a wonderful friend and colleague who had a strong sense of moral obligation and compassion.*

*With these losses is the holding of the future:*
*The embodiment of that future is with my wonderful and beautiful children who allowed me to grow with them and now with their kinder.*

# Contents

*Acknowledgments* — ix
*Preface* — xiii
*List of Illustrations* — xix

## Section One:
## The Problems and Problematics of Studying Practical Research

1 ◆ Introduction. Studying Science: Research as Planning and Practice as Its Object — 3

2 ◆ The Reason of Research: Practice That "Acts" as Desires — 21

## Section Two:
## Historical Traces, Movement of Lines, and Limits in the Making of Practical Research

3 ◆ The Emergence of Science as Changing Everyday Life: Historical Traces and Movements of Lines — 45

4 ◆ Virtue in Secular Saintliness: National Exceptionalism, Science, and Schooling — 65

5 ◆ What Is "Really" Taught as the Problem of Research? The Alchemy of Teaching School Subjects — 85

## Section Three:
## Coming to the Present: Alchemies, Desires, and the Production of Differences in American Practical Research

6 ◆ American Progressivism: Practical Sciences as Desires to Actualize the Future — 109

7 • The Reason of "Systems" and Practical Knowledge: Post–World War II Educational Research and Development   130

8 • Numbers, Desires, and International Student Assessments: Benchmarks and Empirical Evidence   158

9 • Teacher and Teacher Education Research: The Practical Knowledge of Change That Conserves and Divides   184

## Section Four:
## A Method of Study, Critique, and Change

10 • The Impracticality of Practical Research: From Matters of Research to What Matters as Research   207

*Notes*   229
*References*   241
*Index of Names*   267
*Subject Index*   273

Digital materials related to this title can be found on the Fulcrum platform via the following citable URL: https://doi.org/10.3998/mpub.11354413

# Acknowledgments

As the idea for this book began to take shape in 2014, it became part of conversations in different spaces. What appears as a "list" of acknowledgments entails many intellectual encounters that are the luxury of the academic environments in which I have traveled. It's a luxury to engage in the research and writing that includes friendships that has helped to sustain that work.

While the acknowledgments can start almost anywhere, I initially focus on two. Miguel Pereyra, of the University of Granada, Spain, has continually responded to my writings and questions, providing literatures that gave further nuance to my readings, directing attention to the arguments as interventions in the Spanish academic literature, and, finally, arranging for the Spanish translation of the book. Working with Sverker Lindblad, of the University of Gothenburg, Sweden, is another gift. Even riding bikes in Chile or in Door County, Wisconsin is a conversation that moves from scenery and peddling uphill to intellectual matters. Sverker's invitation to join him with the Swedish Science Foundation's commission to analyze the system of reason in the international assessments of student performance, and now with a project on the changing relation of science, policy, and society, gave me the impetus for thinking about numbers and statistics that resurfaces in this argument. Our work has also allowed me to begin collaborating with Daniel Pettersson (Gävle University) and Gun-Britt Wärvick (University of Gothenburg), resulting in conversations that have become a continual current running through the book.

My immersion in the social and psychological sciences for this book was helped through comparative history projects with Daniel Tröhler at the University of Vienna. The initial drafts of ideas in these projects are reshaped and elaborated in the book's chapters on American Progressivism and the mobilizations of postwar sciences. The discussions intersected with a rotating yearly doctoral student seminar with Daniel and David Labaree at Stanford University. Besides the fun of the seminars, I had opportunities to present some of the ideas in this book, and David's comments facilitated thinking further about the arguments that made their way into the book.

While I tend to shy away from institutional analyses, I have the luxury of working at the University of Wisconsin–Madison. It is a research institution whose culture of science has existed for over 100 years, one of the first American public institutions to adopt the German science model in higher education. It is easy to underestimate the value of the institutionalization of intellectual culture and how it can fold into the infrastructure of its administration and departments. This is particularly important in academic cultures and in professional fields that sometimes fall into the balancing of its normalcy, which translates into the feeling of being practical. While I was recently told that I have lived in that academic culture's "golden age," my hope is that the changes occurring to rationalize American universities enable the finding of new ways for that culture to exist as it has for me.

The academic culture is expressed in different and concrete ways in the book through the Wednesday Group, my graduate seminar initially organized by my PhD student Marie Brennan in 1989. Marie felt that I needed this kind of environment to read across the humanities, social theories, and cultural histories for both the collective purpose of the graduate studies and my own thoughts. She was right! The seminar "works" because of the flexibility of the graduate program, which enables students (and me) to move across the campus, and to interact with a range of faculty and literatures brought back into the seminar in ways that otherwise would not be possible. Ideas initially approached in the seminar's readings are dispersed throughout the intellectual organization of the book.

The book's arguments could not have been made without the scholarship done by current, and the collegiality of former, graduate students, with their references often found throughout the arguments of the book. Other colleagues have also been available to comment on the ideas and the historical substance in drafts: Catarina de Silva Martins, University of Porto; Fazal Rizvi, Melbourne University; and Melissa Andrade, Pontificia Universidad Católica de Valparaíso. I owe the each a deep appreciation for their intellectual conversations and collegiality over the years, as I do in particular for Lynda Stone's invitation to give a lecture on the alchemy of school subjects at the University of North Carolina–Chapel Hill, and Julie McCloud's invitation to the Australian Association for Research in Education's History and Education Special Interest Group at the University of Melbourne—experiences that enabled me to try out ideas.

Malin Ideland of Mälmo University, Sweden, graciously arranged for me to spend most of a semester writing while at the university, with a wonderful apartment near the Öresund Bridge and the Baltic Sea. As important, Malin and I participated in a PhD course on the limits of good intentions, a conversation that has also been carried into this book. Dean Anders Linde-Laursen, Associate Dean Sussane Hedenborg, and Anna Jobér were also generous in their conversations and support.

There is also a less visible but important support that was continually there even as I missed self-imposed deadlines in the writing of the book. In the years leading up to the writing of the book, Guorui Fan 范国睿 of East China Normal University, Shanghai, has continually encouraged me, including organizing the book's translation. Shuping Zhang 张淑萍, a PhD student at that time, has also been encouraging and patient with me as I kept promising the text for its translation. Kan Wei 阚维, Beijing Normal University, has continually provided important support over the years.

The support of my department was important in completing the book. Beth Graue, the departmental chair, was instrumental in providing support during a crucial time in writing the book. The department enabled graduate students to help with library research and manuscript preparation that were invaluable. Kai-jung Hsiao has been continually invaluable in tracking down materials, checking references, and providing substantive intellectual comments—all the while with a good sense of humor. Mariam Sedighi provided a deeply appreciated thoughtfulness in the textual and theoretical reading of earlier drafts of the book. Britt Marie Zeidler provided editing for some of the final chapters. Daniel Berman, a history of education PhD student, helped with directing me to readings about religion in American Progressivism.

I wish to thank the following for permission to use their photos, charts, graphs, tables, and reproductions: David Labaree; the Organization for Economic Co-operation and Development; McKinsey & Company; Sage Publishing; and Michel Wlodarczyk, former director of the Folkuniversitet, Umeå, Sweden.

One of my more important academic lifelines comes via the support from Christine Kruger, who has continually provided me with administrative/secretarial assistance that has become more than that—a friendship that has continued for many years.

In writing this book, it is important that I recognize how Lea continually deferred to my work schedule that changed habits in the house. But now, with a bit of irony, that work life is been produced as Lea has started an NGO to alleviate the hunger among children in local schools and their families—work about a condition that we both feel should never exist in any society.

It should be obvious in these acknowledgments that the intellectual debts have no particular geographical location. I am reminded of my son, maybe three or four years old, looking at an airplane in the Madison sky and saying to his mother, "Is that Daddy?"

And there is a continuity of work expressed by my then four-year-old daughter when we lived on Staten Island and I worked at home writing my doctoral thesis. A neighbor asked my daughter what I did. With great assurance, my daughter said, "He is a typist."

I still am.

# Preface

Across different decades, I have been interested in how we think about research and change in what seems to have become more particularly an orthodoxy that the only important research is one that identifies "practical" and "useful" knowledge. Today, practical and useful research is expected to supersede the past and usher in the potentialities and hopes of progress and happiness for all. That sentiment is caught in the often-made comment: "Thanks for telling me about your interesting research! But how can it improve my school, teaching, and society?" It was also captured when a well-known American educational researcher invited me to his house for dinner and told me that the only reason people invite us to give speeches is that they want us to tell them what to do.

Maybe not.

This book maintains the social and political commitments expressed in my colleague's comment that research should contribute to the common good and address social wrongs, but it raises questions about the limits of the assumption of change and knowledge at work in the idea of practical knowledge. What if what seems self-evident about science finding practical knowledge is—when looked at historically—a false prophet? And when I link the historical examination to my own studies of the conduct of research in American schools that give focus to questions of inequity, these question are also raised: What if the orthodoxy of practical research is a particular phenomenon in the human sciences that falls apart when the present is examined? What if the political of what is suggested in change works against its commitments?

These questions guide the analysis that flows through this book. As I read more historically, I realized people have not always thought about knowledge and science as being directly useful in relation to their hopes and aspirations. For many Enlightenment thinkers, algorithmic rules of science were thought as unreasonable for thinking about achieving a moral life. Yet, today, practical knowledge is given by many as the incontrovertible purpose of research.

This book challenges that assumption about science and also the notions of equity and democracy that it implies. This brings to the fore the purpose of this book: tracing historically central principles in the system of reason assembled and concerned to order contemporary research as a practical knowledge for producing change. The historical thinking explores the conditions that make the sciences of change plausible and the limits of that plausibility. The central questions explored are: What is the object of the "practical" knowledge in doing such research? How do these objects change over time? The analysis continually probes the question of "practical research as practical and useful for what?"

Change, while a seemingly innocuous word referring to the good intentions of research, is not merely about producing something different from the present. The book explores how the theories and methods of science are "actors" in the sense of generating rules and standards to reason about people, experience, and change.

The notion of critique that organizes the analysis also serves to outline an alternative approach to research. The mode of analysis suggests a style of reasoning about science, its questions, methods, and historical and empirical interpretive qualities for organizing research. The aim is to unshackle science from the residues that join Cartesian logic with analytical philosophy, and a positivism and empiricism that narrows the questions and phenomena of research.

The book draws from science studies and postfoundational and Foucauldian studies in a manner that "plays" intellectually with their ideas to form a method of study that responds to the phenomena of science as a historical and cultural artifact. I use the word "play" intentionally as a way to think about a flexibility of the mind in reading across literatures and in thinking about how to respond theoretically and empirically to the particular events under study. In doing so, it is important to recognize that while I focus on the limits of how particular notions of reason and science became visible in the European and American Enlightenments, the discussion maintains the Enlightenment's cosmopolitan attitude toward reason and science.

The book enters into multiple conversations about contemporary research, theory, and methods. Among these are the following:

(A) to examine the limits and paradoxes of "practical research," whose orthodoxy is part of the nexus of US educational policy and programs, but also influential internationally if one thinks of global reform efforts, international student assessment programs, and policies that aim to produce more effective schools;
(B) to make visible the often-unexamined way in which knowledge or the system of reason that orders research is political, in the principles generated about what is thought and done in schooling and efforts for reform and change;
(C) to address whether contemporary research concerned with inequality and injustice is sufficient when the epistemic of contemporary research embodies a comparative style of reason that differentiates and divides in efforts to include;
(D) to contribute to science and technologies studies through examining how research "acts" in social arenas through the principles generated about the types of objects recognized, the classifications that give direction to explanations, the problems and evidence necessary for managing and predicting, and the modalities on which change is calculated and administered; and
(E) to suggest an alternative view of science in which historicizing the present is placed in, renews, and (re)visions Enlightenment attitudes about critique as a strategy of change.

## How Does the Book "Think"?

The book is divided into four sections.

*The first section* (chapters 1 and 2) describes the theoretical principles and major conceptual tools that guide the analyses. This section discusses research as political in the sense of Foucault's (1980) notion of power/knowledge and Rancière's (2004) notion of the political as "the partition of the sensible."

*The second section* traces how it is historically possible to think of the human sciences as changing everyday life and people. Science is not approached as a unitary entity, rather, it is historicized as an assemblage and connections of different social and cultural principles that change over time. Explored are the (re)visions of prior religious salvation themes with social and cultural principles in the social and educational sciences into desires about the potentialities of who the child should be; the insertion of time as social and cultural dimensions (the arrow of time) in governing change; and the comparative reasoning that inscribes differences and divisions in efforts at inclusion.

*The third section* explores the concrete movements and historical shifts in science as making kinds of people that become (re)visioned and activated in contemporary studies as the object of practical research. American Progressivism, postwar educational science, the macro quantitative studies of the Organization for Economic Co-operation and Development's (OECD) Programme for International Student Assessment (PISA) and McKinsey & Company's models of school change, and contemporary studies of the micro processes of classroom teaching are explored. The analysis considers the changing principles governing the research in these different time/spaces.

The fourth section, the final chapter, brings together two trajectories of the book. The first trajectory is the paradoxes of practical research; as the title of this book implies, practical research is actually impractical. The research to recognize differences produces social and cultural divisions and inscribes principles of inequality. The impracticality, I will argue, mistakes the elegance of methods about science as the assurances for securing the conditions for the actualization of the undertaken social commitments. The second trajectory is a discussion of the mode of analysis of the book as bringing forth an alternative to thinking about science and change.

A final word about origins. At one level, I can think of the book as part of a long trajectory that began with my dissertation, which drew on the sociology of knowledge and looked at the knowledge conditions of political science and the designing of the school curriculum. I soon found that my work continually looked as much at the sciences related to education and then at the history of the social sciences and the politics of knowledge as they intersected with the history and practices of the modern school. This vision was reflected in my first book on *Paradigms of Educational Research and Evaluation* ([1982] 2017) and in multiple other research projects on the history of history: a cultural, historical sociology of the sciences that required reading more broadly than in education, and eventually reading about the European and American Enlightenments. These various readings are reflected in the arguments performed in this book to understand further the way in which science becomes integral to modern governing and as a productive actor in shaping and fashioning principles of reflection and acting.

One of the ways that I have accidentally learned to move across different intellectual terrains has been through my work with my graduate students and its weekly seminar called the Wednesday Group. The graduate program is organized such that students take courses across the Madison campus. The Wednesday Group is a place where the more interesting readings gained from working with faculties across the campus are brought back to the seminar for us to read closely and collectively. This reading is continually from what is outside of educational literatures and thus not part of the latter's own canons. This reading and the conversations it generated have acted on us collectively—I say this also as important for me—as a beautiful strategy for thinking and pushing the boundaries of intellectual thought that has made for a particular kind of scholarly community spanning multiple decades. The accidental accumulation of readings and conversations, I have realized more and more in recent years, provides me with a space to read literatures that are important to the cutting edges of multiple disciplinary conversations outside of education, which otherwise would be invisible and not possible to locate through typical academic searches.

And a confession. When I started this book approximately six years ago, I thought of it as a straightforward task of collecting some articles that I have written over the past decade, and organizing and editing them to create a flow and coherence to the argument about the limits of what I saw as the doxa of research in education. That hope of creating a collection of past writing soon disappeared and I became engrossed in the subsequent ideas present in this book. My general interests presented in the prior research have been maintained, but they have different elaborations and distinctions. One of this related to science and its orientation to the future. I realized after writing the book that I continually mention how science is not about the present but about making people as the problem of change. These ideas about science, which were buried within the texts, have become a major thesis of the book: the "empiricism" of the social and psychological sciences cannot be adequately understood as merely about what is and the present. The distinctions and classification are orienting and about desires about what people and society should be. While themes of the comparative reasoning of science have been discussed before (Popkewitz 1991, 2008), the book gives explicit attention to (a) how the issues of exclusion and abjects are tied in with the inscription of objectifications in the theories and methods of sciences, and (b) the role of the practical sciences as being about desires about the potentialities of people and society that exclude in its thrust to include, which produces research that is not about understanding the present but about actualizing some future through its technologies. This anticipatory quality is the politics of knowledge in the sciences of change.

Thomas S. Popkewitz<br>
University of Wisconsin–Madison<br>
March 2019

# List of Illustrations

Table 1. Summary of acceptance and rejection of hypotheses 3, 4, and 5 dealing with development and within-child variability and concerning relationships among physical and mental achievement measures in children of low, average, and high intelligence — 151

*Figures*

1. Auguste Rodin's *Gates of Hell* — 24
2. Auguste Rodin's *The Thinker* (*Le Penseur*) — 25
3. Robert Fludd's *Vision of the Triple Soul in the Body, of This World and the Other* — 27
4. Major components of Individually Guided Education — 143
5. Instructional programming model in IGE — 145
6. Multiunit organization of an IGE school of 400–600 students — 146
7. The OECD-Sweden Education Policy Review — 161
8. The OECD Education Policy Review process: Sweden — 167
9. Percentage of 15-year-old students performing at PISA Mathematics Literacy Proficiency Levels 5 and above and below Level 2 — 171
10. Sustained improvers and promising starts — 173
11. Student truancy reported by 15-year-old students and principals 2012, PISA — 176
12. Cycle of enactment and investigation — 194

# Section 1 ♦ The Problems and Problematics of Studying Practical Research

The first section is organized around the central theoretical question of the book, "How can the social sciences become an object of study?" The two chapters are written less to express a review of existing literatures in science studies than to draw on a range of scholarship about knowledge and science to intellectually orient the analyses that follows in subsequent sections.

The discussion's purpose is to create a way to study and rethink the particularly strong, and often overwhelming, belief in contemporary cross-Atlantic sciences that "good" research is meant to develop practical and useful knowledge for changing social institutions and the everyday life of individuals. This belief circulates in contemporary American policy and in large segments of the social sciences that are linked with managing social reforms. It is also expressed explicitly through calls for science to generate the "empirical, scientific evidence" to testify for "what works" for social and personal improvement. The sciences are placed in the service of organizing change that enables people to become productive citizens and children to grow into responsible, economically skilled adults.

This book seeks to problematize these assumptions of research, with the section's two chapters orienting the analyses. The task of this first section is to outline the particular approach to the study of science taken in the book of subjecting the good intentions of research to its own interrogation—that is, to think about the obligation of science to engage in self-reflection about its principles of knowledge and change. What is in question in the first two chapters is how to think about that reflection, making science into an object to study.

The particular approach expressed in the first chapter focuses on science as a historical phenomenon and an expression of the political in modernity. It is historical in the sense that the notions of science are not constant and the conditions of enactment change over time and space. The political is explored through thinking about how the distinctions and classifications of research "act" to partition what is sensible, creating rules and standards that separate the normal and the pathological through ordering and classifying what is known and how that knowing is to occur. The second chapter explores more explicitly how the "reason" of science can be studied as a historical and cultural artifact for an empirical investigation.

Research is viewed as a cultural artifact to think about the conditions that make research possible as a way of seeing, thinking, and acting in human affairs. The arguments explore how research can be studied as a productive "actor" through organizing and generating principles that order change. This understanding of science as an "actor" moves from the institutional and organizational focus on science to a historical discussion about the social epistemologies and constructions of systems of reason that shape and fashion what counts as practical and useful knowledge for changing societies and people.

Three central notions are introduced and subsequently given nuance and distinctions in the following sections: science as making kinds of people; the epistemological/ontological inscriptions in research as desire about the potentialities of what society and individuality should be; and in these inscriptions are exclusions and abjections in efforts to include. The section discusses how these themes instantiate the ontological objects of change that are identified as the practical knowledge of the sciences related to education. I use ontology as does Hacking (2002), not in the discipline of analytic philosophy, but rather to bring new objects into "existence with the historical dynamics of naming and the subsequent use of the name" (26).

The section explores the importance of studying events through maintaining a historicity so as to continually ask how the present is given intelligibility. And that intelligibility entails different historical lines that come together in the present to define the conduct of research. The method is discussed as critique—not as finding fault but as understanding the malleable processes and congealed forms that order and give a natural quality to what is acted on in the present. The discussion also engages in a rethinking of the meaning of methods, the empirical, and the issues of change and human agency, the latter as embodying a central social commitment of modernity. This rethinking, which is embodied in the notion of critique, challenges the orthodoxies that traverse the contemporary social and psychological sciences.

The two chapters are formed in relation to the other and develop in a spiral manner to explore and give nuance, distinctions, and elaborations to the questions that form the historical lines folded into subsequent chapters.

# 1 ♦ Introduction

## Studying Science: Research as Planning and Practice as Its Object

There is an alluring, daunting, and haunting vision of science holding the possibilities of changing everyday life and people. The promise of science is to provide the practical knowledge that enables more effective pathways for social and personal improvement. The sciences related to education, for example, speak about research as necessary for the perfectibility of the schools, but also as making possible how education can enable a good life in a just and equitable society.

This view of science providing practical knowledge is not merely about the present.[1] It was visible in the Enlightenment and became increasingly important with the governing associated with the modern welfare state. With different sets of principles, the 19th-century moral sciences, early 20th-century American Progressive sciences, post–World War II research and development (R&D), and contemporary science are explored in this book as promising practical knowledge to change social institutions, everyday life, and people.

The orthodoxy of practical research has a naturalness today that seems almost unquestionable. The assumptions frame not only the purpose of science but the "reasonable people" who do research. One has only to visit schools of education to hear the common refrain: "How practical is this research for teachers to improve their teaching, to enable every child to learn, and to make the potential of society possible?" If not seen this way, the research(er) is assigned as elitist, relegated to the uselessness of the "ivory tower."

This book is about this doxa for practical research. It argues that the issues of science and social change are more profound, complex, and paradoxical than would be initially suggested with these pronouncements about science providing for social improvement; and all that is needed is the empirical evidence to show "what works." That complexity is historically explored to understand the systems of reason or the principles that order what is "seen" and acted on as the practical knowledge of science; and how that knowledge paradoxically generates differences and divisions about kinds of people as the object of change.

The politics of knowledge to change people is often taken for granted in research. The good intentions of practical research to create a better society, greater personal happiness, and to address social wrongs, embody, I will argue, a complex comparative structuring of differences that was visible in the European and American Enlightenments.[2] Changing people was central to the concern of the 19th-century sciences with the moral disorder of urban populations. The changes were directed at changing the family and the mother's interactions with children; today's sciences speak about social and educational reforms as changing the "mindsets" and "habits of the mind," and as making the globally competent citizen, the professional teacher, and "the lifelong learner." The desires of research to make certain kinds of people have, as I argue, historically generated differences. The optimism of change as the desire inscribed in research produces what Berlant (2011) calls a "cruel optimism," igniting the sense of possibility for transformation that creates its own impossibilities.

These paradoxes historically inscribed in contemporary practical research are the object of this book. The chapters continually ask: "What if the orthodoxies of science having practical knowledge to effect change have little historical evidence to sustain that promise?" "What if the 'scientific evidence' of practice is not merely about facts, evidence, or 'Science,' but about the ordering of conduct that produces differences?" And "what if this doxa of science is—when looked at historically—a false prophet?"

These questions form the currents of the analysis that follow and underlie the title of the book: *The impracticality of practical research*. The exploration focuses on the sociologies and psychologies related to the modern school that emerges in the 19th century. The book explores how configurations of the past travel and become connected as partial reinscriptions, modifications, and amplifications in the present. These continuities and replacements in the present become "ghosts" in contemporary research, unseen but as part of the surface of "the reason" that orders and classifies contemporary research.

The ordering of conduct and the making of differences in the sciences linked to the modern school are ignored in educational studies and, at best, given only a peripheral glance in studies of the social sciences.[3] Unnoticed in studies of schooling and science is how the problem of making the citizen and developing a common ethic of belonging was connected with the schools formed within the new European and American republics in the 19th century. What differentiates the modern common school from earlier educational projects was the importance of science. The new sociologies and psychologies associated with American Progressive education,[4] for example, gave focus to the sciences of pedagogy as replacing moral philosophy. Its concerns were with the moral disorder of urban life and its populations. The sciences' recognition of differences produced differences in fashioning new senses of belonging and "home." The manner of constituting the hope and fears in the sciences performed as the objects of the practical knowledge to the sciences.

The chapters are formed as a historical odyssey about how the objects of changing people are produced. The discussion first traces historically how the idea of science as providing practical knowledge was articulated and continually modified in the long 19th century. The long 19th century gives attention to the uneven historical lines that collide, rearrange, and refold to give intelligibility to events and people.[5] I explore how particular social and cultural principles about people, society, and differences emerge, are arranged, and connected to the surfaces of research to articulate the objects of practical knowledge. This section is followed by moving to the terrains of sciences related to the American school and its pedagogical practices; exploring late 19th-century American Progressivism, the mid-20th century school reform research and development (R&D), and early 21st-century research related to teacher education and international assessments of national school systems.[6] The last section explores how these principles of science and knowledge are put to work as they are assembled in the specific, complex edifices in American educational sciences.

The historical odyssey views the sciences of practical knowledge as a continual series of intersections of the past that folds into the present that is never merely describing the present. The sciences are anticipatory. In particular, the historical explorations of the social and educational sciences involve the coordinating, connecting, and transfiguring of the past with the present in a manner whose "eye" is oriented to the future.

This thinking about science as anticipatory recognizes what gets unnoticed: invoking the idea of change activates desires about what is to become the social and its populations. The desires inscribed are embodied in the theories and methods of research about, for example, children's learning, development, and growth. Such words about changing children, I argue, are not merely about a universal good that research anticipates. The words are given sensibility through connecting the past and present, generating principles about the potentialities of people if research does its job correctly. These categories and distinctions generate utopic visions, visions that appear in the 19th century with phrases about social improvement and ideas about development concerned with changing children.

The focus on desires makes visible that the cognitive work of science has affective dimensions.[7] This affect is explored as desires that are generated through the social and psychological sciences. The desires are built into the very way that schooling and its research is organized epistemologically. If we take a simple expression in educational research about children's learning, learning is about desires directed to what is to be and what teachers and children are to feel: satisfaction, self-esteem, and motivation, all words that embody affect.

But what is obscured in the good intentions and affect is how the hopes of the child learning simultaneously generate fears about the potentiality of the child who is not classified as an effective learner and the danger of not being a productive citizen in the future. This hope and fear is explored as the double gestures of research. If I think historically about the Enlightenment, there was the cosmopolitan gesture that expressed the hope of science producing the enlightened person. But that gesture of hope engendered the gestures of fears about social degeneration and decay that threaten the future. The optimism expressed in the hope, paradoxically, binds itself to situations of profound threats that are confirmed in the optimism. This paradox occurs as the double gestures that exclude and abject in efforts to include in the interstices of research.

The book's analysis interrelates historical, philosophical, and the discursive analyses. The methodological approach studies research as cultural artifacts, asking about the conditions that give the sciences and their notions of change intelligibility. As Hayles (1999) suggests, "culture circulates through science no less than science circulates through culture" (21). The intellectual odyssey is to understand, in different historical spaces, "where what is said and what is done, rules imposed and reason given, the planned and the taken for granted meet and interconnect" (Foucault 1991, 75) as cultural principles in the sciences thought of as practical.

The different layers of the investigation that underlie this book are brought together as the study of social epistemologies—that is, how the rules and standards of reasoning in science are made possible historically. The analysis "plays" with different sets of ideas from the political sociology of knowledge, science and technology studies, and postfoundational and poststructural studies. I use the word "play" to express an intellectual method to think across different fields of research that otherwise would appear as distinctive and historically unrelated. The "playing" is to discipline the various ideas into a form of thinking that responds to the phenomena under scrutiny—the social and education sciences. This "play" is not an eclecticism but a strategy that allows moving between these different but related spaces of scholarship in order to "work" on science as cultural artifacts.

I use practical research as a phrase to give specificity to something often classified as "applied" research," but the notion of "applied" is too generic and, at the same time, misleading in its divisions from "basic research." What is talked about as science as "empirical evidence" and methods to produce practical knowledge are not transcendental concepts to locate realities. They are intricately bound with the conditions that give intelligibility to the knowledge organized to change social life and people.

But there is also a second meaning of practice used in the discussions, drawn from science, postfoundational, and Foucauldian studies.[8] Methodologically, this second notion of practice directs attention to the statements, theories, and methods of research as embodying complex historical conditions that engrave memories about things and people in governing the objects of change. The statements in research reports are viewed as practices, to draw on Stoler's (2009) discussion of the archive, that "animates political energies and expertise, that pulls on some 'social facts' and converts them into qualified knowledge, that attends to some ways of knowing while repelling and refusing others" (30).

I realize that these claims about the paradoxes of the practical sciences go against the grain of contemporary research. I hope that the chapters not only document the structuring conditions of apprehending change and its paradoxes in the doxa of practical research, but also the need to rethink the role of research, critique, and notions of change outside of its current orthodoxies.

## Three Historical Themes Explored in Practical Research

Moving across the different chapters of this book are three themes about the sciences related to education and change: the object of change is changing people; research is anticipatory, embodying desires about actualizing imagined potentialities of society and people; and instantiating comparative principles about people.

First, the object of change in research is explored as the making of kinds of people. When the sciences associated with education are examined historically, the continual objects are modes of living. The object of change, however, is not only the outer behavior but also the interiority or "the soul" of the person. G. Stanley Hall argued at the turn of the 20th century that the psychology of adolescence was to work on "the soul" of the child. Psychology was concerned with the inner moral qualities and characteristics of people that are today expressed as changing people's "dispositions" and "mindsets." Again, the issues at hand are not the particular phrases, but how the phrases are assembled and connected in particular historical grids that govern the possibilities of existence—making of kinds of people. These possibilities are performed as cognition and affect.

It may be asked at this point, "Is not that what schools should do? Are not the modern schools to change children so they become productive, thoughtful citizens of society?" The answer is "Yes, of course." But while this is not necessarily bad, it is always dangerous, and the particular principles ordering and classifying people need to be continually scrutinized.

The importance of this scrutiny emerges more forcefully through the second theme: the research concerned with generating practical knowledge embodies desires. The desires are not personal and psychological, but about making kinds of people and modes of life instantiated in the research. The notion of desire plays with Gilles Deleuze's and Giorgio Agamben's arguments about how the principles of ordering and classifying are about the imagined potentialities of society and people (Deleuze [1968] 1994; Deleuze and Parnet [1977] 1987; Agamben 1999).[9] The principles of desire are affective, linking the cognitive and the aesthetic that perform as attachments to what should be done to shape action and to manage living. Reform-oriented educational research, for example, engenders the desire of making the lifelong learner for the Knowledge Society. The lifelong learner is a kind of person desired for the potentialities of people and kinds of societies that research and programs are to actualize.

The desires are linked often with salvation and redemptive tropes about teacher effectiveness and models of school improvement enabling personal happiness and the betterment of society. In this sense of potentialities, the notion of change embedded in practical research, explored as directed to actualize potentialities, is utopic. Of course, the utopic qualities are not spoken of as such. They are embedded in how things are ordered in a manner that orients thoughts and actions as desires about what should be. The desires are sometimes expressed conceptually as socialization, acculturation, learning, learning outcomes, and the professional teacher who works for social improvement. All these activities are directed to what is to be changed and, implied, what should be.

The third theme explored is the comparative reasoning generated through practical research. The comparative reasoning about kinds of people relates back to the double qualities instantiated in the desires about potentialities. Explored in the research is how fabrications about kinds of people perform as double gestures of the hope of that future that encompasses what is not to be, and thus what is to be excluded, abjected, or cast out as different from spaces of inclusion.[10] Problem-solving, motivation, learning, self-realization, and development, for example, are explored as distinctions in research about the qualities of people. The distinctions engender the people who do not have these qualities—the child who is not self-realized, developed, learning.

Belonging, exclusion, and abjection become part of the same phenomenon in the epistemic ordering of research (see Popkewitz 2008). The double gestures are the imprinting of two seemingly opposite feelings and thoughts performed in the same utterance. School curriculum and research, for example, embody statements about the hope of making children who will participate in society that simultaneously instantiate fears. The fears are of dangers and the dangerous populations abjected from the spaces of belonging: the "backward" child at the turn of the 20th century who later becomes the unmotivated, lazy child who lacks self-esteem and "grit."

The focus on comparative reasoning that orders research historically points to the conditions that make possible the inscriptions of eugenics and the shifting terrains in which racializing populations occurs. When the objects of research are stripped of their feeling of moral entitlements, change embodies the mutual dependencies of the potentialities of to-be and not-to be the "reasonable" child. The production of comparative reason and double gestures to generate differences entails, as Casid (2015) argues, "the colonial machinery of dominance" (122), which I will return to in the last chapter.

Throughout the book, the sciences of change are viewed as emerging in flows of uneven historical lines from the Enlightenment's cosmopolitanism to contemporary research about teacher education, school reform, and international assessments of student performance. The historical lines bring into view notions of progress that are continually activated, (re)visioned, and (re)articulated in practical research. The historical lines form as cultural theses about how people should live. This is expressed in contemporary research to comparatively differentiate the child who is "mathematically able," "scientifically literate," and "problem solving" from others who do not embody these qualities.

The three themes are explored in organizing practical research (making kinds of people, inscribing the present as desires, and the double gestures of potentialities) that produce the spaces of the *political*. This notion of the political operates as what Foucault (1979) gave focus to as "productive power" that becomes important in modernity. This productive notion of power is complementary but different from the idea of sovereign power concerned with how structural agents repress, dominate, and rule over the ruled. While not to discount the possibilities of the exercise of brute force, productive power gives entrances to a different vector in which power operates that cannot be worked through institutions or as structural forces as the origins of power.

> They are practices or operating mechanisms which do not explain power, since they presuppose its relations and are content to "fix" them, as part of a function that is not productive but reproductive. There is no State, only state control, and the same holds for all other cases. (Deleuze [1986] 1988, 75)

*I focus on this concept of productive power because of its centrality in the operation of the social and psychological sciences and modern education.* The production of "desires" in research directs attention to how knowledge "acts" and has a materiality. This intentionality is produced in social affairs through the rules and standards that order reflection and action.[11]

## The Political and to Think Otherwise about Agency

This notion of the political and materiality embodied in the knowledge of research provides a way to rethink one major thesis of contemporary research—that is, how sciences in this study give intentionality and purpose to the human agency inscribed as directing change. In the research examined, the inscription of agency is rendered through the objectifications of people articulated in the theories and modes of analysis that focus on the processes for collaboration, empowerment, and participation. The argument that follows is that this reasoning about agency in the practical sciences is less about agency and freedom than it is about policing the boundaries of the possible as the effects of power.

*Questioning how agency is inscribed in practical research, however, does not to forgo the idea of agency, but allows us to think otherwise about change and agency.* The historical analysis continually explores how the inscription of agency is enclosed and interned by epistemic principles through which experiences are classified and ordered. The a priori identification of the actors as the agents of change in social theories performs to police the boundaries of the existing order and its partitions of what is sensible. It misses how experience is not merely there for research to recoup and explain. Making visible this policing of the boundaries that prescribe agency is to rethink agency and freedom through making fragile the given as the principles of reflection and action, and thus to open up possibilities other than those taken as the order of things.

The concern with the political as productive power does not diminish the importance of the complementary notion of power tied to the politics of representation that organize contemporary struggles for equality. While necessary, however, the politics of representation are not sufficient for considering the effects of power. My concern with productive power is the relation of power/knowledge in the educational sciences. It is to understand historically how a particular style of reason colonizes what constitutes, interns, and encloses what are the impossibilities of its good intentions.

## Against the Orthodoxies of the Present: The "Reason" of Science as Cultural Artifacts

Change, while a seemingly innocuous word of good intentions, brings into existence particular systems of reason in projects of changing human conditions and people in the sciences related to education (see Popkewitz 1991, 2008; Popkewitz, Diaz, and Kirchgasler 2017). I use the phrase *systems of reason* throughout the chapters to excavate the historically formed rules and standards that order the sciences that I discuss. My concern with the "reason" of research brings into view how methods and theories are intertwined to produce what is seen, thought about, and acted on. The focus on *systems* of reason thinks about how the principles generated in research historically produce distinctions, differences, and divisions sedimented as the relation of individuality and society. This use of system is in contrast to the later discussions of systems theory, a particular theory that populates contemporary educational research discussed in the third part of the book. The exploration of systems theory is made intelligible and plausible in the latter part of the 20th century and into today's reform-oriented research in finding practical knowledge.

The rules and standards of the reason that order research, as mentioned earlier, are explored as cultural artifacts. The classifications and distinctions of research become the empirical object of study, examining how they form through the folding together of different historical events. Murphy (2017), for example, traces how theories of the economy, which first appear in the 1930s, work into quantitative measures that come to define how a nation "sees" itself as a macroeconomic output. The measures come to pervade the details of a large range of the valuing of life that are built into the architectures of nation-states and collective environments.

To think about the reason of science as an actor in social life does not discredit people who say things. But while people say things, the statements are not adequately understood outside of the conditions that give intelligibility to thinking and actions. That is, the systems of reason lend a materiality to daily life as an effect of power.

This notion of action and materiality, however, goes against existing canons about the calls for rigorous methodological designs and empirical evidence in assessing social policy and programs. In contemporary school-reform-related research, methods are thought of as the tools used to verify concepts and hypotheses, and as the means for collecting and organizing the facts of the world into meaningful statements. Data are treated as the material facts about what is real, gleaned through rigorous procedures of statistics, or through triangulation in qualitative research to assert the objective nature of statements. The discursive form of writing research reinforces this notion of data as statements about reality. This writing is to eliminate subjectivity by embracing special sections in articles or chapters on methodology.[12] The research/methodology section attests to the reporting as merely excavating the empirical evidence for analysis.

Calls for "empirical evidence," as I will argue, are bound to the epistemic principles or systems of reason through what qualifies as evidence. In the contemporary research under discussion, the notion of science and what counts as "empirical" are given their reason through a constellation of principles generated through systems theories and cybernetics that become visible in the middle of the 20th century to order and classify what is to be known. This is evident when examining the models of change in the international assessments of students' performance in chapter 8. The "evidence" of benchmarks used for establishing standards for successful reforms is drawn from criteria that reference the proper working of the school "system." The "evidence" is what produces the coordination, flow, and feedback mechanisms of the communication patterns and processes directed to changing kinds of people.

The term "empirical" is used intentionally throughout this book when examining research reports. Its use is as an intervention to challenge the more provincial uses of the term related to positivism and its realist philosophical overtones.[13] While I return to the term "empirical" in the following chapter, I do so to think about giving attention to the things occurring in the world.[14] The empirical explores the conditions in which the objectifications about people, differences, and divisions are given intelligibility. Methods as the interrogation, however, are never outside of theory (Popkewitz 2013b, 2013c in press). The empirical in this study directs attention to events as practices that can be scrutinized to understand how multiple historical lines come together, which I speak about as a grid. A grid forms among multiple and different historical lines brought into contact with each other in producing the objects of change: what matters in research as classroom communication, children's learning and participation, teachers' talk, and policies about social and instructional improvement.

The notion of science in this book recognizes the importance of reason and rationality while arguing for the limits of the particular historical variations linked to practical research. Science and the empirical, then, are not transcendental concepts but given meaning and reference through historical practices that form as within a particular style of reasoning. My use of these words is to disrupt the colonization in which principles of positivism and empiricism define science in contemporary research. The colonization is to think that the empirical is solely what methods capture as the reality independent of theory, time, and space.

American economist Paul Krugman spoke of the effects of practical research when examining the sciences of economy at the beginning of the Great Depression at the turn of the 21st century. Economics, he wrote, performs as the current nobility of the human sciences. Its assertions are built on the belief that it had the real world under control and had solved the problems that would prevent the reoccurrence of the failures of the last Great Depression of the 1930s (Krugman 2009, 2010). Yet economists "mistook beauty, clad in impressive-looking mathematics, for truth" (Krugman 2009). The reigning theories of the "rational individuals" who interacted in "perfect markets, this time gussied up with fancy equations," turned a blind eye to the limitations of human rationality, the imperfections of institutions and markets, the irrational and often unpredictable behavior, and the idiosyncratic qualities of markets. The idealizing of markets and romanticizing of the rational individual could not "foresee" the impending depression that began in 2008.

Krugman's observation about economics can be directed to social and educational sciences related to educational reforms and change. The reigning educational research creates symbolic canopies through its impressive-looking technologies that perform ceremonies of codification and standardizations for designing social life. The codification becomes coupled with a language of objectivity about benchmarks, numbers, evidence-based reforms, and teacher effectiveness. The question is whether these symbolic canopies mistake the beauty of the form for the material actualities and turn a blind eye to the paradoxes of practical research.

## Two Intertwined Tasks

Sections 2 and 3 work methodologically to historicize contemporary research. But there are differences in how they are done. The second section asks how it is possible historically to think about and act as if science is to plan and change everyday life. I examine the *uneven* flows, arrangements, and rearrangements to render the object of science as changing everyday life and people. The section explores how particular notions of science emerged in the European and American Enlightenments to alter social conditions and people, bringing into existence narratives of salvation and redemption, of rescuing populations as desires to usher in the future. These comparative practices of differences and divisions are inscribed into the operation of change.

The section is explored through the particular historical lines that come together to think about how a specific knowledge that appears as "useful" and "practical" for changing people. The argument has homologies to Cassirer's ([1932] 1951) study of the Enlightenment, or Dumont's ([1991] 1994) research on German and French modernity. It draws on multiple and interrelated literatures in history, philosophy, cultural studies, and the social sciences. What seem as irreconcilable, contradictory, and heterogeneous actions are seen as intersecting to shape, fashion, and give coherence to today's practical research.

The third section explores the concrete spaces of American research concerned with practical knowledge: Progressive education at the turn of the 20th century, in post–World War II research and development (R&D), and contemporary research on teacher education, curriculum improvement, and international assessments. The analysis is more textually specific in examining research programs. Attention is directed to the manner in which and the conditions under which research generates desires and the double gestures of potentialities. Post–World War II and contemporary educational research, for example, draw attention to a new set of rules and standards in research articulated through systems analysis and cybernetics incorporated into the psychologies of children's learning and teacher education; where research is organized epistemically as "problem solving," statements about benchmarks and standards appear as outcomes that educational research assesses.

The last two chapters explore how systems and cybernetics theories are folded into, congeal, and collide in research on the micro-processes of classroom teaching and the macro-quantitative studies of the Organization for Economic Co-operation and Development's (OECD) Program for International Student Assessment (PISA). I explore principles that are generated to produce the double gestures of exclusion and abjection in efforts to include.

The differences between quantitative analyses represented through numbers and qualitative analyses represented as semantic or contextual qualities disappear when their systems of reason are examined. The differences between the qualitative and quantitative studies in these research programs are technical distinctions about *variations within similarity*; these are concerned with making kinds of people in which the sciences of education recognize differences to unite and make equal "all children" that paradoxically produce differences and divisions.

One important and intertwined element of section 3 is the assumption that research measures and assesses what children learn, in mathematics, science, art and music, for example. This assumption is so pervasive that it performs in the writing about standards for optimal learning, in the benchmarks established in international assessments of student performance, and in the criteria of scientific evidence to affirm "what works" as school reforms, to name a few. Yet when the school curriculum is looked at historically (chapter 4), that assumption falls apart. The school curricula, I argue, are alchemies, or translations and transformations. Curricula are translations of disciplinary spaces of knowledge production (e.g., physics, art, history) into the spaces of schooling.

The alchemy or translations that occur in schooling ironically have nothing to do with learning school subjects. The concepts and classifications of disciplinary knowledge translated into the content of the school curriculum are reworked and revisioned. What is measured and gauged as the effective learning and teaching of school subjects is discussed in section 3; paradoxically, it is not about learning the practices of science and mathematics, for example. The practical knowledge for research to improve learning is linked to curriculum practices that normalize and pathologize the characteristics and capacities of the kinds of people in practical research.

## Writing the Book as an Alternative Register for a Science of Education

The focus on research concerned with generating practical knowledge to organize change is thought of as one of the multiple paradigms or styles of reasoning about science. Like Latour (2004), the study of practical research asks

> my readers to agree to dissociate the sciences—in the plural and in small letters—from Science—in the singular and capitalized. I ask readers to acknowledge that discourse on Science has no direct relation to the life of the sciences, and that the problem of knowledge is posed quite differently,

depending on whether one is brandishing Science or clinging to the twists and turns of the sciences as they are developed. (9–10)

This book treats practical science as one of the twists and turns in the development of the sciences, and in doing so seeks to register a different and alternative notion of science and the theory of change. Science is viewed as critique. It draws on an attitude highlighted in the Enlightenment as the problem of change (Blumenburg [1966] 1983), something that I return to in the final chapter. That attitude is of science as one critique that accepts the Enlightenment's cosmopolitan attitude about reason and science as holding the possibility of freedom in doing things that previously were not possible.

The method is to study practical research as a historical artifact located in the multiplicities of differentiated spatiotemporal relations, "seeking to reconcile genesis and structures to a number of issues embodied in the sciences that pretend to secure the future" (see Deleuze [1968] 1994, 20). This strategy of research, embodied in the notion of critique, engages in the problem of change as the opening up of spaces beyond what exists as its ordering of "things."

This study of research "thinks" about change in a way that makes the matters of concern expressed in research into *concerns about what matters*, to borrow from Latour (2004). Its method directs attention to "what is accepted as authority through a *critique* of the conditions of what is known, what must be done, what may be hoped" (Foucault 1984, 38; my italics). To paraphrase (and maybe misquote) Karl Marx's "Thesis Eleven" in *Theses on Feuerbach* ([1845] 1976), this work engages in the human sciences not only to interpret the world, but to find knowledge that has the possibility to change it (see, e.g., Llewelyn 2004). *That knowledge, I will argue, is not in the prescriptions, codifications, and standardization of practical research, but is found in the interpretative modes that engage and give visibility to the historically given determinations in the contemporary order of things.*

The book's concern with the cultural principles produced by "reason" and their historical enunciations in research enables asking a further question: *"Practical and useful knowledge for what?" "What is actualized in the doing of such research?" "What kinds of people, change, and divisions are embedded in the objects constituted as practical knowledge?"*

I earlier talked about the political. I want to return to this through considering how the statements of research have a materiality. That materiality entails recognizing the statements as social and cultural objects of the world and empirical "things." The rules and standards of reason do not act directly on people, but act as principles in the actions of the self and others by presupposing the freedom to act in one way or another. The particular sets of rules and standards of reason in research or policy enunciate what to know and how to know have a materiality and are no less significant when placed within their historical conditions than other kinds of statements, such as found in the discourses of classrooms.

## Methods as Mode of Thought and the Grammar of the Book

The writing of this book is intellectually indebted to intersecting fields of thought that are often associated with the conduct of poststructural, posthumanist, and postfoundational studies. This indebtedness works into the analysis as a "traveling library":[15] different readings are mobilized as a mode of thought that connects to interpret the present. The indebtedness to these literatures is signaled, in part, through the use of a range of words that bring into existence the epistemological turns taken in this book. The reading across "libraries" requires, at one layer, a closeness to how texts are ordered as a style of reason. This close reading is not to replicate an author but to accomplish a "playfulness" with ideas that can be generative in articulating nuance to thought itself that is not merely the sum of the parts.

This thinking about "traveling libraries" methodologically gives attention to how words are used and the syntax of sentences given form in the narrative. In writing, I tried to be careful about the syntax of sentences to express the theoretical concerns of writing about "reason." When an author (e.g., the American philosopher/psychologist John Dewey or the psychologist Edward Thorndike) is cited as "saying" something, the issue at hand is not the person as author but the historical sensibilities generated through the principles embedded in the statements. What is of interest are the cultural principles activated in the texts; the identifiable forms produced about the potentialities of people, societies, and nations through the categorization that organize desires.

This attention to words, syntax, and grid is evident in the notion of "visibility." Visibility is used not to privilege vision but in two historical ways for studying change. One is to understand how knowledge is not merely cognition but embodies dispositions, affect, and emotions, and how narratives and images bring together the cognitive and the affective in research. Second is to historically think about how particular kinds of phenomena become evident in the possibilities for thinking, seeing, and acting. This is evident in the emergence of child studies and its concept of adolescence in American Progressive Education at the turn of the 20th century. It is again explored in how systems and cybernetics theories that emerged after World War II are connected and (re)visioned in contemporary teacher practice research. Systems theory is viewed as part of a traveling library to think about children, schooling, and society in education. This concern with the theoretical use of words is evident with the notions of "produce," drawing on the Foucauldian sense of the relation of power as generating principles structuring what is seen, said, and acted on.

Central to the discussion is a particular notion of history, the idea of historicizing to interpret the conditions that make the present possible. Historicizing directs attention to thinking about the grids, or multiple and different historical lines, that come together in particular times and spaces to produce the objects of change. In thinking this way, the problem of research is to consider the intersections of various technologies of measurement, theories, and cultural, institutional, and social practices that travel in uneven historical lines but connect in particular times and spaces. Conceptual distinctions that create analytical distinctions between cognition and affect, knowledge and emotion, and epistemology and ontology in many ways elide these historical complexities.

I realize that the argument often brings unfamiliar words, but the unfamiliarity is important for unthinking what has been naturalized and taken for granted as the objects of our social world. To paraphrase Albert Einstein, "We cannot solve our problems with the same thinking we used when we created them." I have, though, tried throughout the text to make clear how and why particular words are used as a way of interrogating the phenomena of research.

This questioning of practical research is sometimes challenged as "elitist," related to "the ivory tower" discussed earlier. The term "elitism" operates as an intellectual McCarthyism that simultaneously censors as it enacts a politics of knowledge. It is forgotten that the "non-elitist" language that is called for was once part of highly specialized theories (culture, knowledge transfer, learning, and documentation). The previous specialized language becomes so naturalized that the words and theories have no need for explanation. The salvation and redemptive themes that seem "non-elitism are embodied in what is promised by practical research. But as this book explores, the making of things as natural has limits and potential dangers in conserving what is.

My focus is primarily on American historical settings, although at times I will explore similarities and differences from other historical spaces. The questions of social epistemology, however, are not merely about the US and "the West" but have possibilities for unsettling the dichotomies of West and Others through exploring intersections, traveling, and translation that are not reducible to such dichotomies (see Zhao 2015, 2018; Popkewitz, Khurshad, and Zhao 2014; Wu 2013).

A further note about the reading of the argument of this book and its grammar. The argument is pursued in a spiral manner. The principles of the sciences investigated are continually developed, given nuances, expanded, and changed in relation to different times/spaces. While each chapter has its own integrity of argument and phenomena under scrutiny, the intellectual foci and manner in which the arguments pursued are formed in continual reference to what preceded it. Thus, the beginning is in fact a beginning as a flow in an expanding development of thought, although that flow is intellectual rather than chronological.

## 2 ◆ The Reason of Research

### Practice That "Acts" as Desires

This book begins with a simple observation: people have not always thought about knowledge as being practical and useful in relation to their hopes and aspirations. Nor have people always thought of knowledge as having the purpose of calculating how to plan everyday life or, even less so, as being useful for changing people. Practical research, though, comes in a variety of forms, sometimes as pragmatic knowledge, sometimes as instrumental knowledge, sometimes in qualitative research, and other times in quantitative research. Yet these different varieties of research express the possibilities of knowledge that directly capture what people do and how to produce processes of change.

The historical exploration of the book is about the emergence of and the possibilities of science as having practical knowledge to change social conditions and people. Science, in the analysis, is viewed as an "actor." By actor, I explore the principles generated in the theories and methods of research that shape and fashion what is "reasonable" to say, think, feel, and act on. Change is explored in the sciences as the inscriptions of objectifications that represent and identify kinds of people comparatively. And that desire for change is about the potentialities—that is, the qualities and characteristics of what people and society should be. These desires are expressed in what seems as natural to science; that is, to enable social improvement, human development, and learning. Change becomes functionally the desires about people and society that research is to realize. The study of science, then, is not asking about the governing "by institutions, prescribed by ideology, guided by pragmatic circumstances," but about the objectifications of research as having historically "their own specific regularities, logic, strategy, self-evidence and 'reason'" (Foucault 1991, 75).

The method of study, discussed in the first section, is the *social epistemology of science*—examining the rules and standards of reason that order and classify what is seen and acted on (Popkewitz 1991, 2014a). The *social* directs attention to the historical conditions that make the ways of seeing and acting "practically" (Popkewitz 1991, 2008, 2014b). The second section focuses on distinctions and classifications that allow for the possibility of studying research as a cultural artifact. The third section discusses how the theories and methods of research generate desires about kinds of people that research actualizes. The final section explores the method for examining the knowledge of research—that is, how to think and give an empirical substantiation of how research generates principles for ordering and classifying change.

Research is thought of as a social epistemology that engages in understanding the intersection of multiple historical practices that come together and render present research plausible. The theories, concepts, and technologies of research are turned into sites to understand "where what is said and what is done, rules imposed and reasons given, the planned and the taken for granted meet and interconnect" (Foucault 1991, 75).

## The Reason of "Reason": Knowledge as an Object of Study

While appearing as a single entity, what counts as practical research is formed through a complex assemblage of ideas, concepts, and principles that produce the objects and how those objects are known through research. I use an analogy: "practice" and "practical" research are like the ingredients of a cake. The cake is made possible through the mixture of different ingredients that are not "seen" when the cake comes out of the oven. The cake is a cognitive and affective objectification, acted on like a singular object, and affected through the desires and affect generated. Second, this mobilization of desire as the experience of the cake is not inherent to its objectification. To someone raised in a culture where sugar is not used so extensively as in American bakeries, the same affect and desires are not created.

If I continue with the analogy of the recipe,[1] practical knowledge and research are formed at the interstices of other "ingredients" in different historical spaces. The desire to make the creative child, the expert teacher, and the nurturing family as objects of research activates a grid of particular assemblages and connections. These "ingredients," or more accurately the principles given as the "nature" of the child, collective belonging, and change, are brought into social and psychological theories and methods as the identities and representations of people. These objectifications, which provide identities to people, are like recipes. They are formed in historical grids that give intelligibility to the objects to be "acted" on. The grid is filled with "ingredients" that form a complex, but unstable, edifice in the making up of kinds of people.

The study of "reason" enables us to think about what is thought, talked about, and done as not the result of a pure logic or rationality, but instead as historically instantiated. This historical quality of reason can be initially explored through art and through Auguste Rodin's sculpture of *The Thinker* at the turn of the 20th century (figs. 1 and 2). *The Thinker* is not merely the product of a sculptor's imagination and creativity. Embodied in sculpture is a network of ideas, narratives, and ways of thinking about the past, present, and future that is important in making possible the modern sciences.

The initial bronze casting was placed above a doorway depicting Dante's *The Gates of Hell*, but it was recast multiple times as a singular and independent statue.[2] The initial sculpture of *The Thinker* was outside the doorway and interpreted as looking down to reflect on human existence, which was influenced but outside of the world ordained by God.

*The Thinker* can be read as capturing the cross-Atlantic Enlightenment's cosmopolitanism, a notion of the universality of human reason as a force of change. While this "rational" eye is visible earlier than the Enlightenment (Casid 2015), the enlightened "eye" of thought can be imagined in the sculpture as more of the Enlightenment's acts of contemplation than of the reason of theology. The mediation is the human observations of the world that include even thinking about purgatory.

This "looking" into purgatory had significance within broader arenas than just of science and art. There were social and diverse theological discussions that focused on the possibilities of human thought and science guided by divine insight for the interventions in the perfection of society and the amelioration of social ills (Greek 1992). The "seeing" is for determining the facts of the world that differentiate truth from falsehood. The thinker has his back to purgatory, possibly providing a gaze of humanity that becomes capable of reflecting autonomously on the theological.

*The Thinker*, particularly as a singular sculpture, gives expression to an Enlightenment notion of human agency as existing in seeking the perfec-

Fig. 1. Auguste Rodin's *The Gates of Hell*. Photo courtesy of David Labaree, Stanford University.

Fig. 2. Auguste Rodin's *The Thinker* (*Le Penseur*).

tion of the earthly world (fig. 2). That perfection is signified in the idea of progress and human agency. While discussed more fully in the following chapter, agency and progress bring into existence salvation themes that articulate desires and potentialities about society and people in the long 19th century. The notions of agency and progress were connected to the application of human reason in thinking about change, replacing the preordained and the determinism of the theological world. Progress engaged reason to move the objective order of institutions into the realm of subjectivity, with subjectivity administered in the name of the nation and freedom (Pocock 2003). Reflections of the past and codifications of the present were placed in a sequential and irreversible "arrow of time" in which intentionality could be brought into the actuality of becoming.

Rodin's sculpture can be contrasted to a different historical artifact of thought in Robert Fludd's (Robertus de Fluctibus) drawing of *Vision of the Triple Soul in the Body, of This World and the Other* (1619) (fig. 3). The diagram of the mind embodies the Thomist logic of the taxonomic order, a classificatory ordering of things in a progression of differences that follows universal rules of thought and things given by God. The taxonomies of the Swedish Carl von Linnés (Linnaeus) in the 18th century, often thought of as a precursor to modern science, expresses this Thomist logic in reasoning about nature, animals, and differences in humans. Linnaeus created a system of naming, classifying, and ordering plants and animals in a hierarchy of organisms with shared characteristics in order to find the rules of existence provided by God. Linnaeus's classificatory scheme is still used today.

Time in Fludd's drawing was not about earthly change and progress but about the universal, eternal necessity of existence defined through the Holy Bible (see, e.g., Le Goff [1985] 1988). Whereas the reason of time resides in the humanity of Rodin's *The Thinker*, Fludd's faculties of thought emanate from God. The latter's taxonomies are deductive and classificatory realms that identify the validity, clarity, orderliness, and consistency of an eternal time that fulfills human's final destiny.

The different systems of reason given intelligibility to Rodin's *The Thinker* and Fludd's drawing of *Vision of the Triple Soul* are not purely of the interiority of the mind or logic, but the effects of particular historical assemblages and connections that form as grids in which the rules and standards of reason are produced. I used the notion of grid to think about the porousness rather than the determinate character of what is formed. What follows, then, is an exploration of particular historical intersections

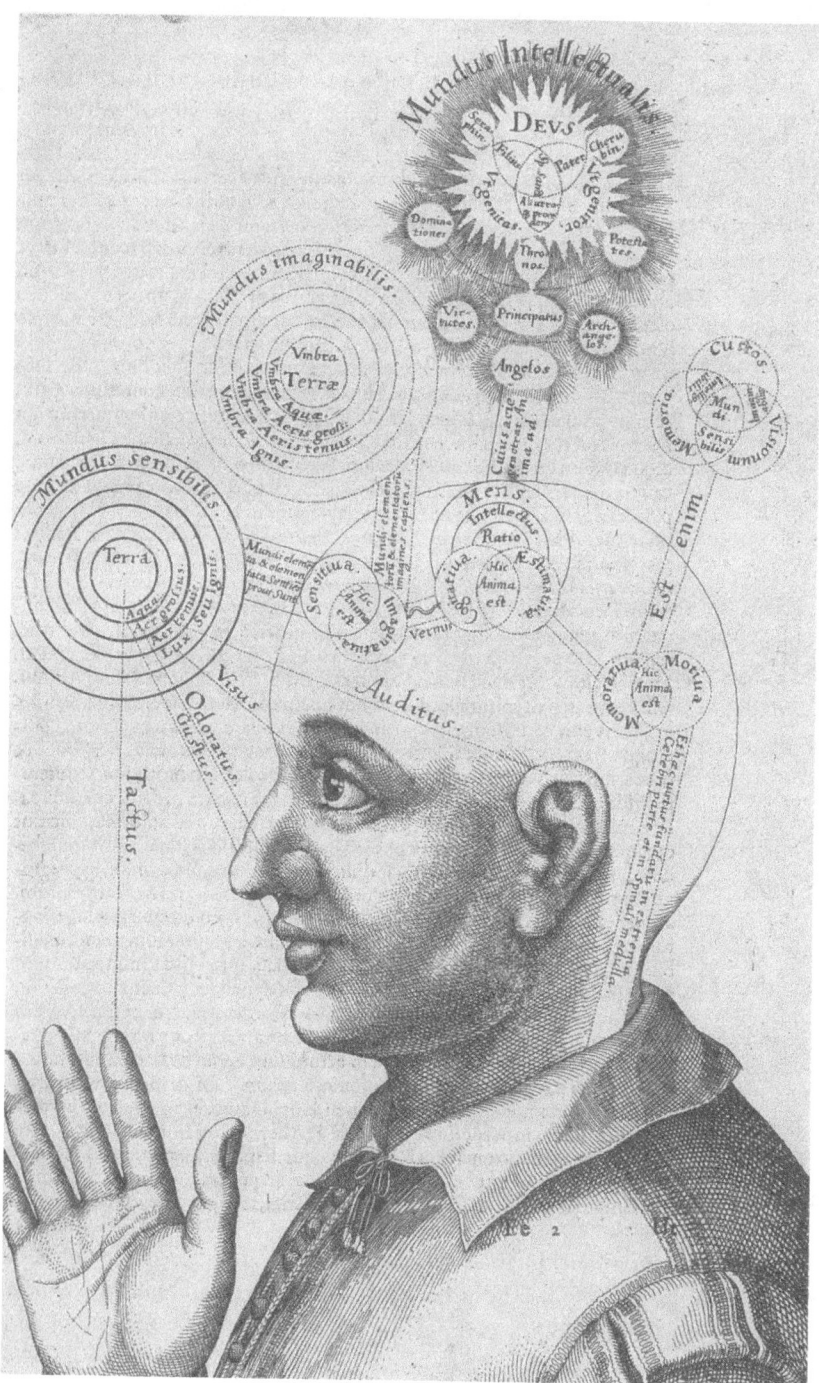

Fig. 3. Robert Fludd's *Vision of the Triple Soul in the Body, of This World and the Other* (1619). Reprinted by permission from Tankens Bilder, Utställningen ingår I Programmet för Stockholm—Europas Kulturhuvudstad 1998. Lokal Programmarrangör Folkuniversitetet.

that mediate between different principles whose historical intersections form as the reason in which the objects of practical knowledge are made knowable in research.

My use of drawing and sculpture to talk about the reason of science might, at this point, seem incongruous. They are placed together to think about reason to recognize that early science and art were directly connected to establish the objects of classification and reflection (Daston and Galison 2010; Daston and Lunbeck 2011). But as significant for this discussion, the illustration of the mind in Fludd's drawing and the Linnaeus's taxonomies of animals and plants reference a particular grid of historical lines that are not only that of the artist or scientist. They embody different rules and standards of reason from Rodin's *The Thinker*. The drawing and sculpture are a pedagogical device to think about the reason of science as not being something in and of itself.

To talk about human reasoning, science, and the European Enlightenment is not to suggest that people did not "reason" before or in other historical spaces. Christopher Columbus and Hernán Cortés coming to the Americas differentiated "natives" by whether they could "reason" to find God and accept the salvation message of the Church. If they did not accept Christianity, they were "savages without reason." No longer leaving reason to God or the heritage of one's birth, human reason was given a particular autonomous and universal quality by the Enlightenment. "Reason" was something to acquire to guide the discovery and determination of truth (Cassirer [1932] 1951, 13).

## Making Kinds of People: Desires and the Arrow of Time

The discussion on art and science as systems of reason provides an entrance into a particular quality of the human sciences that forms in the textured planes of the reason of contemporary practical knowledge. That quality, as discussed previously, is making kinds of people in the social and psychological sciences. This becomes obvious in education once it is said. The discourses of educational research, teacher education, and the more general public discourses about the modern school are about making kinds of people. The language may be about children learning or the child "growing" and "developing" as an educated person. But when notions of growth and development, even learning, are examined, they are about changes in people that are effected through schooling. But that change is not only about the present but involves desires about who the child becomes.

The desire to change people was written into the formation of the republics in Europe and North America. The creation of the republics gave recognition to education as important for government. The desired person called the citizen was a particular mode of living that entailed the participation needed for government to function (Cruikshank 1999; Wood 1991). While distinctions have existed among German, French, British, and American sciences of pedagogy, the different sites of intervention and planning are the interior of the child (see, e.g., Ó 2003; Horlacher 2015). French and Portuguese pedagogies at the turn of the twentieth century, for example, observed and "registered" the inner physical and moral life in order to map the spirituality of "the human soul" as the educated subject who contributed to social life (Ó, Martins, and Paz 2013). The American Progressive psychologies such as the child studies of G. Stanley Hall spoke of science as providing the cultural principles necessary for collective belonging. Science was to provide these cultural principles through the "more laborious method of observation, description, and induction" that would enable "conquering nature" and developing the "reason, true morality, religion, sympathy, love, and esthetic enjoyment" of the child (Hall [1904] 1928, vii).[3]

The production of desires enables us to think that the abstractions about people that populate research are not merely there for research to recoup the qualities and characteristics of people's "nature." The objectifications of people situated in research entail identifiable forms that generate possibilities for codification and administration. The creative child, for example, is a particular way of thinking, differentiating, and ordering who the child is and should be; a comparative way of thinking about the child who also is not "creative" that appears in the 19th century as a concept of science. The concept, however, does not have sharply delineated lines but multiple and mobile lines that are rearranged and reinscribed in different cultural and social edifices (see, e.g., Martins 2017, 2018).

The mobility in the classifications of kinds of people is not only about "thinking" but what occurs as a materiality. That double of thought and materiality has resonance with the idea of fabrication. Fabrication entails two seemingly different and oppositional meanings: to fictionalize and to manufacture. The "adolescent," for example, was a fiction brought into turn-of-the-20th-century child studies. The notion of the child was to think about, classify, and plan for producing the moral development of the new urban populations that were coming into mass schooling. It both embodied a philosophical ideal of the "adult" that the adolescent was to become and, at the same time, thinking of "youth" as a period of transition where the deviances and moral disorder of urban life can be controlled. The fictions for thinking about a person as an adolescent (but also a youth, a worker, or a welfare recipient) loop into everyday life and assume a materiality through theories, programs, and stories, among others. This brings into view the second nuance of fabrication as manufacturing. The classifications become determinant categories about people that are taken as real. The classifications are no longer only used to think about people; rather, the categories work their ways into what teachers, children, and family do and the degrees of freedom available.

### The Arrow of Time That Is Not! An Arrow That Accumulates Desires

The making of kinds of people entails the generation of desires that research is to actualize. Desires are expressed about potentialities of kinds of people to be *realized*. As I discuss later, research about the characteristics of teacher expertise as participation, collaboration, and competence are not empirical substances (Popkewitz 2018b). The statistical equivalences and comparisons of international assessments of student performance in science and mathematics, for example, are not merely statistical analyses about nations and their development. The measures are not "measures" but a priori assumptions of the potentialities calculated as if they did exist to think about their realization.

This concern with desires might have seemed misplaced at first glance, particularly when talking about science as a form of knowledge. The rituals of the social and psychological sciences pronounce disinterest because the concern is about "what works" and "empirical evidence," which are installed to rule out such notions of desire and potentiality. When desires are studied in the realms of the contemporary psychologies, they are given as an empirical substance to understand as personal fantasies or as utopian thoughts in what are otherwise considered as not properly scientific. But these separations of science as concerned only with the objectifications of the world are historically misleading. As Daston and Galison (2010) argued, the notion of scientific objectivity is an elusive concept. It has existed with different epistemic forms since the late 18th century from which what is observed is never merely about recouping the real world.

In the following, the inscription of desires are examined as performed in a temporal grid. That grid connects the past and present to mark what is anticipated as the potentialities of people and society. Research is discussed as expressing the flows of different temporalities in "the arrow of time," appearing as in an irreversible, regular time. The arrow, however, is no arrow. Concepts like development, action, and problem solving instantiate multiple temporalities of the past as they are folded into and rearticulated in the present that anticipates its future.[4]

## The Intersection of Multiple Temporalities

Progress is one of the central concepts that inscribe time in thinking about human history and change. The notion of progress is given visibility in the Enlightenment, when it was discussed as a social notion in relation to the differing development of civilizations placed in a continuum of value associated with the modern. Time is also an element of subjectification—that is, how individuals give meaning to experience and the trajectories of one's life. Cultural changes in the 19th century, for example, made it possible to think of one's life as a planned trajectory of biography in "the arrow of time." This planning of life was articulated in the idea of people having careers, a word that previously described racetracks for horses (Bledstein 1976). The idea of a career, however, was not only about an individual planning a life but was intertwined with the emergence of the expertise of professional theories for codifying and standardizing who people were and could be as a course of life.

The seeming directionalities of planning in the arrow of time entail a complex intersection of multiple temporalities. The future becomes part of a present that simultaneously includes the past. The reasonableness given to people and events is never in solitude, but collectively formed within historical conditions. The past in the present is what Judith Butler (1993) spoke about as the historical "I"; that is, speaking and thinking are performed through prior conceptions and classifications that give intelligibility to what is said. It is in this sense of the past connected to the present that objectifications of people are given visibility in reconfigured spaces that generate potentialities. Change in research functions as technologies to actualize those possibilities.

The enunciating of complex temporal points as potentialities can be explored in the Middle-School Mathematics and the Institutional Setting of Teaching (MIST) project (Cobb et al. 2013). MIST is a thoughtful and well-articulated research program about practical knowledge in the design of educational systems. The research is designed to improve the quality of mathematics instruction and thus to change schools and their populations.[5] The designing process is called a "theory of action" in which practical knowledge is generated to actualize the school's "systems improvement." Improvement involves calculating, codifying, standardizing, and administering the change in relation to five interrelated components of the educational system. The interventions are identified as

> five interrelated components: curriculum materials and associated instructional guidance instruments, such as curriculum frameworks; pull-out teacher professional development and school-based teacher collaborative meetings; mathematics coaches' practices in supporting teachers' learning; school leaders' practices as instructional leaders in mathematics; and district leaders' practices in supporting the development of school-level capacity for instructional improvement. (Cobb et al. 2013, 321)

Governing the spaces of instructional change in the MIST project is organized through the boundaries ordered by the concepts and distinctions of systems theory, a way of thinking about social change discussed in the third section of this book. Systems theory articulates the design of the research as particular plans for action and solutions that occur at the intersections of a wide range of literature on educational research, reform, and school improvement (change).

The school as a system is a particular abstraction about the relation of mind and machine (cybernetics) applied in the social and psychological sciences in the middle of the 20th century (chapter 7), and then transformed in contemporary research to organize change (chapters 8 and 9). The system's connections, distinctions, and correlations in the research about teacher characteristics, school resources, and children's activities perform as the principles that articulate the potentialities of what should be, which is often also spoken about as children's growth and development.

At first glance, the components of the school systems' improvement appear as self-evident and reasonable, especially when read within current literature about curriculum reform, research, and instructional improvement.

The systems categories in MIST are similar to those associated with the international comparisons in PISA models for professional development and in the literature about teacher reflection and school-based teacher development (see, e.g., Matsumura and Wang 2014). The research views the school as a system of interrelated components whose harmony allows for its efficiency. These components relate to teacher development, children's learning, and school leadership. The research invokes words like "action," "improving instruction," and "design" as concepts about how these components can be brought into an anticipated relation that is hypothesized as what the school system should be. Change consists of activities done to accomplish something that is not now present and is about the potentialities-to-be in the future.

The systems theory that organizes the research connects with the school alchemy to articulate the work of change. Mentioned in the previous chapter and explored in chapter 5, alchemy is an analogy to the medieval practices to consider how the school curriculum transports and transforms knowledge formed in one social space (the disciplinary structuring of science or mathematics) into the space of schooling. The school curriculum is the recalculation and settlement into historical sets of principles drawn from psychologies of learning that are not derived from understanding science or mathematics. The psychologies are sciences about making kinds of people that connect the norms and values of the potentialities of the individual and daily life as something to achieve that is not there yet.

The desire about the teacher as an agent of change in the MIST project is seen and acted on as the objectifications of people—teachers, children, families, and school leaders. These objectifications function through the alchemy as philosophical universals connected to liberal theories about association, participation, interpersonal relations, and values about collective belonging. The assembly of these universal qualities become the possibilities of the systems theory. Change is the realization of the desires embodied in the alchemy of MIST, expressed as the "argumentative grammar" of the research.

Systems theory performs in the research not as a theory in and of itself. The theory is assembled in a complex coordinate with psychologies, pedagogical knowledge, and cultural principles about belonging. A grid is formed for judging the directions given to change as the "uncharted territory [that are formulated to] implement improvement strategies" (Cobb et al. 2013, 322). Normalized are particular kinds of people that are embodied in the classification of the mathematically able child and the effective teacher.

The reason of research and change explored in subsequent chapters joins the alchemy of school subjects whose representations and identities become the objects of governing.[6]

## Time as the Faustian Bargain in Becoming

The arrow of time in research appears as the wholesale awareness of change, the future, and history, with a Faustian desire for the knowledge of becoming, rather than being. The Faustian becoming brings the relation of the past and the present as giving direction to the future that science anticipates. Research rearticulates and (re)visons John Stuart Mills's expression: "the idea of comparing one's own age with former ages, or with our notion of those which are yet to come, had occurred to philosophers; but it never before was itself the dominant idea of any age" (Eksteins 1985, 3).

The Faustian becoming and change are spoken of as the necessity of social improvement, a mark in contemporary research of its commitments to change. That mark is one that was given visibility in the 19th century as an imagined future that could be engineered. Social improvement was a radical idea to think about how a society could progress as it moved forward from past to present while simultaneously giving a presence to what could be in the future (Hetherington 2001). This idea of social improvement was placed in narratives of progress and the stages of development in time.

While the idea of improvement is a constant refrain in educational reform and research literature, its imprint in thinking about change can be elucidated through the notion of change as social improvement attached to the factory in the 19th century. The factory was discussed as having a utopic quality of an imagined future that was simultaneously evoked for capitalist and socialist notions of modernization. The practice of social improvement was heterotopic in the sense of what was novel and different in organizing what was possible for the future. Today, the inscriptions of social improvement erase the activations of the politics of that knowledge, spoken about as the "principled and constructive response to current demands" through "engineering, likening social investigations to agriculture, industry and medicine" (Burkhardt and Schoenfeld 2003, 3). The future seems unencumbered with historicity. It is now obtained through the pathways for change for individual well-being and modernization.

The problem at hand, then, is the paradox of science. The ideas of practical and useful knowledge generated by science appear as descriptions of human affairs, but those descriptions are the ordering of the past brought into the present that constitutes desires of what should become. Humanity and its kinds of people are brought into sequences in which the past provides templates connected and assembled in the present as the double potentialities of people. *This actualizing potentialities of kinds of people, in one sense, becomes the operational definition of change in the research examined throughout this book.*

## Inscriptions of Desire: The Double Gestures of Exclusion and Abjection in Efforts to Include

If inscriptions of potentialities about people were all that there was regarding the problem of "the reason" of a practical science, then the questions and the politics of research are simple enough: How can the social ideals be identified and placed as the ordering principles of the research concerns with education—its curriculum, the psychologies of learning, or the pedagogical knowledge required for teaching? In fact, this assumption that research identifies the pathways to achieve the ideals of education forms a basis of the alchemy of school subjects discussed earlier.

### The Paradox of the Comparative Reason of Change

The desires as the double gestures of potentialities were initially explored in the previous chapter. Research renders what is observable as a comparative style of reasoning. The impulses to enact the hope of the future contains within its construction fears about the dangers to and the effects of dangerous populations on that future. The double gestures structuring hope entail the optimism that actions can change things and people and repair social inequities so that the dreams of the present can be actualized. But the normativity that constitutes that optimism generates the threats of the dangers constituted in that optimism. The potentialities that fold into the objectifications of what the child and society should be are qualities that work against those potentialities, *what the child is-not-to-be*.

The paradoxes of the double gestures in research instantiate a continuum of values between the normal and the pathological. The recognition and production of differences are bound, for example, to categories of the child as the "backward" urban immigrant and the racialized child at the turn of the 20th century who were classified as lazy and today's urban and socially disadvantaged child. The child recognized to rectify social wrongs performed as distinctions that produced difference (Popkewitz [1998] 2017b).

The comparative ordering is part of particular displacements in trajectories of science that were visible in the debates of the French Enlightenment's philosophes and are still visible today. The cosmopolitanism that expressed human reason and science to bring about human perfection embodied a particular mode of life associated with moral cultivation and the continuum that differentiated the advanced from other less advanced civilizations. Immanuel Kant's ([1784] 1970) "Idea for a Universal History with a Cosmopolitan Purpose" placed the moral perfection of humankind in a temporality that was directed to the future progress that was enabled through reason and science. Kant argued that

> we are cultivated to a high degree by art and science. We are civilized to the point of excess in all kinds of social courtesies and proprieties. But we are still a long way from the point where we could consider ourselves morally mature. (49)

The Enlightenment's universal reason of cosmopolitanism, however, enunciated double gestures. The civilized and civilizations in the English, French, and American Enlightenments placed and differentiated people in the regulated "arrow" of the time of progress. That optimism of progress traveled simultaneously with fears of degeneration and decay. The earlier Renaissance equation of degeneracy and diversity increasingly led the observations of the elaborated symbols of corruption that were taken up in the Enlightenment. As Chamberlin and Gilman (1985) suggest, "Hope was looked after by progress and seemed as the tenor of the times, but fear was contagious" (xiii). The Enlightenment projected degeneracy on the lower categories of the taxonomies of humankind rather than, as previously held, on the doctrinal opponents in sectarian disputes among religious groups (Boon 1985, 25). To "civilize" endowed what was common to all human beings that was, in fact, a particular historicity about the potentiality-to-be and the potentiality-not-to-be. Humanity was placed in a continuum of value and hierarchy that ordered and divided people, races, and their civilizations. The comparativeness and social differentiations historically connect cosmopolitanism and liberalism to colonialization in complex intersections that relate external and internal spatializing of divisions (Lowe 2015).

There is little talk today in education about the civilized and noncivilized; "we" are more civilized than that. The double gestures as the comparative relation of hope and fear, discussed in later chapters, are embodied in the sociology and psychology of American Progressive sciences, (re)visioned in the post–World War II years, and again, *with different connections*, in contemporary reform-oriented educational research. Distinctions between the civilized as the potentialities-to-be and the uncivilized as the potentialities-not-to-be are explored as inscribed in developmental norms and notions of learning/learners. The ordering of development differentiates, for example, those who master concepts from those who have misconceptions about concepts, and those who succeed because they are motivated from those who "fail" because of their lack of "motivation," self-esteem, efficacy, or because of their "family fragility." The failures are about "uncivilized" moral disorder given as the psychological qualities of children and populations that form determinant categories about kinds of people who are "at-risk" and the disadvantaged in comparison to the unspoken norms.

## Ontological Determinism, Differences, and Precautionary Actions

Epistemologically, comparativeness is formed through an ontological determinism. The representations and identities of people are objectified as stable configurations resting there for research to give direction to them—the professional teacher, the creative child, the lifelong learner, and the "at-risk" child. The objectifications about "reasonable" kinds of people are projected as having universal qualities from which comparisons are drawn and differences produced (Popkewitz 2018a). Today, the "at-risk" child is a kind of person recognized as different but to be included. The recognition of differences produces distinctions that divide the potentialities of those belonging to the spaces of normalcy and those outside and abjected: the immigrant, the ethnic, and the child embodied in the achievement "gap" and "left behind."

The objectifications in research are studied as entailing a Cartesian separation of the reflective mind and the objectifications represented as ontological identities to be administered. Categories of human kinds as "creative," "disadvantaged," and the "professional" are abstractions that seem separate from the observing subject. The abstractions about people and society appear as ahistorical and transcendent classifications for reflection and administration.[7] For example, teacher education research, discussed in chapter 9, is designed to take the philosophical ideal of the professional teacher as an ideal abstraction to create measures for its realization. Data from studies of classroom communications are organized into hierarchies of development for the attainment of that philosophical ideal. When scrutinized, the hierarchies of development are comparative about the qualities, capabilities, and characteristics that are placed in stages and scales of differences that are expressed as the objectifications of the teacher as "professional."

Comparative reason is displayed in the arrow of time and generates a moral order from which differences are formed. The stages and scales of teacher development perform as the hierarchy of development in which the teacher research identifies the pathways for the novice teacher to move to the professional teacher, defined in contemporary research as having a common pedagogical knowledge.

Practical research, as I explore, entails precautionary or preemptive actions—that is, responses to an affective and anticipated threat that is not fully articulated (Massumi 2007). Practical knowledge is the grounds for finding solutions to the problems that arise if an action is not taken, expressed in one report on the importance of helping adolescents not to become sexually promiscuous and delinquent. The desire for precautionary or preemptive actions instantiates fears of the imagined future. The precautionary and preemptive programs are engendered, on the one hand, as fears of the populations, and, on the other, as rescue and redemption to include as the potentialities that constitute "humanity."[8]

## On Method: Concluding the Opening of Thought

The objects and "usefulness" of practical research are explored as a historical particularity of science in the subsequent chapters. I reverse current interests in practical knowledge understood as the evidence needed to bring about change and, instead, engage particular historical instantiations of science as mobile configurations through which the objects of practical knowledge become plausible and perform as desires. Studied are the shifting principles that give intelligibility to practical knowledge as a strategy for governing the change of schools and people.

The methods of the analyses in the chapters explore multiple historical lines as they overlap, assemble, connect, and disconnect with the past to give intelligibility to singular events. Each of the historical articulations of research as changing people requires the excavation of the multiple historical practices that come together and settle with a fragility in ordering what is "seen" and acted on as the objects of schooling (see Popkewitz, Franklin, and Pereyra 2001; Popkewitz 2011a, 2013a, 2013b). The method in the following chapters is to engage historically that

> at every moment, the world is what it is: the fact that its practices and objects are exceptional. That they are surrounded by emptiness does mean that they are surrounded by some truth which no one has grasped to date. The figures the kaleidoscope will produce in the future will be neither more nor less true than earlier ones. There is . . . no repressed and no return of the repressed, there is nothing unsaid clamoring to be heard. (Veyne [1971] 1998, 176)

Attention is directed to how objects of reflection and action in educational research have historically come into being and change (or disappear) over times/spaces. Childhood, for example, is not treated as an ontological fact or a substance of experience for people to help children grow and develop as moral and responsible humans. Instead, the concern is with conditions of knowledge that make possible children (but also families, communities, and teachers) as kinds of people (see Foucault [1971] 1977; Popkewitz 1997a; Popkewitz and Brennan 1998).[9] It is often forgotten that childhood, for example, is a historical event that becomes visible as a way to think and act by the late 18th century to differentiate children from adults, and to think about the family as morally responsible for who the child is and should become (Steedman 1995). Historicizing the child as an object of reflection and action in practical research inquires into the specific ways that the child is (re)visioned as a cultural thesis about kinds of people and differences (e.g., Ariès 1962; Hultqvist and Dahlberg 2001; Lesko 2001).

There is a second meaning of practice in the discussion that is drawn from the *practical turn* in science, postfoundational studies, and Foucauldian studies.[10] While the literature on the study of practices is diverse (Rouse 2007), my use of "practice" focuses on the historical activities whose articulations can be studied as events and as cultural artifacts. The objectifications of the child as an adolescent, youth, or creative learner are treated as practices, in the sense they can be interrogated as cultural artifacts to understand the conditions that make it possible to think about kinds of people in these ways.

To think about practical research as an event—that is, to think about how the rules and standards of reason construct the objects of reflection and action—decenters the subject. The purpose of this decentering of the subject, however, is not to eliminate the subject or to forego the importance of the notion of agency.

> The subject is absolutely indispensable. I don't destroy the subject; I situate it. That is to say, I believe that at a certain level both of experience and of philosophical and scientific discourse one cannot get along without the notion of subject. It is a question of knowing where it comes from and how it functions. (Derrida 1972, 271)

Methodologically, this notion of practice and the decentering of the subject directs attention to research as the statements, theories, and methods of research as events; that is, thinking about research as a historian views the building of the New York's Empire State Building, the Great Depression of the 1930s, or the American Declaration of Independence. The classifications of the child as a learner or "at-risk" are taken as the objects to understand the complex historical events whose conditions engrave memories about things and bodies in governing what is done, said, and felt as the objects of change.

The study of events entails exploring the multiplicities of historical lines that are irreducible to one another, but which come from countless transformations in forming a grid that gives intelligibility to particular moments. The rules and standards that govern reason do "not exist apart from the practice that is applied to it; its existence is not indicated by any concrete aspect" (Veyne [1971] 1998, 155).

The study is empirical. Being empirical is, in the sense of Deleuze and Parnet ([1977] 1987), paraphrasing the philosopher Alfred North Whitehead, to view what are given as the objects of the world. Being empirical is historically examining the statements that order and classify the objectifications that form the knowledge acted on in science. The objectifications that represent and identify people are abstractions to be explained rather than taken as the origin to provide explanations. The statements made about schooling, learning, teachers, and children become the empirical objects to understand the conditions of their possibility.

This engagement in history is not something spoken about as the past having a concrete, localized specificity that historians (but also social scientists) call context. This notion of context is a historicism that tells of accounts of the past through chronicling the "objective substances" and "facts" derived from specific documents of archives that themselves become the ontological objects studied as the origin of historical narratives (see Popkewitz 2013a).

The social epistemology of practical research is an attempt to relocate the problem of change and agency while not simultaneously universalizing, essentializing, and dividing people. The approach accounts for the rules and standards that order the present in order to make possible alternatives other than those that are already taken as seemingly inevitable.

Change is possible, I will argue, not by forecasting the future but by denaturalizing what is taken as natural and thus opening spaces to make alternatives possible that are outside of what is given as the order of things. In approaching this book as an alternative method of study of the human condition, the project is not merely intellectual but engages what is the political in modernity. It is a method of critique. To borrow from Stoler (2016),

> Critique here is not about "fault finding" and judgment but about restoring the forms that occlusion takes and the questions that its effects may lead us to ask. Thus, the effort is to understand that occlusion is an ongoing, malleable process, sometimes in a form already congealed and seemingly over as it acts on the present, making of us unwittingly compliant observers, nearly always belated in identifying just how it works. (14)

The designing of alternatives is itself embedded in a political theory related to democracy, one debated in the European Enlightenment. At that time and in the present, the sciences, often said through different ideological positions, have largely operated on the assumption that people could not "reason" and needed guardians, to borrow from Kant or from Vladimir Lenin's vanguard of society. This book is written in a different strain of the Enlightenment. Change should not rest in the inscriptions of an expertise that pretends to know the future, its kinds of people, and the paths for its realization.

# Section 2 • Historical Traces, Movement of Lines, and Limits in the Making of Practical Research

This section is about three historical themes that connect to the conditions that make possible practical knowledge as an object of research and change: the object of change is about changing people; research is oriented to potentialities about society and people; and the potentialities embody a comparative style of reasoning that produces differences and divisions.

Chapter 3, a genealogy, explores the historical question: How is science as planning human experience and changing daily life made possible? This intention of science has not always been the case. The chapters in this section trace how the purpose of science to change people is given its "reasonableness." I use "trace" to consider complex historical principles that are *partially re-inscribed, modified, displaced,* and *amplified* over time in forming the practical sciences of the present. Central to the discussion is the European (and North American) Enlightenments' cosmopolitanism as a historical condition that gives visibility to the reason of science traveling into modern governing, and that brings into view different historical lines about human history, agency, and progress that are connected and assembled in the theories and methods of the practical (or applied) sciences.

The particular reasoning about the potentialities of society and people embedded in research is explored in chapter 4. The issue undertaken is how desires "act" in research not as a psychological quality of the individual but are generated through the "reason" of change whose object is perfecting the individual and social life. This reasoning about science and change brings the earlier notions of social time, human history, progress, and agency into narratives of salvation and redemption in orienting science to the future and a comparative style of reasoning that generates exclusions and abjection in the efforts to include.

Chapter 5 continues thinking about the research principles that organize change in making different kinds of people. It examines a particular condition of research related to schools: what I call the alchemy of teaching school subjects such as science, mathematics, art, and music in the modern school. The notion of alchemy draws an analogy to the medieval alchemists who sought to translate base metals into gold. In the school, the curriculum performs as an alchemy, moving disciplinary projects into the cultural and social spaces of the school.

This alchemy chapter explores American research related to schools from the turn of the 20th century to the 21st century. That research assumes that what schools teach and measure are about the name given to school subjects, such as children's learning of science. Chapter 5 argues that the research is erected as a chimera, a beautiful illusion built on historically faulty assumptions.

Each chapter in this section has a recurring theme about the object of change as making people that simultaneously produces differences and divisions. This theme is continually extended, refolded into the specific historical analyses. Explored are how principles are generated, and how nuance and distinctions are given in a manner that research is never merely about the present. The classifications and ordering of the practical sciences generate desires about potentialities about what is to be. There is also the reoccurring exploration about how the reasoning of research paradoxically differentiates, divides, and excludes in the very principles of inclusion.

# 3 • The Emergence of Science as Changing Everyday Life

## Historical Traces and Movements of Lines

This chapter asks how it becomes possible to think of science as generating practical knowledge. More particularly, it asks about the possibility of thinking about science as planning human experience and changing everyday life; assumptions that are re-assembled with different historical lines in contemporary American research about change. The historical odyssey recognizes that there is nothing "natural" or inevitable in this notion of science and planning change (Popkewitz 2006). Historically, science as the "planning people" emerged from a series of accidents that came together as ways of seeing, acting, and thinking. The early 20th-century psychology of Wilhelm Wundt in Germany, Edward Titchener in England, and the American William James, in contrast, did not think of psychology as providing explanations for everyday conduct or as a force in the planning of the future.

I begin the chapter exploring a particular set of principles that enables "seeing" the potentiality of directly intervening and changing everyday life, what I refer to in the first section as "the homeless mind." Visible in the long 19th century[1] is a form of consciousness about human history that enables theories and "concepts" about people and change to appear as external to the immediacies of daily life, such as the abstractions of society, populations, and childhood. These abstractions appear without a "home," yet they are capable of looping back into daily life to govern experience. The homeless mind entails a mode of reflection that folds into the making of modern science and its notions of independent "empirical" entities. The second section pursues the contours of the methods of calculative judgments instantiated in the cosmopolitanism of the European (and North

American) Enlightenments.[2] The third section focuses on the Enlightenment's cosmopolitanism as making possible the idea of human agency in the design of change. This notion of agency, however, is historically located in particular enclosures of science in which theories inscribe the actors responsible for change.[3] In the final section, I pursue how the search for progress in science generates utopic visions[4] that, paradoxically, differentiate, divide, and exclude in the very principles of inclusion.

I use the notion of historical traces in this discussion for two reasons. First, the enormous range of phenomena entails a multiplicity of historical lines in forming the events that are not possible to explore in a single chapter.[5] The chapter's strategy is, therefore, to explore traces that serve to mark the uneven multiplicity of historical lines that are amplified, (re)visioned, and reinscribed as a single plane of consistency in contemporary practical research.[6] The historical discussion is modestly genealogical in relation to the historical task undertaken, yet hopefully it makes visible how multiple historical lines come together and connect (and disconnect from its past configuration) in the present. Second, the historical discussion "decenters the subject," not to eliminate the human subject but to explore how particular kinds of knowledge emerge and "act" to constitute experience and intern and enclose the possibilities of the agential subject.

## The Possibilities of Reflection about Change: "The Homeless Mind"

The modern school and the sciences have an indebtedness to the Enlightenment's cosmopolitanism (see, e.g., Popkewitz 2008). Cosmopolitanism, however, is not used as distinctive doctrine. Cosmopolitanism is a historical notion that directs attention to the emergence of theories and practices about people as having their own history, development, and change that becomes accessible to plan through human reason and rationality (science).[7] It embodied a mode of "reasoning" that inscribed a universal "nature" of humanity. That universality was expressed through abstractions that simultaneously embodied images and narratives of the nature of society and the individuals who were open to intervention and change. Cosmopolitanism in the spaces of Europe and the Americas brings into view the concern with planning and changing everyday life through theories whose abstractions provide an order in the arrow of time.

The radicalism of the Enlightenment's cosmopolitanism was the privileging of human reason and science in establishing a particular relation between collective belonging, daily life, and change. Traces in the debates over rationalism (René Descartes, Baruch Spinoza, and Gottfried Wilhelm Leibniz) and empiricism (John Locke, George Berkeley, and David Hume) that organized philosophical discussions of science in the 17th and 18th centuries, while different in their starting points, were homologous in reflecting on the Enlightenment's hopes of progress through inscribing a temporal order to human life. Cosmopolitanism was given as a universal mode of reason that made possible liberal ideas about "open and free debate in an equitable economy: economy in its classical sense of the principles for people to manage and safeguard the moral good of community and human happiness" (Gaonkar 2001, 8).[8]

Cosmopolitanism is usually associated with the European Enlightenments but I want to explore it first in a particular consciousness for thinking about the world and self in processes of change—qualities I call "the homeless mind."[9] The homeless mind entails a way of thinking about collective belonging that forms through abstractions that objectify people and events. The quality of "mind" entails separating the viewing subject from the objects as a means of reflection. This quality of consciousness can be understood historically as making possible the methodologies of modern science and research, which are designed to perform as the practical knowledge to effect change (see Casid 2015; Daston and Lunbeck 2011).

## Objectifying the World as a Method of Change

"The homeless mind" of cosmopolitanism is a particular quality of reflection in which the mind connects with the external objects of social life to think about everyday life and human experience. Abstractions about human life are given as conceptualizations about people as stable entities. The object of social life is given an autonomous quality that is outside of the self but serves to understand the self and the world. The significance of the abstractions about people is that they appear as having no specificity or historical place of belonging, thus their "homelessness."

The abstractions are "homeless" in the sense of giving reference to universal qualities of human experiences that seem to have no geographical location. The quality of this homelessness is a distancing technology that makes it possible to think historically about the causes organizing human life, such as social forces, society, bureaucracy, capitalism, and socialism.

Concepts about groups of people as populations of workers, the citizen, and learners are "homeless" distinctions. I discuss this below in relation to a Cartesian logic. The abstractions perform as devices for the mind to reflect and act on the peculiarities of the given "nature" of human life, ordering collective belonging and individual attachments; and which can be mobilized to consider change-in-time about their development and growth.

The significance of the distancing technologies is that abstractions about people and events are theories that form as determinate categories or objectifications to understand and interpret, such as the naming of things as organizations, institutions, society, and populations. The abstractions about people stand as objects "seen" and talked about as being outside any particularities of experience but they serve to explain experience.

The technologies of distancing are important to the making of modern science (see, e.g., Bledstein 1976; Daston and Galison 2010; Shapin 1994).[10] Daston and Lunbeck (2011), for example, explore the emergence of observing experience as a distancing technique in the making of the scientific self between 1600 and 1800. The disciplining of the "eye" embodied in scientific observations was registered in notebooks. The notebook became a register of the eye to organize things and events into discrete parts, producing a mosaic that was more than what was observed. Scientific observations, when registered, were "forms of 'learned experience' that had to be crystallized out of vernacular practices and conceptualized as evidence and proof" to "calibrate perception and judgment" that remade both the body and the soul of the observer (Daston and Lunbeck 2011, 3–5). Scientific observation became a way of reflecting on objects that separated the observer from the object so that the observer became someone "who 'no longer reasons; he registers'" (Daston and Lunbeck 2011, 4).

The distancing and the "homelessness" of the abstractions (and their theories) about kinds of people, however, is only part of the phenomena at work. The "homelessness" of the conceptualizations, however, holds the potential of looping back to order "experience" and the planning of change. Concepts like the citizen, society, immigrant, gender, and race function, for example, to order reflection and differentiate between kinds of people that have material effects as they move into theories, programs, and stories, among others. This materiality was spoken about earlier as the two nuances of fabrication.

The "homelessness" is significant, then, not only as distancing technology. The objectifications that represent and identify people, society, and populations arise from their historical conditions and can loop back to interpret the experiences of what people do, how they do it, and why (see, e.g., Scott 1991). Further, the objectifications of children as "youth" or "adolescent" entail particular historical lines that form as folds that act in a grid or as a "recipe." The categories are abstractions that have "no home" but are given homes by people placing individuality within the spaces formed through the objectifications, such as "being" a worker, a citizen of a nation, and a learner. As the lines form as determinant categories about people, the abstractions are apparatuses for reflection and planning. The planning entails individuals organizing their lives and careers as trajectories, for example, for success and self-fulfillment.

To return to the previous chapter's discussion of Robert Fludd's *Vision of the Triple Soul in the Body, of This World and the Other* (1619), the drawing of the mind gave expression to a Thomist logic in which there was no sense of what today is thought of as human history. Cosmopolitan notions of human agency, science, and progress were not possible as abstractions to organize reflection about human conditions. To have cosmopolitanism as the embodiment of "reason" required different conditions, ones that gave humans their own history, one separate from that of God and Nature.[11]

What makes "the homeless mind" different from Robert Fludd is the idea of humans having their own history. Reason "sees" the abstractions about society or populations as spaces of action. The kinds of abstractions about people, collective belonging, and human history become a method of calculating the "nature" given to the experiences of everyday life and worked into the possibilities of what is useful knowledge. Human nature stands, paradoxically, outside of history itself; yet the objectifications of people are given identifiable forms through the complex edifices in which they are arranged. The forms given to experience don't rest in place but give direction to think of the potentialities of change in the immediacies and intimacies of one's life.

The historical peculiarity of the homeless mind is illustrated with the abstractions of society and populations. Abstractions about society appear in the 18th century, for example, as structures or forces that have no "home." Society is an abstraction that has no particular specificity but in fact emerges in a particular historical space and serves as a secure anchor to think about people, collective belonging, and human history. It provides coordinates about what to notice, order, and classify for thinking about the organization of humans and their development.

The word "society" was connected to guilds and associations in the Renaissance. By the middle of the 18th century, however, society becomes an abstraction that objectifies patterns of life as universal distinctions about what holds people's collective life together. Society, for example, becomes an important abstraction in the emergence of the social sciences from 1750 to 1850 (Wagner, Wittrock, and Whitley 1994). The invention of childhood, as well, is an abstraction that is not merely a reflection about social life but also about kinds of people. The abstraction appears in the late 1700s and early 1800s as the search for the lost realm and the dislocation of the adult's past (Steedman 1995; also see Ariès 1962; Dekker 2010).

The objectification of social life through abstractions like society works as a mode of reflection about the world and "self" that seems transcendental and ahistorical—"homeless"—and also is localized as a knowledge to think about one's relations, meanings, obligations, and responsibilities. Society, for example, is a conceptualization that instantiates a moral order and political authority that is objectified, differentiating, for example, "civil society" from the state.

Concomitantly, the abstractions about human life offer possibilities for acting on daily life in relation to the universalized spaces generated through the abstractions. Society, for example, serves as a concept to structure cognition through turning it back on the world. It becomes a determinant category to measure, codify, and standardize the properties of programs and theories about people, and to organize how people categorize and differentiate experience. This looping is evident in the discussion prior to the French Revolution. The Encyclopedists' writing in the late 18th century expressed this notion of the relation of the social and the individual as important to the formation of democracy. Embedded in the notion of equality was the abstraction of society. The Encyclopedists posed the issue of inequality in the inconsistency among measurements, institutions, inheritance laws, taxation, and market regulations. These inconsistencies were perceived as the greatest obstacle to making a single people (Scott 1998, 32).

It is important to reiterate that my focus on the historical instantiation of "the homeless mind" is not to say that abstractions did not exist prior to this or that representational forms were only a property of the long 19th century. For example, one could think of the Kingdom of God as having symbolic qualities that performed as abstractions of universalistic pretensions, but they were different from those of the homeless mind. The Kingdom of God told a history of humans through a universalist and theologically oriented time. The individual's relation to God in Lutheran traditions, for example, elaborated on 17th-century pietistic notions of personal awakening and commitment, and introduced the self as an agent and object of change. That agency was in finding the grace of God and not as a citizen finding progress in "the city on the hill."[12]

The homeless mind attends to how abstractions and the objectifications of people inscribe memory of a shared history that is not only reflective but material. Concepts of society and the child, for example, enter into and "act" in the everyday life of the family and community through pedagogical, medical, social, and political discourses. Further, the abstractions explored as being activated in research as a comparative system that generates differences about what kinds of people are outside the boundaries of society and childhood, and thus outside of belonging.

## The "Mind" and Its Apprehension of Change: Cartesian Logic

Cartesian logic, which has a strong presence in modern positivism and empiricism, can be thought of as possible within the contours of the consciousness of "the homeless mind." Cartesian logic is a theory of knowledge that desires to make visible the inherent nature of humankind and provide explicit procedures of justification and belief in order to obtain that truth. Reason is considered as the natural property of the mind, creating concepts that perform as the methods of interrogation and identification. The mind orders the things of the world and the "self" as objects that appear as external to the self, but nevertheless the mind can apprehend and conceptualize for understanding and change.[13] The rationality and scientific method, within this view of research, requires "for the subject to get outside of itself to perform the very self-reflection that is to distinguish rational judgment" to produce "the very ability to differentiate, sight or perception" that becomes "the battleground and the saving sense" (Casid 2015, 122).

This mode of thinking forms abstractions about the human condition that pass through the consciousness of the subject to apprehend the universal qualities of human nature, and to guide action for social change. The abstractions are thus "given" transcendental qualities. Abstractions about social and individual life function as conceptual apparatus or "frameworks" to express the universal human qualities that research identifies and orders the planning of interventions (in education, it is called instruction).

Important to this "reasoning" is the objectification of things of the world; people are made into ontological "facts" to be classified and ordered as the origin of reflection and change. Abstractions about society, populations, and the child as the learner are such objectifications. Research on the school curriculum, for example, starts with psychological objectifications, such as the child as learner; the methods are used to find better and more efficient processes to realize desires, which are expressed as achievement.

"The homeless mind" thus operates as a method of thought that codifies and standardizes abstractions that form research methods. The abstractions about "the nature of learning" perform as theoretical entities to calculate and standardize as if they did exist to say something about cultural and social life. The empirical becomes the historical agent of "human nature" in which the philosophical universal is named and measured as the effects of the abstraction.[14]

Theories and methods (and the inscribed ontology and epistemology) become analytically distinct and different in the processes of science. Methods develop finer distinctions and add nuance through giving "empirical" substances that enable articulation from the philosophical ideals embodied in the theories of research. The empirical is not merely there for the researcher to access reality to gain its facts as data.

This observation about methods and theory does not suggest a logically deductive and tautological process. Rather, it suggests how what constitutes methods is a theoretical and historical practice bounded through different contingent qualities that fold back into research to constitute what is useful and practical. The "homelessness" of the conceptualizations that works into theories about society and people is never separated from daily life itself. The abstractions hold the potential of looping back to order "experience," differences, and the planning of change. Concepts like the citizen, society, immigrant, gender, and race function as abstractions whose representations and identities generate double gestures, which are always dangerous. The objectifications hold the potential to materialize as the ontological objects for reflection and action that, paradoxically, excludes and abjects in the process of inclusion.

### Modern Poetry and Abstractions Performed in the Immediacy of One's Experience

This mode of seeing or consciousness about science is not only about science. Poetry required an individual to recognize distant, abstract, and seemingly unrelated phenomena to find meaning, memory, and feelings in everyday life (see, e.g., Daston and Lunbeck 2011; Rancière [1998] 2004b). Ancient Greek poetry, for example, was nonrepresentational, nonsignifying, and nonmetaphorical (Rancière [1998] 2004b, 10). The correspondence to the physical world was understood as a model for beauty, truth and the good, in which metaphors are not central. It was expressed through mimesis, the imitation of life or nature written fantastically about everyday life. For Plato, Aristotle, and Homer, it was the art of composing fables that represented the aggregation of a certain type of individual for imitation.

By the 19th century, different epistemic forms were noticeable. Although I have focused on science, the qualities of the homeless mind are inscribed in poetic representations. This change in poetry is often presented as nineteenth-century Romantic poetry, a reaction to the Enlightenment's concerns with science and rationality. Yet if Romanticism's "seeing" is viewed as displacements and (re)visioning of surfaces associated with "the homeless mind," a different form is identified as its possibilities. Romantic poetry embodied particular kinds of abstractions, different from those of science, but they connected the objects of nature and society with the immediacy of one's experience, feelings, and emotions. The "I" of the poem is produced as echoes that act with subjectivity. The abstractions in a poem about a tumultuous storm is given as the expression of experience of a traveler who passes through a certain territory. The words work to "coincide with things, utterances with visions" that bring experiences as a way of provoking particular feelings and emotions. The traveling of the individual brings into existence "some relationship with the 'we' of the community" (Rancière [1998] 2004b, 12).

The homeless mind that transverses science and poetry points to the emergence of a mode of reflection and action that enters into contemporary life. This section gives attention to how a particular way of reasoning about society, people, and change that entails particular technologies of distancing the intimacies of face-to-face relations for reflection, acting, and entering into the creation of experiences. Central to this process was the production of objectifications of people and events whose calculations and standardizations form to organize the knowledge of change.

The relations posited between abstractions and the immediacies of everyday life have particular contours important in the constellations through which contemporary practical research is produced. The general qualities of "the homeless mind" traverse diverse registers of thought that are continually (re)configured. My interest is how continual modifications, inscriptions, and their amplifications intern and enclose particular epistemic principles that link human history, agency, and change to the objectifications that represent kinds of people.

## Science as a Prophetic Text and the Idea of Progress

This chapter began with the particular qualities of the homeless mind and how it's woven into notions of progress, theories of change, development, and agency for acting to produce change. Science was "the prophetic text" that recast time as a social dimension of human development that had a past, present, and potentialities given to the future. *The temporal ordering of progress was framed through the objectifications of people* that inscribed philosophical ideals of the characteristics and capacities of people as a humanism in which people acted and their agency was inscribed in the ordering of change. The revelatory qualities of science embodied old theological metaphysics of certainty in its search for the universals of human nature and uncertainty in how earthly pursuits can actualize that perfection. Agency, as I will argue below, was in finding the pathways to perfection of the human condition.

### Science, Agency, and Prophetic Text of Progress

Cosmopolitan reason gave twin focus to a humanism and progress that has residues in the present. The Renaissance's concern with people as actors and agents of change (Bhambra 2007) was brought into new spaces of reflection as humanism was linked with cosmopolitan reason. It connected ideas of people as actors in daily life to theories of social affairs and the political forms of government for intervening and planning to effect change. Political theories of citizens, for example, assigned particular rules and standards for the kind of person upon whose agency that government was dependent. The reflective technologies posited existence within sites for pursuing people's own and collective well-being.

The agentic hope for cosmopolitan knowledge was as the positivist force for change. It was embodied in political theories of the English and American philosopher and political theorist Thomas Paine and the French Marquis de Condorcet (Jones 2008). Paine and Condorcet both subscribed to a new form of republicanism, forged out of three major political and intellectual developments in the last third of the eighteenth century. The first was a more confident belief in the control over chance and the future through the coming together of the collection of vital statistics and the mathematics of probability. The second was the great impetus given to the growth of positive future-oriented conceptions of commercial society embodied in the publication of Adam Smith's *Wealth of Nations* in 1776, and in France, the liberal reforms attempted by the Turgot ministry of 1774–1776. The third was the radicalization of the understanding of each of these starting points visualized in the American and French Revolutions. (62)

Humanism and its notion of agency entailed debate in the Enlightenment about whether the public could be taught to understand the laws of human nature that would eliminate obstacles to change (Broman 2012, 203). Jean-Jacques Rousseau's *Emile*, for example, saw the public's education as necessary so there was no permanent social barrier to the social order based on the natural order. Condorcet, a French philosopher and mathematician influential in the rationalism of the Enlightenment, wanted, like Rousseau, to abolish hereditary elites but recognize differential talents. Education would provide the basic tools of reasoning and scientific knowledge that would advance the Enlightenment's rationalization of society, but also identify those who are not able to have that kind of reasoning.

This agency of humanism was initially found in the philosophies given the name of the moral sciences in late 18th and early 19th century. Science served as the prophetic text that, in the hope of the Enlightenment, would serve the interests of all humanity. Immanuel Kant's ([1784] 1970) *Was ist Aufklärung*, for example, talked about the philosopher as the guardian of the moral development and order of society. The philosopher's duty was to acquire the necessary knowledge to guide that development. The Scottish Enlightenment, influential in the construction of the modern American school,[15] sought to have the philosopher construct a bridge over the gap between the written records of the past and the unrecorded origins of society, which otherwise was divinely given and belonged only to Providence (Poovey 1998, 215).

The objects of reason and agency in the moral sciences are illustrated in the work of Hume and his contemporaries in the 17th century. Hume did not see science as providing useful and practical knowledge. Against philosophical rationalists, Hume thought that knowledge was formed directly from objects perceived in experience, or from abstract reasoning derived from experience. This empiricism, however, was only worthwhile if bound to human judgments and wisdom. For Hume and other political economists, notions of equity and "equivalence between objects were less questions of knowledge than of *justice*," for instance, with respect to the law governing market exchange and for deciding "if an item were of satisfactory *quality*" (Desrosières [1993] 1998, 199, italics in original).

Human intentionality and purpose that performs as agency is defined through the objectifications given in the representations and identities of the sciences. The homeless mind, as a historical formation about human consciousness, makes possible the means of assessing that agency and the properties of the humanism that went against prevailing social and theological determinisms. That agency was ordered and classified through the theories whose abstractions became the objects of change itself. The agency was directed to the future, named as progress that linked the past and present to the future through human action. The sciences, however, reassembled the revelatory qualities that previously were assigned to the theological realms, with the certainty in religious thought brought into history as human "nature." The reason reserved to science would generate the basic truths of nature and society on which the progress of society depended.

### The Paradoxical Cosmopolitan Reason of Certainty in the Desire for Change

The principles that ordered the cosmopolitan reason discussed above entailed paradoxical qualities of certainty and uncertainty/determinism and indeterminism in the desire for change. The cosmopolitanism embodied the older theological metaphysics of certainty in its search for the universals of human nature. Carl Becker (1932) gave focus to this when he wrote about the philosophers of the Enlightenment as moving the universal Heavenly City to the earthly rules of nature that ordered "The City of Man." Inspired by philosophers who contributed to the idea of secularization *but* influenced by Scholastic rationalism, God's certainty was reinscribed into "human" nature and the Enlightenment's search for the universal qualities of human reason. Philosophical curiosity, and later the human sciences, was directed by "the postulate of the radically new foundation of cognitive certainty and the project of the regulated procedures of all cognitive acts" (Blumenberg [1966] 1983, 404).

But as a note of caution pursued in later chapters, this break with religion is not a foolproof as it sounds. There were debates about, for example, the role of Christian ethics in science, the speculative or empirical qualities of the sciences, and the relation of subjectivity and objectivity in the methods of the psychological and social sciences (see, e.g., Haskell 1977; Herman 1995; Ross 1991; Shapin 1994; Silva and Slaughter 1984).

What were called the moral sciences (or moral philosophy) in the 19th century were to introduce precision into the knowledge of human affairs. Descartes, in the spirit of the Enlightenment of the next century, gave attention to generating knowledge about the processes that are to achieve justice and happiness (Blumenburg [1966] 1983). Descartes's positivism helped codify and standardize the order of everyday life to achieve a functional order in the pursuit of progress. Condorcet thought science, for example, would replace the "prejudices planted by superstition and tyranny" (Jones 2008, 62). The guarantor of change was people's ability to exercise ever-increasing control over both natural and social environments. The later 19th century's deductive qualities of positivism and inductive qualities of empiricism aimed to access the objects of the world and enable the continuity of movement toward humanity's progress (Foucault 2008, 12, 19). But the guardian of that ability and its "reason" was organized by the philosophies. Kant argued for the importance of establishing principles of evolution and the progress of mankind that gave justification to the social and moral perfection of human nature and even human happiness.

While mathematics that assigned rigid rules and standards was thought of as unreasonable in the 18th century, statistics began to take on new notions of reason in its inscription in science in the 19th century. Probability theories provided ways in which to think about knowledge that could be used to monitor and govern populations (see Hacking 1990; Porter 1995). The numbers generated through statistics performed as a means to visualize and connect phenomena (such as populations of people) through the abstraction of probability theories (see, e.g., Hacking 1990).

## Progress as "the Arrow of Time" That Has a Future

If science performed as a prophetic text in the 19th century, the idea of progress provided its directionality. Time was given its own uniqueness as ordering the regularity and irreversibility of processes in human development and the growth of institutions, populations, and civilizations. What happened in the past was believed to be not merely actual but necessary in the present. Enlightenment ideas of progress gave time as an essential social element in its humanism, having a linear, nonreversible, and, in some instances, dialectical movement. Marc Bloch ([1949] 1953), a founder of the French Annales school of history, recounted the emergence of modern history as a social time that told about the advancement of civilizations, with history tracing the movement from Egyptian pyramids through Greece and Rome as material evidence of humanity's evolution. He remarked that up to the 18th century people wrote graffiti on pyramids when they rode past them in the desert. The pyramids were merely rocks in the sand that held no teleological or historical value for telling about who people were or what they could become. By the 19th century, the idea of modern history, or what might be called historicism, become reason's telling of the events of the past as a tale of humanity's development whose evolution could be traced from the people of Ancient Egypt, through Greece and the Romans, to the present.

### Times as Development and Utopic Potentialities

History could "tell" not only about who people have become but about who they should be. Past, present, and future were placed into a relation with each other through a notion of regular, irreversible human development. Human reflection could "see" the past as no longer the source of wisdom, but rather as something to be overcome or to learn from to effect the Enlightenment's hope of progress. This ordering of time gives possibility of a science of social improvement and knowledge useful for change. The past was no longer mysterious but connected to the present and its potentialities (see Popkewitz 2013c; Popkewitz, Franklin, and Pereyra 2001).

Time as a sequence telling of human development gave the present utopic potentialities as possibilities to bring into being (see, e.g., Heilbron, Magnusson, and Wittrock 1998). Models of human affairs focused on the processes of social improvement that embodied an unknown future obtained from a prefigured world of the present (Hetherington 2001, 59). Discourses of social improvement in the 19th century, for example, were placed in utopian narratives in projects of social engineering (Hetherington 2001). The desire for social improvement, however, fixed the idea of improvement within the context of the objectifications of the solid, stable, and dependable present. Neoclassical art, for example, was envisioned for a newly emerging society that was organized along capitalist and democratic principles. Neoclassical art was imagined as a replica of the ancient past whose geometric symmetry and formalism modeled the social order.

Time as development was also placed in the planning of the human interior in the late 18th century, although emerging from different lines than those of human history (Steedman 1995). The theological "soul" was reconceptualized as the interior of the individual. The interior of the child was given a history that could become an object of the new sciences of childhood. In the late 19th century, G. Stanley Hall's ([1893] 1924) studies of childhood, influential in the formation of American education, placed youth in a temporalization of experience (Lesko 2001). Youth was cast as a particular kind of person in time who represented the moral panic about the degeneration of the future that required proper administration to act in civilized and responsible ways. The moral panic was grounded in racialized, gendered, and class distinctions.

Time as the ordering of human events in a sequence of past/present/future (Tega 2008) became a reflective practice to establish the autonomy and authority of knowledge—the practical and useful knowledge that contributed to the consciousness associated with "the homeless mind." Static time found in natural history's taxonomies of species, like in the biologist Linnaeus's *Systema Naturae* (1735), was shifted to the idea of evolution later embodied in Charles Darwin's *On the Origin of Species* (1859). Empiricism instantiated time in the belief of learning directly from what was present and from experimental effects for understanding the present and creating pathways for the future perfection of human life (Blumenberg [1966] 1983, 410).

The inscription of human time in which agency, progress, and change were given form can be contrasted to time in Medieval "reason." In the latter, time was static, with an ascribed unity that guaranteed an already determined future. If approached as epistemic differences, nothing was "new" or unfamiliar in the reason of Medieval thought. It was a closed universe that was given and eternally ordered by God. To be aware and "conscious" was to acknowledge the universality of time for the ordering of all things necessary for the finding of grace. Medieval texts, for example, were devoted to the memory practices of monastic culture (Danziger 2008, 104).[16] The texts chronicled the sacred narratives and parables in the Bible remembered as holy sacraments to be relived in the body and the soul. St. Augustine's autobiography was told through reminiscences of his personal progression from sinner to devout believer. His reflections embodied a Neo-Platonic memory that had a didactic function to help others find a path to God that ultimately remained mysterious.

The disciplining of time was important to the making of the scientific "self." Experimental sciences held the observer as external to a predetermined system of representation located in dimensions of the past and present, a quality spoken earlier as related to "the homeless mind." Representations of nature appear free of time, but they move in a linear progression that advances toward an anticipated future. Measurement in physics, Schrader (2012) argues, becomes a copying mechanism that gives special ontological presence to objects of nature through the presumed tracing of time in a manner that erases human intelligence from the measurement process. An autonomy and authority to knowledge is established through erasing human intelligence in the methods of measurements.

The ordering of time introduces regularity or the arrow of time into social processes that make it possible to think of progress, human agency, and social improvement as processes of change. The inscriptions of the arrow of time ordered human events in a sequence of past/present/future. The reflective practices of science are to map human development. Agency is functionally defined as that knowledge useful and practical for actualizing the processes of change in a temporal flow. This notion of "agency" finds its way into contemporary teacher education research and international assessment of student performance, as discussed in chapters 7 and 8.

### Progress as the Temporal Ordering of Settled Relations

The ideas of progress and agency are worked into the humanism put into service in the social and psychological sciences. A particular historical set of principles encloses and interns the knowledge that is generated as "practical." The linking of cosmopolitan reason and progress opened up new human possibilities that science was to actualize. While it took a long time, with uneven development and multiple configurations to get to contemporary notions of improvement, the past articulations of humanism, history, agency, and progress formed as traces that are partially activated in defining the objects for useful and practical knowledge.

Progress, at least in the historical conditions described, gave a temporal ordering to a settled relation of past, present, and future. The reason of science was to generate the basic truths of nature and society on which the progress of society depended (Broman 2012, 203). The settled order enclosed and interned the possibilities of social improvement, what constituted agency, and institutional and personal development. The objectifications of people functioned as the abstractions placed in sequences in time whose outcomes were given in statements about progress (see Nisbet 1980).

As Nisbet (1980) reminds us, the notion of progress was not new. The Greeks, for example, had a conception of the world that did not place people at the center of the stage or as the axis of society around humanity. There was no philosophy of biological change or cultural improvement of humanity; living things had their own laws of cause, mechanism, and a fixed succession of stages and purposes. For the Greek Stoics, reason was the act of memory that liberated one's own being. Knowing oneself meant knowing the past that was drawn from the wisdom given by the gods (Foucault 2005, 468). The mind preoccupied with the future was considered as consumed by forgetting, filled with hubris, and incapable of action.

Not so with the modern notion of progress. Time is a dimension of life and human development in the research concerned with change. Instantiated are multiple temporalities that engage the past in the present to inscribe potentialities given to the future.

Progress linking the past and present to the future through human action assumed revelatory qualities in the social and psychological sciences. Revelation was a term used in religious discussions in the 19th century that was (re)iterated in the modes of reflection necessary in the new republican forms of democracy.[17] Reforms of government and society were to make visible the latent, inherent provision of progress. The object of change, with some counternarratives, was to find the conditions of a true universal knowledge that would reform society and bring it into line with reason and nature.

Even though there was a settled order to what constituted development, there were different cultural principles in the theoretical and methodological practices when comparing British, German, French, and American social sciences (see Levine 1995; Horlacher 2015). American pedagogical psychology, for example, was formed as an applied science, whereas German pedagogical psychology was less practical and more philosophical (Depaepe 1987). German pedagogues were concerned with the *Geist* or spirit of the nation and the *Bildung* that differentiated its sciences from those of the US and Switzerland, where Calvinism and republican ideals reigned (Tröhler 2011).

While these amalgamations of principles about humanism, time, progress, and agency may seem far away, maybe even irrelevant, in current education research and children's learning, they are closer than they might seem. *What is historically significant in the temporal ordering of progress was the objectifications of people that generated principles as desires in the organization of knowledge itself.*

## Science and Its Double Gestures: Fears in the Panacea for Equality

The paradoxes of the reason that effect humanism, agency, and progress were discussed as the settled order that theoretically inscribed their possibilities. The paradox is also in the double qualities of desires as generating the potentialities-to-be that simultaneously embodied principles about the potentialities-not-to-be, about fears of the qualities and characteristics of particular populations in research. The comparative qualities of this reason of science has a homology to debates called the Quarrel of the Ancients and the Moderns, which were about the nature of people who were and who could be civilized. The 15th–16th century European Renaissance and into 18th-century England and France saw the rediscovery of ancient texts that invoked debates about whether there was a continuum that differentiated less advanced from more advanced civilizations. The debates gave rise to the idea of "the modern" and whether the present superseded the Ancient Greeks in art, oratory, poetry, and science. The literary and artistic debates in the Académie Française, for example, differentiated "the modern" and civilized person through distinctions and rules of politeness, refinement, manners, and decencies between people and their degree of being "civilized" (Passavant 2000).

The comparativeness in the Enlightenment's themes of progress expressed fears of decay and degeneration. Degeneracy was projected on the lower categories of the taxonomies of humankind. Comparative qualities were embedded in legal codes that mirrored customs and practices to differentiate people while creating a nationally inclusive community (Scott 1998, 90). Certain populations were considered dangerous to the development of civilization, in contrast to prior classifications of doctrinal opponents in the religious wars (Boon 1985).

> The Enlightenment view of legal codes was less to mirror the distinctive customs and practices of a people than to create a cultural community by

codifying and generalizing the most rational of those customs and suppressing the more obscure and barbaric ones. (Scott 1998, 90)

Social theories made the arbitrariness of difference necessary and inevitable (Rancière 2004c, 305). The new treatises of the Enlightenment, the positivist science of Auguste Comte, and the new sociologies, for example, were given as a necessary order through which differences in people were defined. Thomas Paine saw a future in which there would no longer be "an age going to the workhouse and . . . to the gallows" and in which "the loss of a breadwinner, orphans, single parenthood, unemployment, sickness would be relieved by right" (quoted in Jones 2008, 59). The recognition of differences to make people equal, paradoxically, generated principles that distinguished and differentiated the normal and pathological.

Time as a stable, singular phenomenon stabilizes the objectifications to enunciate principles of difference among people. The ordering of vision connects and is reassembled in the 19th century. Casid (2015), for example, explores how the development of rational vision before the Enlightenment was a method to manage fear, desire, and attachment that makes colonialism possible. Related to the earlier discussion of "the homeless mind," the subject of rational vision produced through projection machines appears as an ordering of vision to distance the self from the objects being observed in the 1600s. The distancing mechanism projects desires as a mirror of the self that imitates and differentiates to abject in what Casid (2015, 122) calls "the colonial machinery of dominance." Cultural memory and "proof" of the Enlightenment's belief in the universality of its "reason" (Bhambra 2007, 27) provide this rational vision of mirrors in the adaptive education of colonialism in Africa, and the early 20th century US social studies curriculum that comparatively differentiated the qualities and characteristics of people (C. Kirchgasler 2017; Lybarger 1987; Madeira 2005).

The theories disclosed differences in the ethos that differentiated workers, artisans, and racial groups from the unspoken norms of civility. Differences were inscribed in Europe and the US as notions of poverty and the poor were replaced with concepts of workers, employees, and citizens who had social as well as political rights in the early 20th century (Nowotny 1991). Differences in people and the state of their rehabilitation cast those outside of normalcy as "incapable of ever acquiring a taste for the philosophers' goods—and even of understanding the language in which their enjoyment is expounded" (Rancière [1983] 2004a, 204).

## The Past in the Practicalities and Potentialities of the Present

It seems natural today to say that research provides useful and practical knowledge to fulfill social obligations and utopic dreams—articulated in language about social betterment, individual freedom, social participation, and the correction of social wrongs. These commitments, however important, are enacted through grids of particular historical practice and effects of power that give intelligibility to notions of change.

This chapter focused on historical lines that come together to produce a particular way of reasoning about human development, change, and agency instantiated in the social and educational sciences, what I initially gave focus to through "the homeless mind." I explored historical principles that form a grid through which "the homeless mind" sees and acts, articulating *the temporal ordering of progress. A directionality is given to change as the arrow of time, with agency framed through connecting the old theological metaphysics of certainty. Revelation is found in the search for the universals of human nature to be achieved.* The desire to change human conditions in these assembled principles brought into existence double gestures about the potentialities of people as hierarchies of differences and divisions among people.

How these principles are (re)visioned and operate as the objects of practical and useful knowledge is explored in later chapters.

# 4 ◆ Virtue in Secular Saintliness

## National Exceptionalism, Science, and Schooling

The chapter continues to explore the particular epistemic principles that are historically connected and (re)visioned with contemporary practical research. One of the connections is the inscription of time—time oriented as potentialities of kinds of people that research will provide the pathways to actualize. Science becomes the agent for organizing the spaces or territories of becoming. This chapter focuses on the relation of time and desires as embodied in salvation and redemptive themes that travel in research. The salvation themes are offered as the means of perfecting individual and social life. They are spoken about as the exceptionalism of the nation and its population, and more recently as the skills and knowledge necessary for participation and global competence explored in the third section of the book.

I place salvation themes with those of redemption to focus on how the inscriptions of desires perform affectively as pathways to rescuing nation and its progress. They function in the attachments of the personal to collective belonging and "home." The themes are of rescue and redemption through changing the interiority of individuals. Prior notions of "the soul" are brought into the sciences of pedagogy, now reassembled and connected as the salvation theme of the professional concerned with improving human conditions and the characteristics of people in liberal theories about the pursuit of happiness. And the idea of improvement and its salvation themes are not merely about the child, but the relations of the child with the family and community. The object of change is about moral order and problem solving as "revelation," a theme discussed initially in the previous chapter and again in American Progressive education and sciences (chapter 7).

This chapter places salvific and redemptive themes as generated in a multiplicity of social and cultural principles inscribed in the production of desires. The salvation and redemptive themes are no longer about religion but about affective elements of science that project cultural principles of optimism with fears of degeneration if there is not preemptive action. For example, if research does not find a pathway to improve science and mathematics teaching, then the nation will fall from grace as the Knowledge Society; nations who do not improve in international ranking will never be able to become "average" and receive the benefits of that grace.[1]

The discussion considers first how religious narratives of salvation are translated into seemingly transcendental, ahistorical principles linking individuality to the collective belonging of the nation. The second section focuses historically on the rhetorical form of the American Jeremiad as salvation and redemptive narratives in the social and education sciences. The sciences simultaneously express fears about the fall of the nation with an optimism about its rebuilding as "the temple" envisioned by the Enlightenment's universal dreams of human perfectibility. The third and fourth sections give attention to the redemptive narratives as directed to the human interior or the soul; transformations of religious conceptions into secular, worldly modes of living in finding perfection; and the "soul" conceptualized through psychological categories of motivation, engagement, and "well-being" in contemporary sciences. The practical knowledge of science, explored in the fifth section, functions as a redemptive force to liberate the child that has the double qualities of optimism and fears. That redemptive force, discussed in the sixth and seven sections, is bound through the 19th century Social Question and its 20th century revisioning that gives attention to the undoing of moral disorders and rescuing the dangerous child and its community.

## Virtue in Secular Saintliness: National Exceptionalism, Science, and Schooling

The inscription of salvific themes in cosmopolitanism goes against a central thesis of the European Enlightenment. That Enlightenment thesis is that the mysticism of religion, tradition, and the parochialism of the nation was replaced with the universalism of human reason. Concepts of the citizen, human agency, bureaucracy, and science are given as examples of the importance of secularization in modern societies. Secularization is expressed indirectly through the "homeless mind," which appears as the trust in the mind to apprehend the objects of the world and to act on those objects to produce change; that is, trust is built into the objectivity given to science that includes standardized knowledge (e.g., numbers and statistics). Yet, as this chapter argues, secularization obscures how religious themes (but not necessarily theology) connect with and are (re)visioned in the production of desires in notions of progress and change.[2]

The plausibility of a secularization thesis lies in the (re)visioning of theological desires into a humanism that privileges principles about human agency. To counter the evil, social chaos, and immorality that were assigned to the Church by the Enlightenment, the philosophes created an image of virtue in secular saintliness. Virtue was given in the application of human reason and change that enabled agency and change in earthly conditions. Agency was brought into existence through concepts of freedom, liberty, and the right of individuals.

The "humanism" of the Enlightenment, however, was not a break as such from previous theological concerns, but it transformed the Christian doctrine of salvation into a project of universal human emancipation. The centering of human agency in the Enlightenments overlapped with the religious beliefs of the Moravian brothers, the Puritans, the Wesleyans, and the Pietists, for example. The Enlightenment's narratives reassembled Stoic ideas with Reformation and Counter-Reformation notions of salvation in the political theories of the republican citizen (see, e.g., Caride 2015; Horlacher 2015; Tröhler 2011). The idea of agency was connected with the idea of progress, the latter as "a secular version of the Christian belief in providence" (Gray 2002, xiii). The righteousness of conduct, paradoxically, for both Enlightenment philosophers and their critics was not about what one did but about what one believed in regard to the power of universal reason and healing (Jones 2008).

The intersection of religion, political theory, and science in the Enlightenment brought into view questions from at least as early as the late 17th century. Questions were raised about how science could help to understand God's direct (and indirect) intervention in daily life. John Locke and Isaac Newton, for example, saw providence as expressed in nature's design whose laws would be revealed by science (see, e.g., Jones 2008).

This folding of salvation themes as connecting and disconnecting religion with the state is evident in cultural histories of the American and French Revolutions (Bell 2001; Marx 2003; Wood 1991). The salvation and redemptive themes gave the nation exceptional political and social character.[3] The new American nation, for example, was proclaimed as "the

City on the Hill" that resettled Protestant religious narratives in projecting the righteousness of the new nation in the perfection of humanity (Ferguson 1997, 21).

While all nations generate narratives of their own exceptionalism, the particular narratives of American exceptionalism told of the providential uniqueness of its republican form of government. Those coming to America found religious freedom in the New World. The phrase New World was a biblical phrase about God's chosen place used by Puritans during the 17th century. It was given a new iteration with the forming of the nation. The land that would serve God's elect for "the day of God's judgment" and the Puritan "utopian moral grace on earth" was transformed into the saga of the nation escaping the evils and disfigurements of Old World traditions. The new nation, drawing from the language of Puritan sermons, was the "errand into the wilderness" to enact the dream of a society that had the providential character of the Garden of Eden (Jehlen 1986; Miller 1953; Ross 1991). This foundation story of the nation was recast at the end of the 19th century as a second creation built in harmony with God's first Creation (Nye 2003).

The epic narrative of the nation was one of loss and reclaiming. The nation provided the difference between light and darkness. The nation reclaimed the utopian past that was lost in the corruptions and traditions of the Old World, Europe. The American republic appeared as redeeming that loss through the evangelical piety embodied in its political form. Thomas Paine wrote at the start of the War of Independence (1776) that the people of the nation were throwing off Old World prejudices and adopting new liberal, enlightened, and rational ideas. "The mind once enlightened cannot again become dark," wrote Paine (cited in Wood 1991, 191).

The citizens of the nation embodied the moral universalism that differentiated those not as reasoned or those without reason; for example, slaves, indigenous people, and later particular immigrant populations. School textbooks of the 19th century told the tale of American exceptionalism as the most advanced civilization. America was given as the home of the chosen people, a radical "otherness" in which the nation's citizens were the "racially elect" differentiated from others who had fallen from moral grace (Glaude 2000; Low 1982; Wong and Chang 1998).

The culture of redemption and salvation is not merely of the past. It is reassembled and transfigured to connect in the practical knowledge of research discussed in the second part of the book. Contemporary reform-oriented research on teacher practices, for example, articulates salvific narratives that appear in the discourses of teaching as a helping profession whose purpose is "human improvement." The latter is an affective locution that embodies notions of an expertise in the service of the universalistic cosmopolitan liberal values about human fulfillment.

## Populism and Desire: The American Jeremiad

The culture of salvation and redemption joins with a particular populism inscribed in the social and education sciences. This populism embodies the redemptive form of the "American Jeremiad" in political rhetoric (Bercovitch 1978). A Hebrew prophet of the 7th century BCE who predicted the destruction of the Temple, Jeremiah's prophetic injunctions were reconstituted in New England Puritan sermons to convey a duality. The sermons were practical and spiritual guides that wedded theology to politics as progress toward the Kingdom of God. In contrast to the European Jeremiad whose skepticism decried the sins of the people, the American Jeremiad was optimistic: it joined intellectual and political critiques with assertions that social progress brought spiritual redemption in its creation of human happiness.

Embedded in the Jeremiad's optimism about progress, however, were social critiques that depicted decay and degeneration related to the moral disorder produced through industrialization and urbanization. The crises of unbridled capitalism, the perceived breakdown of moral order in urban life, and the brutality of modern warfare coupled with the struggle over slavery in the American Civil War, among others, cast doubt on the prior American narrative of the idyllic reincarnation of a biblical Garden of Eden (see, e.g., Menand 2001). In this scenario of the Jeremiad,

> the Industrial Revolution was not repelled but embraced; it was often seen not as an intrusion but as an offering of possibility. It brought miseries but also innovations. It did not overturn the natural world, it seemed to coexist with it. (Rothstein 2011)

The duality of hope and fear in the American Jeremiad linked moral and political prescriptions for the public good to the achievements, competence, and salvation of the individual. While this will be explored further in American Progressivism (chapter 6), science was to offer practical advice on the social development of the child and family that contained the millennial vision of the "New World." In the new sociologies, for example, was a perspective that the millennial world would come about through human efforts of "disinterested benevolence," an 18th-century religious term brought into the reform activities of the next century. "Disinterested benevolence" described the selfless giving of one's time and energy to social concerns (Greek 1992). The religious mission worked with public reforms as an evangelical effort to build orphanages, provide free medical dispensaries, organize professional services like social work, and host day camps for urban children to create a moral and virtuous public.

That image of hope and tranquility gave expression to the poetry of a European Jewish immigrant, Emma Lazarus. Placed today on the plaque at the foot of the Statue of Liberty, the site that symbolically stood where many Europeans saw the shores of the United States for the first time, the poem epitomized what was seen by many immigrants as the hope of the new land and nation. Lazarus wrote of the United States:

> Give me your tired, your poor,
> your huddled masses yearning to breathe free,
> The wretched refuse of your teeming shore,
> Send these, the homeless, tempest-tossed, to me:
> I lift my lamp beside the golden door.

The moral purpose of Progressive reforms redesigned Protestant agrarian values as principles for Americanizing its "others" defined as the urban populations. The moral disorder and the plight of the immigrants and the poor were different sides of the same coin articulated in the American Jeremiad in policy issues and the new social and education sciences.

## Systematic Reflection as the Revelation of Potentialities

The expertise of science expressed a populism of American Progressive political and social movements. The early 19th century American Jacksonian populism was an agrarian revolt against big business, professional knowledge, and government through evangelical hopes for the new millennialism. The populism of Progressivism that replaced the Jacksonian movements was of the expertise of "disinterested benevolence" whose redemptive power would bring forth the possibilities and innovation of the millennial vision.

The optimism of progress and social critiques that depicted social and moral decay and degeneration was taken up in political, social, and religious institutions, with science viewed as a method of purification and redemption (Nye 2003; Boyer 1978; Greek 1992). Science was spoken of as the great panacea for equality (Sklansky 2002). The new human sciences were elixirs of hope that embodied a millennial belief in rational knowledge to achieve justice and happiness (Blumenberg [1966] 1983). Calvinist salvific themes in America were (re)visioned into ideas for civic processes of social and personal betterment.[4] New institutions of health, employment, and education tied scientific expertise to organizing subjectivities for understanding experience (see, e.g., Scott 1991).

Progress was individualized and made part of each person's self-actualization. Inscribed in the psychological discourses discussed later were political principles. These principles were of science making kinds of people whose thoughts, reason, and feelings would enable them to act wisely and autonomously in the new systems of participation on which government was dependent. The enlightened and virtuous citizen of the American republic was labeled as civilized by the inner characteristics of being reasonable, tolerant, honest, virtuous, and candid (Glaude 2000, 195). The new citizen (or the "new man," a term that circulated into the early 20th century) connected the scopes and aspirations of social principles with the personal and subjective capacities of individuals.

Reflection in the pursuit of progress (re)visioned revelation as the prophetic vision of democracy. Previous church conceptions of revelation were transferred to strategies that produced personal self-reflection and the inner self-guided moral development of the individual.[5] John Adams, for example, a signer of the US Declaration of Independence and the second president, described the nation as spiritual fulfillment through evoking the Enlightenment. He discussed education as the inculcation of reason. The learning to reason would create "new habitual principles" and recall "the lost images of virtue" that will overcome vice, with the mind "cultivated like a garden, with barbarous weeds eliminated and enlightened fruits raised" (Wood 1993, 190). The method of reason in the new republic was revelatory.

Education was a process of revelation of the prophetic vision of democracy. The school inscribed the prophetic vision as part of the inner qualities of the child. The psychologies of pedagogy were envisioned as empirical building blocks in forming a new ethical person (Popkewitz 2009). An educational text, *The New American Citizen* (Dole 1891), made the basis of the citizen as the "consideration of the public good, the welfare of the nation, or the interest of mankind," and traced the idea of government and ethics to its religious basis for producing the "patriotic emotion and moral enthusiasm" of the child (v). The problem of professional knowledge was to act on the behaviors of individuals. Conduct was ordered by the rules and standards of reason by which individuals applied problem-solving skills in the areas of health, sexuality, and good ethical living.

Earlier notions of revelation were made into the promise of the sciences to rationalize the processes of childhood by the turn of the 20th century. Theories and technologies of pedagogy focused on those individuals whose dispositions could actively respond to the collective social needs of the workplace, the family, hygiene, and politics. The domestic science movement, for example, was designed to bring scientific principles into organizing the home, shaping the moral habits of the families of working-class women and their practices in childrearing.

The very notion of democratic dialogue and reason was expressed in American Progressive sciences and reforms as a form of revelation, likened to its origin in Christianity.[6] John Dewey's pragmatism viewed democracy as similar to the reasoning found in Christianity (see, e.g., Childs 1956). Dewey ([1893] 1975) spoke of democracy by drawing on the contemporary religious discussions of revelation. Revelation was the opening of the individual's mind to "uncover and discover" and to "bring home its truth to the consciousness of the individual" (5). Dewey's pragmatism, for example, emphasized the relation of the rationality of science, the qualities of the democratic citizen, and a generalized Protestant notion of salvation. The secular language of children's learning and development embodied the self-watchfulness of the individual, as historically analogous with the pursuit of "signs of grace." The focus was on the "soul," now classified as the mind, learning, problem solving, and intelligent action.

## Social Science as "Liberating the Human Spirit"

Science as the arbiter of the good and the moral replaced the earlier national epic of reclaiming the past and the pastoral New World. Science would produce progress through systematic public provision, coherent public policy, and rational government intervention (Rueschemeyer and Skocpol 1996; see also, e.g., Popkewitz 1992, 1993). The knowledge systems of science acted as the modern oracle that decoded and recoded social affairs so that subjects could act with agency (Popkewitz 1991).

Scientific reflection as "revelation" inscribed a specific Western messianic tradition of redemption in the social sciences. Science and technology were imbued with values that universalized the history and future of the nation as transhistorical and transnational in its modes of living and promise of the ideal of democracy.[7] The moral grace of the nation was defined as "an inventive people" in the "Great Experiment for promoting human happiness" (Nye 1999). Samuel Morse's telegraph transmitter, Thomas Edison's 1880 lightbulbs, and the Connecticut clock were seen as the embodiment of the culture of democracy.

The redemptive and salvific principles joined the social with modes of living in the formation of the American common school. Education was the preparation for a conversion experience that gave the individual moral behavior. Drawing on John Calvin's notion of curriculum vitæ or "a course of life," pedagogy was the "converting ordinance." It was written with an evangelizing and calculated design on the souls of their readers—with the "soul" rewritten into theories of the child and citizen as actors and agents with the role of community to create collective belonging and "home."

Pedagogy was the technology of change. The Connectionist psychology of Edward L. Thorndike, for example, joined the hope of education in developing "the moral, political, and economic health of the republic." The virtues would lay the foundation to restore the moral order of the city. That restoring embodied fears about absorbing the Irish, Greek, Italian, and Jewish immigrants and their "foreign" radical ideas that could produce anarchy (Joncich 1968, 46). The child study movement, as well, enabled systems of pedagogical scrutiny and assessment to differentiate, classify, and normalize children according to notions of development.

Inscribed were the salvific themes of science that enabled people to act wisely and autonomously in the new democratic systems. The US Department of the Interior's Bureau of Education wove the promises and prophecies of progress with Old and New Testament themes into the pedagogical constructions. Education was to produce the self-reliance and self-motivation of the child as "the founding [of] a civilization" that expressed the "character in the American people" (US Government Printing Office 1874, 13).

The themes of salvation and redemption were enacted in the rhetorical form of the Jeremiad. The problems of moral disorder and deviance were decried while at the same time heralding an optimism of knowledge generated that was practical for ushering in the future. The new scientific universities at the turn of the 20th century embodied this duality of the Jeremiad. They were modeled after the German universities to provide institutional "homes" for the production of knowledge to identify the conditions that produced the social wrongs and to guide change for both the state and civil society. The university, which had been built on the British (Irish) Cardinal Newman model of education to reproduce knowledge for the adornment of the mind, was expanded to include the university as a site for the scientific production of knowledge. The university was to provide the expertise necessary for change, and its scientific disciplines in "service to the democratic ideal" (see, e.g., McCarthy 1912).

The sciences were to design people who embodied conceptions of the common good and the citizen. The object of science was the design of the self: folding religious themes into theories of social belonging, individuality, and change as desires about the future. Previously, design was based on evidence of intelligence or purposefulness in nature to prove the existence of God (Reuben 1996, 31). The personality was formed through the applications of techniques of self-watchfulness in the private pursuit of the "signs of grace" represented in the construction of the self. Early colonial travelogues and the church's ideas of conversion and civilizing "the heathen" embodied this design of the self (see Hirst 1994; Todorov 1984).

The religious revivals of the first revelation prior to the American Revolution were revisioned as a millennial language of the nation that visualized elements of Puritan theology as the problem of designing human affairs and people. The Christian millennial belief that the proper object of study was God was reassembled into narratives of the new republic as the Enlightenment's cosmopolitanism that (re)visioned the universality of religious morality as the basis for a common mankind (Schlereth 1977, 56). William Rainey Harper, the first president of the new University of Chicago, argued that the mission of the university was to be the guardian of civic virtue, democracy, and progress. He likened the role of the university to that of a priest "whose great duty is to enlarge the vision of his followers." Harper continued that to unlock "the inner secrets of the soul of humanity (not a single man), of mankind (not a nation) [that] are the subjects of study and of proclamation" (Harper 1905, 27).

Unlocking the secrets of the soul of humanity was anticipatory, with science generating desires about the self that inscribed social "needs" and cultural priorities. The psychologies and sociologies concerned with urban reform, for example, focused on children's attitudes, abilities, and emotions as interventions in making of kinds of people. For instance, Albion Small, a former Baptist minister who started the Department of Sociology at the new Rockefeller-funded University of Chicago,[8] gave attention to the sociology of urban reform and the school. The school, for Small, was to use social theory that embodied redemptive qualities as the desire of change. The significance of the school curriculum was its promise to design social progress. Social psychology was "the science of assisting youth to organize their contacts with reality . . . for both thought and action" (Small 1896, 178). The teacher held the key to the future of society through remaking the inner qualities of the child.

> Sociology knows no means for the amelioration or reform of society more radical than those of which teachers hold the leverage. The teacher . . . will read his success only in the record of men and women who go from the school eager to explore wider and deeper these social relations, and zealous to do their part in making a better future. (Small 1896, 184)

The redemptive quality of science, however, was not only found in the United States. The new psychological sciences in Russia, Germany, and Sweden at the turn of the century, for example, reconstituted the Enlightenment's belief in the "reason" of the individual as the motor of change (Hultqvist 1998; Rueschemeyer and Skocpol 1996). In the United States, the social sciences embodied the secular promise of the nation that escaped the historical burden of the past and held the hope of fabricating a future cosmopolitan citizen who would truly be a universal model for the world (see Popkewitz 2008). The objects of the sciences and practical and useful knowledge were anticipatory of that future.

Contemporary notions of design maintain the revelatory qualities in the planning of teaching and learning. They portray an open sensibility that brings into existence democratic participation and human agency. Planning is portrayed as the natural expression of a democracy that develops objective knowledge derived from the "evidence" of rigorous data. That knowledge serves the democratic ideal by delineating the conditions under which universal rules and standards of reason organize debate and conflict among different social interests. The democracy expressed, however, is not only about participation. It embodies a utopian quality about the proper planning of society as the reason and "reasonable (and unreasonable) people," the former enabling the fulfillment of a utopian future.

## (Re)Visioning "the Soul"

Religious notions of the soul and salvation were brought into designing the citizen who performed "good works" and embodied civic virtue. Joined was "the health of the soul and the regeneration of the Christian and the virtuous citizen, exultation of the divine and the celebration of design" (Ferguson 1997, 43). The "soul" as the object of scientific knowledge assembled the universalism of the Enlightenment's cosmopolitan reason with various sects of Protestantism and the desire for moral order in what Bellah (1975) calls "civil religion." The Puritans, for example, attached ethical techniques of the individual's self-monitoring and control—consciousness and self-consciousness—to finding the status and attributes of the inner soul. The self-monitoring ethical techniques pursued "signs of grace," the gift of God's love, and mercy in the individual.

The "soul" as the object of change was the knowledge useful in "awakening" and the "quickening" of moral sensibilities.[9] The joining of biblical and Enlightenment narratives in the design of the political body was expressed by John Adams. The settlement of America, Adams said, was "the opening of a grand scene and design in Providence for the illumination of the ignorant, and the emancipation of the slavish part of mankind all over the earth" (cited in Wood 1991, 191). The state was evidence of "divine sanction." The Puritans' biblical interpretation of America as "the light of the world" was brought into political, social, and economic narratives, written into the formulations of the Declaration of Independence and the Constitution (McKnight 2003, 19).

The soul was the pedagogical inscription of virtue in the new schooling of the 19th century, which, in what might seem counterintuitive, initially deployed the catechism style of the confessional. Schooling provided for moral and civic virtues by producing agents capable of self-guided rational action for the public good. In Sweden, the catechism of Martin Luther's "Table of Duties," for example, ordered the modernization of schooling until the 1800s (Lindmark 2011). Heavily influenced by the Scottish Enlightenment, Swedish moral philosophers presented the common duties of "man" and the civic virtues as doctrines of knowing one's duties to God, the individual, and neighbors. The "Table of Duties" was founded upon a patriarchal relationship between God and mankind as a father–child relationship, in which the weak and sinful child needed education and guidance. The catechism of the "Tables" instructed how husbands, wives, children, and common people learned moral virtue and obedience to the patriarchal hierarchy of the estates. The search for perfection also harbored fears about harnessing passions and self-interest that would work against the common good.

During the early part of the 19th century, teacher preparation was an awakening—in search of perfection through enabling the teacher to profess her Christian sincerity. Teaching was an apprenticeship that consecrated one's devotion to work and to expressing Christian sincerity, in which inspiration was given priority over specific classroom teaching competencies. Teacher education was a "civilizing process" that was directed to the "soul." The teacher had to be rescued first in order to rescue the child.

The teacher of the modern school was expected to be committed to general ideals of service, to be trained scientifically, and to be professionally ambitious. The principal of the first normal school in the US (1839), Cyrus Peirce, viewed teacher education as a "calling." The school was organized as a divinity school with teachers as its "dedicated missionaries" (Pierce and Swift [1926] 1969). The curriculum was focused on recitation of content as well as music lessons. The moral character of the teacher was the object of knowledge rather than training in skills or techniques (Mattingly 1977).

The salvific themes of saving the soul were important in the social and psychological sciences at the turn of the 20th century.[10] The administration of the self, as Foucault (1979, 1989) argued, reenacted the early interest of the church in the opening of the soul for inspection, scrutiny, and regulation. European and North American sciences directed their knowledge to activate the individual application of self-watchfulness to instantiate the spiritual/moral life. The American Social Gospel movement, for example, sought to bring Christian ethics into social policy and the social sciences in the late 19th century. The ideas linked salvific themes to progress and Christian ethics. Moral redemptive concerns were merged with ideas drawn from science, social planning, and welfare policies.

The sociology related to American Progressive education brought the providentialism of cosmopolitanism into liberal political theories, science, and the project of educating. Lester Frank Ward, one of the founders of

American sociology, thought of science as a way to artificially change urban social conditions and people.[11] Change was directed to "the soul" of the citizen whose processes of reasoning would embody republican virtues. The knowledge generated by the sciences was directed as an awakening that drew previous religious sensitivities into the making of the citizen. Ward said, for example, that government progress required education to identify the processes "of acquainting every member of society more thoroughly with the special nature of the institution, and awakening him to a more vivid conception of his personal interest in its management" (1883, 243).

Whether calling those notions of awakening as "stimulus/response" (Edward L. Thorndike), "intelligent action" (John Dewey), or "adolescence" (G. Stanley Hall), the site of change in the sciences was everyday life and the soul of the child. The psychological sciences would provide the child with a higher unity of the moral good through principles of thought and action.

The soul was placed into psychological languages as the human sciences replaced moral philosophy in the 19th century (see, e.g., O'Donnell 1985). Science, for G. Stanley Hall ([1904] 1928), would change the unwashed and sinful soul in order to bring the purity of the spirit into being. The child study movement embodied a romantic desire of building the organic values of a pastoral community into an increasingly specialized and mechanized urban, industrial, scientific civilization (Ross 1972, 335–37). Hall's ([1904] 1928) studies of the adolescent were a strategy to reconcile faith and reason, Christian belief and the "Enlightenment's empiricism" in the making of an American society. The psychic development of the child's "soul" was expressed through Calvinist language of finding "the missing links" to fulfill human destiny in achieving "the beautiful, and the true social, moral and religious good."

Child psychology was a disciplining of the teacher's eye through observations of students that allowed for the quickening of moral sensibilities. Hall's *Adolescence: Its Psychology and Its Relation to Physiology, Anthropology, Sociology, Sex, Crime, Religion, and Education* ([1904] 1928) embodied new distinctions and attributes about learning, behaviors, attitudes, motivation, and personality to order the processes of change. Youth was cast as a particular kind of person who represented the moral panic about the degeneration of the future with attention on those teenagers who might fail to act in civilized and responsible ways.

While one might think that the salvific themes of the 19th century are historical relics, there are homologies of prophetic texts in contemporary research. Modern psychology celebrates its movement from the soul to the mind as the triumph of science. The concept of the "mind," however, was meant to satisfy the new scripture of science by replacing metaphysical notions (Danziger 1997; Reed 1997). Ignored, however, is how religious confessional practices were transferred to the realm of personal self-reflection and self-criticism (Gorski 1999). Previous pastoral concerns about personal salvation and redemption were tied to personal development and "fulfillment," words that signaled religious motifs but placed in secular discourses of science and rational progress.

Today, the utopic principles are embodied in contemporary social and psychological sciences. The soul is spoken today through the cognitive and affective psychologies of children's learning, motivation, and "grit" as the salvific themes of effective, successful teacher and child school practices (see, e.g., Popkewitz and Kirchgasler 2014; C. Kirchgasler 2018). Salvific themes of the future are expressed, as argued in later chapters, in the calls for reforms based on *scientific evidence, what works,* and *useful knowledge.* The salvific quality is iterated in a report of contemporary teacher education reforms about the need for teachers to embody "the soul" of the nation (National Commission on Teaching and America's Future 2003). Change is narrated as the dispositions desired in changing "the habits of mind and character appropriate for learning and embodying this identity" of the expert teacher (Grossman et al. 2009, 2060), another name but expressing "the soul" as the object of contemporary practical knowledge.

The redemptive kind of person that appears in policy, programs, and research is what is called "the lifelong learner" (Fejes and Nicoll 2007). The lifelong learner is an individual who is entrepreneurial, a decentralized citizen who is active, self-motivated, self-governing, flexible, participatory, and problem solving (for comparative discussions of child-centered, constructivist pedagogies, see Hultqvist 1998; Hunter 1994; Walkerdine 1988; on its ties to Progressive education, see Gee 1999).

This "lifelong learner" is an abstraction about a kind of person and the desire of the potentialities of a kind of person directed to reconstituting the soul. The operative metaphors of progress and redemption are no longer derived from socially collective norms, common roles, and fixed identities that organize American Progressive educational research. The reforms reconstruct the American liberal image of the participatory and collaborative teacher and child. The redemptive theme is today spoken about as the empowerment of teachers and children. The kind of person is given universal qualities that seem outside of their historical conditions: one who can solve problems, is capable of responding flexibility to the problems that have no clear set of boundaries or singular answers, and who participates in the construction of knowledge as active individuals who produce, modify, and integrate ideas.

## Redemption's "Others": Inscriptions of Exclusions and Abjections in Inclusions

If American Progressivism is examined as an event that brings to the surface particular epistemic forms rather than as the creation of institutions, there is a marked set of articulations that become visible. The different and diverse social and political movements bring into view parameters of the "homeless mind" in which science becomes the sacred knowledge. Public policy, social institutions, and change are designed through bringing rationality and efficiency to government, social institutions, and the school to organize the thought and action of the "reasonable child."

While this is more extensively discussed in chapter 6, my intent here is to describe the inscriptions of salvific and redemptive themes as desires in science. The redemptive themes of American Progressivism were directed to the Social Question of the moral disorder in the conditions and populations of urban life. The object of the theories and methods of the new sciences of the urban sociologies and psychologies of the child were to reform urban life and to change those social and cultural differences that produced the urban "deviances."[12]

The redemptive themes were related to a religious shift about poverty that earlier was bound to the English workhouse (poorhouse) tradition of saving the soul of the sinner for their moral failures to focusing on the conditions that produced the moral disorder and deviance. The settlement houses that provided a variety of social services as well as cultural and educational programs to the poor were influential in American social and educational thought and sciences. New distinctions of differences in social thought and science embodied the displacements and reinscriptions to identify the populations that called for redemptive processes, such as populational categories of the working classes and the idea of human rights that recognize different populations for inclusion.

The Social Question provided ordering and classifications of the sciences that were to undo the moral deviancies of urban populations and identify what today might be called "what works" as reforms. The sociologies and psychologies directed to education entailed programs of disciplining and training the political and social capacities of those populations placed in registers of the Social Question about deviance (Hunter 1994, 152–63). Pedagogy, the psychologies of learning, and the curriculum were moral technologies. They were not to merely inculcating obedience but also shaping personality through the child's emulation of the teacher, pastoral techniques to encourage self-knowledge and to enhance the feeling of sympathetic identification, through establishing the links between virtue, honesty, self-denial, and a purified pleasure (Rose 1989, 223).

Cultural theses about the dangerous populations of urban life, which often included eugenics, instantiated social fears of difference as biological necessities. The fear of "the urban hothouse" in G. Stanley Hall's ([1904] 1928) child studies spoke of the danger of "the losing of the soul" of the child. Hall's talk of the "urban hothouse" articulated a threat to the Enlightenment's hope of developing the providential character of the nation. The darkness represented the urban conditions and people: immigrants and racialized groups.[13]

The making of the child and family embodied salvific themes that (re)visioned not only the child and family but also the identity of the teacher. The "civilizing" practices of teacher education that appear in universities were practices to replace the unredeemed urban family and community as the primary influences in socializing children. The discourses of teacher education reconstituted the identities of urban teachers who had traditionally come from blue-collar and ethnic backgrounds. Professionalization became a tool for reshaping the lines of authority in school administration, for weeding out those of less desirable ethnic and social origins through requirements for higher education, and for instilling a sense of loyalty not to the community, but to the school principal, superintendent, and educational professoriat (Murphy 1990, 23). Professional knowledge separated urban teachers from their local community and the political alliances that carried "radical" social ideas brought from Europe. The reform projects that professionalized teacher education were intended to provide a route to occupational autonomy and status that negated familiar conceptions of teaching but also local and communal attachments (Mattingly 1977).

The expertise of the teacher becomes instantiated today through the images and narratives of the useful and practical knowledge generated in the sociologies and psychologies of the child, as discussed in later chapters. The research directed to teacher and education reform locates the soul of the teacher in personifications of professionalism and the professional.[14] The redemptive agent is the "teachers' knowledge, their professional values and commitments, and the social resources of practice" (Cohen 1995, 16).

The good intentions embodied in the reforms discussed are not to be dismissed. Rather, the discussion and analysis has been to scrutinize the concrete instantiation of redemptive culture and the comparative principles generated that simultaneously position the qualities of the child as inside and outside of reason. The salvation and redemptive narratives can be understood as disqualifying certain ways of being that do not fit the universalized norms. While learning theories and studies of child development were intended to increase individual freedom through education, the distinctions, differentiations, and divisions in the reason of the child work simultaneously to exclude and abject.

## Populism, the New Clothes of the American Jeremiad, and the Objects of Change

There is a continual populism in social and educational research. That populism occurs in science as providing salvific themes of democracy, empowerment, and participation that entail the inscription of desires that interns and encloses its agency. Populism has its affect formed through the political rhetoric of American Jeremiad and has the new clothes of science, discussed previously as in the statements about the modern university and science being "in the service of the democratic ideal." That ideal was intended to bring Enlightenment principles of reason and science into republican notions of civic virtue and the common good enacted through education and the common school. What was initially the duty of philosophy to acquire the necessary knowledge for teaching all citizens to think for themselves was replaced with the duty of science as the paradoxical arbiter of the real and the processes that enable the child to become the responsible adult in determined realities.

Populism and its foundational commitments are not at issue. What is at issue are the particular and concrete systems of reason through which these commitments are rendered into objects of observation and made observable. The sciences examined had two qualities in which the inscriptions of salvation and redemption were assembled and connected to research whose object is educational change. First was science as the telling of the basic truths of nature and society on which the progress depended. This notion of science ordered the practical knowledge in designing models of curriculum into the content of pedagogical knowledge, while eliding the translation and transformation that occur. Second, the school curriculum embodied a generalized and universal philosophical ideal of science when organizing instruction about what children do and should think in navigating everyday life. Children were to think and act "rationally." That rationality, however, was a fiction about how science orders thought, discussed in the next chapter as the translation of disciplinary fields of knowledge through the alchemy of curriculum. The object of children's problem solving organized as the psychologies of learning and teaching, for example, inscribed the rules and standards of the philosophical ideals as "the nature" of the interior of the child. That renaming did not change the object of change as "the soul."

If I move to the present, contemporary discussions about useful knowledge lose sight of the historical conditions in which the redemptive culture is productive of desires. This chapter examined how salvific and redemptive themes were assembled in the sciences as secular themes, what Scheler ([1924] 1980) erroneously posed as separated in a manner that distinguishes modernity. The salvific and redemptive themes generate principles about potentialities in the governing of the soul.

The desires of salvation and redemption are utopic visions about their potentialities as doubles of exclusions and inclusions. The paradoxes are not explicit but are embodied in how science produces cultural theses about who children are and should be—and who is not that kind of child.

Certainty/uncertainty and determinacy/indeterminacy rear their heads with salvation and redemptive themes as desires. Since the 19th century, the twin notions of science are expressive of capturing what is real and as the pedagogical processes to rationally order learning for children to use the psychological models of problem solving for assessing experience against the inscribed "real world." The redemptive theme in which agency is to be enacted, paradoxically at least for liberal political theories, is the application of that knowledge that locates individuals within the bounded structures of existent theories for achieving their potentialities and that of society.

Research, it was argued, embodies conversion processes that are not describing "what works." Practical and useful knowledge is practical as that knowledge which provides references to the system of reason in which it operates. Redemptive change joins political rationalities with those of the social sciences as the promise of the future in the present.

# 5 ◆ What Is "Really" Taught as the Problem of Research?

## The Alchemy of Teaching School Subjects

In American research related to education, a glaring assumption continually appears over time. The assumption is that school research and assessments measure children's learning of what is named as school subjects—children are learning science, mathematics, art, music, and history, among others. That presupposition travels from the 19th century formation of the modern school into today's research about the teacher, teacher education, and international assessments (see Kliebard 1986). Today, outcomes of learning come with the presumption that school subjects represent the cognitive fields on which they are named. The object of educational research is formed on this assumption. The goal of research is to identify the pedagogical knowledge useful to enable more effective teaching, efficient children's learning, and better understandings of the relation of family and community that ensures children's success.

The pervasiveness of the belief that what is assessed is what is named in school subjects has a long history expressed in contemporary programs and research as "benchmarks and curriculum standards," the label given to the content of school subjects that students are to know. Practical knowledge is the "scientific evidence" that affirms "what works" among school programs for children to access that knowledge. Teacher research reaffirms this doxa through identifying the "high-leverage practices" and "ambitious" teaching that are defined as ensuring children's learning the knowledge necessary for their future participation. The criteria of the successful teacher are given as knowing the research about the psychological understanding of children's development and learning (Tucker 2018).

While I return to benchmarks, empirical evidence, and other such research classifications in subsequent chapters, I foreshadow those discussions by paraphrasing a question raised in the first chapter, "What if this faith in research identifying the knowledge useful for teaching of school subjects is a false prophet?" In particular, I ask: "What if the namesake given to school subjects is a chimera, a beautiful illusion built historically on flawed assumptions?" "What if what is measured in the curriculum is not for understanding science, mathematics, or music, but something else?" If the objects of practical research are a beautiful illusion built on historically faulty assumptions, what is the object and desires of practical research?

This chapter historically explores this assumption about what is taught through the analogy to the Medieval alchemies. The school curriculum, like Medieval alchemies, are translation instruments to turn the cognitive disciplines and expressive arts into school practices. To say that schooling involves alchemies and translations is not to say these are necessarily bad. The pedagogical reworking of disciplinary knowledge into school subjects is necessary as children are not physicists, mathematicians, or professional artists. *What is at stake, however, is not the existence of alchemies but the rules and standards of the transformations/translations into the curriculum.*

I argue that modern school subjects are inventions concerned with social and cultural differences and moral disorder, and not with learning art, mathematics, science, or music. The first section historically explores the idea of the alchemy of school subjects as making kinds of people. With the salvation themes about preparing the child for the future society, the object of the school curriculum is ordering conduct that connects daily life with the norms and values of collective belonging. The second section discusses the educational psychologies as alchemic tools of translation. The psychologies are concerned with the interior of the child and the struggling for the soul. To develop a continual theme from prior chapters, the third section explores the alchemy of the curriculum that travels in the sciences of children's learning school subjects as cultural theories of differences, expressed as the urban Social Question at the turn of the 20th century. The final section turns to the inscriptions of desires and potentialities generated in research about school subjects. The objectifications of the child are placed in a temporal ordering of the arrow of time and the production of differences in the post–World War II sciences of the curriculum and pedagogy. The chapter concludes by asking what is "really" taught and measured as the practical knowledge of the research on teaching and learning. The alchemic qualities of the curriculum provide a background for the subsequent chapters in the movements from American Progressivism, post–World War II educational sciences, and contemporary international student performance assessments and teacher education research. In each historical instance, the practical knowledge of the sciences of the school pedagogy takes for granted the translation tools of the curriculum in its research.

## The Alchemy: Curriculum as Translations

The complexities of the movements and translations of disciplinary practices into the school can be thought of as alchemical processes. The sixteenth- and seventeenth-century alchemists and occult practitioners attempted to turn base metals into pure gold through the catalyst of the Philosopher's Stone in Medieval Europe, the ultimate knowledge from which to understand the perfection by which God produced the world. Like an alchemy, the curriculum is today's philosopher's stone, talked about as social improvement and individuals' reaching their potential (Popkewitz 2004, 2008).

The practices of the sciences, mathematics, music, and art exist within particular social and institutional spaces that are fundamentally different. Scientific fields, such as physics, biology, and sociology, have particular epistemic machineries, routines, and cultural and social patterns in the production of knowledge (see, e.g., Knorr Cetina 1999). The school curriculum combines with the psychologies of education as translation devices that displace these disciplinary spaces and remake them into identifiable territorial coordinates connected to the school.

### The Translation Work for School "Content Knowledge"

The travels of disciplinary knowledge into the modern, mass school require work, but that work is designed for tasks different from those of being a scientist or an artist. Entering the spaces of the school entails new sets of categories and distinctions to visualize science or mathematics as a school subject. This visualization is never merely a copy of the original. No good scientist, for example, would break the tasks of the laboratory into cognitive knowledge, skills, and affect—as happens when the laboratory travels into curricular benchmarks that represent standards to achieve in teaching science, for example. To talk about children's learning school subjects is to engage in a range of theories, stories, and narratives that connect with the organization of time and space that is peculiar to schools and quite different from the practices in disciplinary fields.

This translation work is like a moving truck filled with photographs as snapshots of how a disciplinary field "looks." The photographs serve as the artifacts that once existed in the architectural spaces that locate the laboratories, disciplinary machinery, and offices of physics or biology, for example. On the way to the new buildings related to schools, there is a lot of navigation and reimagining that occurs in crossing different streets and the meeting of different intersections, including schools of education, school textbooks, learning psychologies, and even state and local educational rules for operating and assessing schools.

The alchemy works at the interstices of curriculum and pedagogy to enact practices of how children are to know as the objects of the translations. While analytically seemingly distinct, the curriculum creates "modeling" principles configured in the architectural spaces of schools and in the administrative categories and time dimensions of classroom practices. These principles form as the origin of educational research examined in section 3.

The work of translating disciplinary fields for use in the different space of schooling is illustrated in the American *Next Generation Science Standards. For State, By States.*[1] The standards direct attention to organizing the content statements of four different sciences for school instruction. The content knowledge is defined as being specific to each of the sciences, such as "to investigate and compare the motion of objects." That particular content, however, is configured through "crosscutting concepts" among disciplines. The crosscutting concepts bring the propositions and generalizations of science into pedagogical thinking as universal distinctions and categories for organizing children's "learning."

The crosscutting of different scientific machineries is revisioned with the intentionalities of psychologies created for administering educational conduct. The *Next Generation Science Standards*, for example, are statements about learning to "develop an in-depth understanding of content and develop key skills" of science. The psychological distinctions revision the concepts of science to be part of the ordering of the conduct of children's "communication, collaboration, inquiry, problem solving, and flexibility."

To return to the analogy of a recipe, the statements about "in-depth understanding" revision the original cognitive field of knowledge into a grid of "ingredients" oriented to principles about the conduct of conduct. The recipe for the translation and transformation of the cognitive disciplines and arts are cultural and social practices in which the curriculum knowledge is treated as stable edifices, abstracted out of their spaces of realization. This movement into the space of schooling can be thought of as a process of deterritorializing the social and cultural practices of science, for example, and the reterritorializing into cultural spaces of schooling. These latter spaces are where the content performs as generating cultural theses about childhood, growth, and development that have little to do with the practices of science.[2]

Statements that appear as the content of "scientific knowledge" are assembled as creative acts that do not replicate its original disciplinary qualities that entail continual explorations, debate, and revisions. The "crosscutting" concepts of the *Next Generation Science Standards* are abstractions for children's learning, such as explaining volcanic eruptions or the notational practices in reading music. The statements of the curriculum are less about learning science than about making kinds of people. Scientific literacy across international textbooks, for example, has no commonality regarding what constitutes "literacy" (McEneaney 2003b). The construction of scientific literacy is directed to cultural theses about the citizen of the nation.

The translation that occurs in the school curriculum is often defined as the question asked by Herbert Spencer of "What knowledge is of most worth?" (see Popkewitz 1998). This Spencerian question directs attention to the selection, organization, and evaluation of school knowledge. It is important to recognize that the Spencerian question in the school curriculum is a social and political question about what a child is to be as a citizen, worker, parent, and member of a community. It is not about what science and mathematics are!

The Spencerian question performs to deterritorialize and reterritorialize disciplinary practices. The school curriculum and research focuses on the selection of disciplinary "photos" that serve as representations. The representations are classified as the "content" knowledge or bodies of knowledge that children should know.

The translations entail the analytical distinctions between "content" and "methods" that create the Cartesian dualism in the curriculum models. The theories, concepts, generalizations, and propositions taken from disciplinary fields are objectifications in the curriculum, defined as realities (e.g., how gravity affects a falling body or how the American Civil War reunited a divided nation). The representations of society, populations, and individuals given in studies of the natural and social sciences, for example, inscribe Cartesian logic in ordering and classifying the representations of human and natural conditions. The representations are calculated as passing through the consciousness of the student to apprehend the universal qualities of human nature and its differences. The objectifications about nature and populations become the origin of reflection and change, given as ontological "facts" about people and society.

The objectification in the curriculum becomes "the realities" to order experience as an encounter of relating the self and the social.

### The Translation Work as Conversions to Psychology

Psychology gives visualization to what knowledge to learn in school subjects; that is, the learning sciences translate disciplinary fields into modes of living, what earlier was expressed in science education standards as students' "communication, collaboration, inquiry, problem solving, and flexibility." The social and psychological distinctions express desired modes of living of students whose conduct "will serve them throughout their educational and professional lives."[3] The distinctions are not those of the practices of science.

This realizing of potentialities is called children's use of the categories and propositions for modeling their everyday life. The empirical world is thought of as captured through the methods that apply concepts and generalizations to order and assess the world. Empirical evidence verifies the facts as the data that testifies to the truthfulness or the falsity of statements. When contemporary science education is examined internationally, problem solving is the method used to learn the majesty of the procedures and styles of arguments as the expertise to apply to daily life (McEneaney 2003a). The knowledge of science is taken as authoritative for children to learn the majesty of science for managing the natural world and their own worlds—a crystallization of knowledge that has very different qualities from those of the working of the sciences.

The folding of disciplinary knowledge into psychology brings a new intentionality to school practices. Research identifies the psychological characteristics (e.g., motivation) that enable the child to identify disciplinary representations accurately as narratives that tell about people, events, and nature. The goal of research on teaching is to identify methods as retrieval practices about the true and the real, and to identify the dispositions and "habits of the mind" that govern what is classified as "the effective teacher," a particular kind of person discussed in chapter 9.

The reflective practices generated about the methods of teaching are not generic or about pure thought. The reflection is spatially bound and organized by the social/psychological distinctions talked about as "firsthand exploration and investigation and inquiry/process skills" (National Science Teachers Association 2002, 4). Concepts to be learned become the object of instruction, with children's "readiness" and "age-appropriate learning," for example, as the measures of how children are successfully performing the tasks of learning.

Methods of learning are the alchemic processes to access and enable the internalization and utilization of the concepts and generalizations. Concepts, generalizations, and the axioms of disciplinary knowledge are made into analytical "things" or "entities" that are given access through social and learning psychologies. Methods appear as distinct from the representations given as the curriculum content. Learning is the ordering, classifying, and codifying of the events of the world through the practices and representations given in the curriculum. Learning sciences operationalize the abstractions in the curriculum that are expressed as salvation themes: to enable the child to realize the potentialities in daily life.

## The Alchemy and the Sightless Sight

The distinctions and differentiations in pedagogy are not just about finding the best ways to teach. The epistemological principles that translate school subjects embody cultural theses about how to "see," think, and act. The concepts and classifications of the cognitive disciplines enter into the theories, programs, stories, and imagination of school to order thought and have a material existence. School subjects in the modern school were connected in sociologies and psychologies as distinctions that "act" in generating principles about how childhood, family, and community are seen, but also the degrees of freedom in which people are to "see" and act themselves (Popkewitz [1987] 2018b).

The materiality of the alchemy in ordering conduct can be explored in the teaching of Euclidean geometry in mathematics education (see

Andrade-Molina and Valero 2015). Temporal and ontological distinctions of Euclidean space direct children to use its spatialization to model and assess their world. Learning Euclidean geometry functions as a rationality to order, understand, and see life as a two-dimensional space that is objectified as outside of experience and subjectivity. This space for subjectification is a flat and transcendental conception of the complexities of contemporary life.

The placing of one's self in the two-dimensional space of Euclidean geometry inscribes *"the eye" of a sightless body*, as argued by Andrade-Molina and Valero (2015). That "eye" entails a paradox of a certain form of knowing and the objects possible to "see."

The *sightless body* becomes, in effect, sight itself as the translation principles of the curriculum reterritorialize the knowledge through which the self is to understand and makes possible what is seen and felt as experience. For example, the psychological principles of child studies that are inscribed in the formation of art education particularized ways of seeing children's drawing in relation to notions of child growth and development (Martins 2014, 2015, 2017, 2018). Analyses of children's art and drawings were not about art per se, but about a way of reasoning about who the child is and how they might develop in the school. The image of the developing child organized the categories of drawing as the process of children making art that was not about art. The drawing was about the child's processes of "finding" the inner qualities that allow for normal development. "Finding" the child through art was related to cultural distinctions about normal and abnormal development that differentiated what was and was not "art."

Historically, the school as the disciplining and ordering of conduct is not a surprising observation. Schooling and its research, as developed in subsequent chapters, historically connects the scope and aspirations of public powers with the personal and subjective capacities of individuals. Schools have long been places to make children into kinds of adults—kinds of people and society that would not be if children do not attend schools. Education was central in the cultural production of the kind of individual necessary for governing and government. Prior to the modern school and its pedagogical sciences, the education in historical and geographical skills in the German-speaking Habsburg Empire's royal crown lands in the latter part of the 18th century were affective practices. The goal of instruction was to create an affiliation with "the fatherland" and the shaping of "righteous Christians" (Winandy 2019, 88).

The pedagogical knowledge in teacher education are formed with the distinctions and classifications generated through the alchemy of school subjects. With the introduction of "normal schools" in the middle of the 19th century, the professionalization of the teacher was concerned with "awakening" the moral character, replacing the prior emphasis on training in communication skills and the standard techniques of teaching (Lee 2019; Mattingly 1975). School subjects were reasoned about as the teacher learning about the child through organizing classroom lessons and observing the child through the new psychologies of child development. The object of observation was to change the modes of living and the internal qualities of the child, later spoken about as the appropriate attitudes, motivation, and "civic" virtues to participate in society (for a historical discussion, see Popkewitz [1987] 2018b; and for contemporary revisioning, Popkewitz and Kirchgasler 2014).

The translation technologies of the curriculum were a practice of the ordering of conduct in the disciplining of the body and mind. While I explore school subjects related to science, mathematics, and the arts below, physical education in multiple societies became a school subject through narratives about the regulation of citizens in forming an efficient, healthy, and productive society. Physical education acts to discipline children and their bodies. Sport activities and the movement of bodies in Brazilian schools, for example, embody cultural norms that simultaneously create social stability and progress, particularly through the work of teachers (Ilha 2017).

As expressed earlier, what is important in the alchemy is not that there is one. What is important is how alchemies presuppose and (re)visualize the ontological objects of social and educational research. The alchemical presuppositions produce the object of practical knowledge in research to be making of different kinds of people. That object of practical knowledge elides the paradoxes of its system of reasoning about the potentialities of people and society. The salvation narratives, for example, travel within seemingly neutral terms about providing effective strategies for making science accessible and relevant for various racial and immigrant groups (see C. Kirchgasler 2018). The salvation themes are rendered invisible through the focus on processes as the enactments of teacher effectiveness. Occluded are the alchemic practices that inscribe cultural theses and differences in the making of people.

The site of the "sightless body" embodied in the alchemy, as I argue in following chapters, is part of the folding and refolding of historical lines that occupy contemporary research. Research talks about children's learning and teacher effectiveness but the object of change is making people and "the soul." In one sense, this object is not so hidden. In an important call for reforming teacher education, it is argued that teachers "need to understand the person, the spirit, of every child and find a way to nurture that spirit" (Darling-Hammond 2006, 310). The principles of "spirit" direct attention to psychological distinctions between capabilities and abilities that, I argue, differentiate and divide along cultural criteria of moral order/disorder (Popkewitz 2008).

## Psychology as Translator, the Soul as the Pedagogical Object

When talking about school "subjects," there are two overlapping meanings in the work of the alchemy. One meaning is about the translation of external knowledge systems into school subjects—the content selected, organized, and assessed about what children are to know. The other meaning of school subjects is concerned with how the curriculum produces "the reason" for seeing the child as subject and object in making "reasonable people." That reasonable person is articulated with different psychological names, but the qualities referred to are those of the "soul." The soul refers to qualities of the interior of the child that are observed and administered by pedagogical practices and the pedagogical sciences.

Psychology is the magisterial knowledge of the modern school curriculum. The psychologies that inhabit educational spaces are edifices of different assemblages. The assemblages in the psychologies of education are inventions to give direction to questions of moral development. The soul is the object of "the practical knowledge" for learning school subjects. Along with the concern for moral development and "the soul" is the Cartesian logic that travels in curriculum models as the particular kind of analytics for the translations of disciplinary knowledge.

If I return to the prior discussion of the relation of Spencerian questions in curriculum models, there is a vacated space in research on pedagogical knowledge and psychology. It is vacated in the sense that names given for school subjects are taken as the material substance to effect what is done and assessed as "learning" science, mathematics, and so on. Elided is any exploration of what science, mathematics, or music are as fields of social practices and the integrity of the translation models in relation to the school alchemy.

The vacated spaces are illustrated through Jerome Bruner's *The Process of Education* (1960), a canonical text of the American New Curriculum reforms of the post–World War II era. The text summarizes a meeting about school reform sponsored by the American National Science Foundation that was attended by scientists, social scientists, and educators at Woods Hole, a leading scientific institution. Other than identifying the participants as famous scientists and mathematicians, *The Process of Education* entails statements about the school curriculum related to the pedagogical models to enact teaching that have been freed from any thinking about science and the social sciences as fields of knowledge. The discussion focuses on the conduct of instruction, the modes of thinking and acting "rationally" that were related to generalized philosophical characteristics of who the child should be. The various scientific and mathematic fields of knowledge are reduced in the text to a singular unified field of the concepts, generalizations, and epistemic ordering of the processes of schooling. That unification and universalizing were distinctions organized through criteria of cognitive psychology. Science is folded into and given meaning as the property of learning theories to enable the interiorizing of what is seen as the representational content.

As argued earlier, the sciences of schooling were designed as technologies to act on the spirit and the body of children and the young (Ó 2003). The emergence of scientific psychologies of the curriculum in the 19th century (the same moment when mass schooling was institutionalized in the republics that dotted Europe and the Americas) was tied to questions about moral development and making of the "good" citizen. The theological interest of the early Church in rescuing the soul, discussed earlier, was (re)visioned, reassembled, and connected in pedagogy as the strategy of ordering personal self-reflection, self-criticism, and the inner self or "soul" that guided the moral development.[4] The object of the educational psychologies are questions of moral order linked to the conduct of the child that, in effect, becomes a trilogy about change that includes family and "community," joining individuality with norms of collective belonging and the social (see, e.g., Rose 1989; Cohen-Cole 2014).

Questions of the psychologies of children's learning and the school curriculum become interrelated. If I return to the idea of adolescence that appeared in the child studies of G. Stanley Hall ([1893] 1924), this notion of childhood is a fabrication, a fiction and a manufacturing of the child. Adolescence was a way to think about childhood as a transition to adulthood. It was directed to the different populations of children and their families who were entering the urban common school during the decades around the turn of the 20th century. Adolescence in child psychology gave focus to designing the soul of child, the family, and the community of the urban Eastern and Southern European immigrants and African Americans who migrated from the South at the turn of the century (Bloch et al. 2003).[5]

While Hall did talk about the child's soul, contemporary psychology's language is about the mind, development, and growth. But the object remains the interest in governing the soul through distinctions about children's capabilities, sensitivities, and dispositions as qualities to administer and change. Stripped of the affect and the moral certitude in contemporary reforms, changing the teachers' "habits of the mind," the disposition of "nurturing" teacher activists, and "weeding out" bad teachers (see chapter 9) does not erase the focus on the interiority of the teacher and child: the interior that goes under the name of the "soul."

The curriculum principles of the alchemy connected to research make their object the soul of the child, but they are also about differences—the desires of who the child is and should be are also about the qualities and characteristics of the child who does not "fit," the child who is abjected from the designed cultural spaces. The alchemic principles about kinds of people and differences become the performative object of practical and useful knowledge explored in subsequent chapters about educational research.

## The Alchemy and "the Social Question" of Urban Difference

I began the chapter with thinking about the school curriculum as analogous to alchemy, revisioning disciplinary practices into particular images, words, ideas, and experiences recalculated through psychologies of learning, children's motivation, and problem solving.

At this point, I turn to the recognition and enactment of the school curriculum as embodying principles that produce a continuum of values about normalcy and pathology. The pedagogical distinctions and pedagogical sciences produce selective processes that differentiate and divide the qualities and characteristics of children as social and cultural capabilities. Paz (2017), for example, argues that the idea of genius in the middle of the nineteenth century was about the student's soul and body. The gifted (or creative) child had a special soul, the result of a gift—from either heaven or earth. For instance, Portuguese music education focused on the students' relationship with time and space to convey social values as psychology transferred religious confessional practices to the realm of personal self-reflection and self-criticism. Such values were the dispositions of studying, of acquiring knowledge that linked individuality with participatory norms in the new republican form of governing.

The distinctions and differences were generated in a comparative style of reasoning about people. This production of differences was articulated in the Social Question, Protestant reforms on both sides of the Atlantic that were concerned with urban poverty in, for example, American Progressive education (chapter 6). Crossing institutional contexts and embedded in the theories and methods of the social sciences were Protestant salvific and redemptive themes about intervention in social life to mitigate the economic dislocations and the moral disorder associated with urbanization and industrialization (Rodgers 1998).

American Progressive education, the Social Question, and research connected with the formations of school subjects that embodied a paradox. The paradox is the double gestures of the Social Question. There was the gesture of the hope of making productive citizens among the newly arrived immigrants and African Americans in northern cities. The social sciences were to liberate urban populations from existing social conditions through producing self-managed and responsible urban children, families, and "communities" (Popkewitz 2008). That gesture of hope simultaneously generated the gesture that expressed fears about the populations that threaten that hope. While I discuss this more fully in the next chapter, suffice to say here that new distinctions appear to differentiate kinds of people through the new social and psychological sciences.

The mapping of knowledge, differences, and the Social Question in the modern, common school did not only occur in the US. The teaching of modern English literature in British mass schooling, for example, emerged through two different historical movements that differentiated themselves from the prior educative "cultivating" aspects of writing or reading (Hunter 1988). First was the teaching of English literature for the public administration of social problems. Mass schooling was opened to the "inarticulate and illiterate" child of the working classes. English literature was taught to develop a cosmopolitan outlook within the hierarchy of the existing social structure. Second, the subject of English was related to the governmental provisions for social welfare. The narrative structures and ethical messages of literary texts were to help the reader become the moral agent who embodied cosmopolitan values and its notions of "civility." The purpose of making the literature relevant to the everyday experiences of working-class children was to create affective dimensions to the rules and standards for moral conduct that the child would practice in daily life.

The sciences embodied theories and technologies concerned with the measurement of differences in the nature of people. The measurement of differences in scientific ability, for example, occurred at the moment when the American high school science became stratified into distinct levels (K. Kirchgasler 2017). Related to social Darwinism and Lamarckian notions of inherited differences and race, pedagogical categories in the general science movement during the 1920s measured scientific ability through social science techniques brought into psychology, such as the developmental scale, the standardized test, and the home survey. The psychologies adapted instruction for seeing children as belonging to different populations. Psychometric tests scaled differences along a continuum of values constituted as norms differentiating the good, rational American citizen from children seen as belonging to populations with "unscientific minds." The translations of science into psychological processes positioned children in developmental scales that ordered racial and ethnic distinctions alongside stages of mental maturity.

If I juxtapose the formation of science to music education, they appear to be subjects that express different priorities about learning and knowledge—one that gives priority to the aesthetics of appreciation and performance as being different from the striving for order in the worlds given in mathematics and science. Music education enters into the world of schooling, however, with homologous principles about cultural distinctions and differences in science education. Introduced in the 1830s, American music curriculum marked fears of moral decay and degeneration, with mass education civilizing the child (Gustafson 2009). Horace Mann's 1844 "Report to the Boston School Committee" supported vocal instruction classes as a practice in which the harmony of song was the model for the child's own self-regulation in society. Vocal instruction provided regimens to stimulate the circulation that would serve to prevent poor health among urban populations. The singing of proper songs would regulate the moral conditions of urban life with a "higher" calling related to the nation and eliminate the emotionalism of taverns and revival meetings.

Music appreciation joined vocal instruction in the curriculum by the beginning of the 20th century as a civilizing practice. Physiological psychology about the proper amount of stimulation for the brain and body was coupled with notions of musical aesthetics, religious beliefs, and civic virtue. Singing, for example, gave expression to the home life of industriousness and patriotism that was set against racial stereotypes of Blacks and immigrants. Minstrelsy, a satiric version of Black music and spirituals, was contrasted with the complexity of the music of European "civilization." A medical expert in the 1920s, employed by the Philadelphia High School for Girls, described jazz as causing disease in young girls and society as a whole. Choral music in Portuguese education was considered "hygienically, intellectually, morally and disciplinarily" beneficial to the child's health (Paz 2017, 6).

Psychology ordered the selection and organization of music education. Psychometric tests were developed to differentiate musical ability in the 1920s. The scaling of musical response in the classroom classified listening habits with age-appropriate behavior. A scale compared immature or primitive human development with that of a fully endowed capacity that corresponded to race and nationality. The progression of musical knowledge outlined in teacher manuals calculated music as a form of psychometrics associated with psychoacoustics. The "attentive listener" embodied the cosmopolitan values of the civilized life. That child was contrasted with the distracted listener. Carl Seashore, a psychology researcher, claimed that a full 10 percent of children tested for musical talent were unfit for musical appreciation. In teaching manuals, the child who did not learn to listen to the music in a particular way was classified as "distracted," a determinate category bound to moral and social distinctions about the child as a drifter, a name caller, a gang joiner, a juvenile offender, a joke maker, or a potential religious fanatic, someone with acute emotional stress and an intense interest in sex.

The assembly of psychology with the curriculum articulated salvific themes that embodied desires about the double qualities of potentialities. The desires embodied in the sociological, economic, and psychological research are invoked as dispositions of the potentiality of a child to become *creative*, *innovative*, and *independent*. The distinctions refer to universal properties of the mind as potentialities to be actualized. The universal qualities, however, are not universal and transcendent of time/space. The distinctions are bound to a particular style of reasoning that engendered double gestures in theories of learning, communication, and differences that order the pedagogical practices (see, e.g., Valero 2017).

## School Subjects and Desires of Different Kinds of People

The alchemy, I have argued, generates desires about the potentialities that school research is to actualize. These potentialities have been explored as double gestures: the hope of the child who becomes the good citizen is intertwined with the fears about the child who does not embody "the reasonableness" of the good citizen. The potentialities to-be and the potentialities not-to-be coexist and are experienced within the same statements about the child, family, and communities in the spaces of the school curriculum and its research.

The double of potentialities are inscribed in the alchemy of the school curriculum and research as projections of the arrow of time. Mathematics education reform and research in the post–World War II years, for example, asserted that mathematics was the "Queen and Servant of the sciences" (School Mathematics Study Group 1963, 7). The mathematically able child in curriculum research and reforms embodied redemptive discourses about being prepared for "democracy" in uncertain futures (Yolcu and Popkewitz 2018). The uncertain future, however, had a clear temporal sequence that had little to do with being mathematically able. Instead, it reflected generalized cultural principles about immoral conduct. Learning mathematics would enable children to get a good job, make rational choices, and contribute to society's well-being.

Mathematics was given as integral to the scientific production of technological, economic, and social progress (Diaz 2017; also, Valero 2017). Learning mathematics and science was given as that of pure rationalities whose objectivity and detachment transcended social and political arenas; and, thus, they could be technically applied for modeling, calculating, and predicting the unknown.

The curriculum for teaching school subjects was to design particular kinds of people—coordinating and activating double gestures and differences. Diaz (2017) explores, for example, how the seemingly simple and innocuous mathematics equal sign (=) in the school curriculum became part of the discourses connected with political theories of "equivalence." The actual principles generated in school mathematics, however, were fabrications that embodied cultural theses about people and differences. Contemporary curriculum reforms and its research give attention to the general cultural dispositions of the child, such as problem solving, collaboration, and innovation, and being logical, creative, independent, self-sufficient, responsible, and innovative. The qualities and characteristics give reference to ordering the proper and improper modes of life whose dispositions are about the potentialities of "the good citizen" and about the child who is different, unequal, and does not possess collaborative or self-sufficient modes of living.

Pedagogical discourses and research focused on children "possessing mathematics" and "doing mathematics" are not only about changing the child but also are desires that leach into a trilogy as the object of change—the child connected with what family and society to secure the social and moral order.

The pursuit of a life was a desire about potentialities that inscribed differences. The differences were embodied in the phrase "all children" to indicate the concern for equality. The hope in "mathematics for all," for example, is to address social problems, technological advancement, social inclusion, and economic growth. This hope is taken as a "tool of modern life" (College Entrance Examination Board, cited in Diaz 2017, 29).

The paradox of invoking "all" is the unity constitutive of the continuum of value between the normal and pathological. "All children" functions as a pivot point to distinguish two kinds of human beings in the standards and research concerned with school change: those who have all the cosmopolitan capabilities to learn math and their disadvantaged others. The qualities and characteristics of "all children" become the criteria from which differences in kinds of person are recognized and divisions inscribed, such as, or not, problem solving, rational thinking, and collaborating.

This production of difference in the unity of "all children" today is defined as the social commitment to correct social wrongs. Notions of ability and differences travel into present-day science education reforms and research, for example, to adapt science instruction for diverse subgroups. The adaption produces new distinctions and exclusions to recognize diversity. In the 1920, differences were expressed as

> the science teacher of today [must] realize that his place in the democracy is that of bringing this unassimilated material into at least as close harmony with the original stock of the nation as it is possible to do. (George W. Hunter, *General Science Quarterly* [1922]: 526, as cited in K. Kirchgasler 2017, 91)

Today, differences are given new distinctions:

In America, it should be possible, even essential, to elevate the achievement of low-performing at-risk groups while simultaneously lifting the ceiling of achievement for our future innovators. (National Science Board [2010], referenced in *Next Generation Science Standards*, 2013, cited in K. Kirchgasler 2017, 91)

The distinctions are not only about language. The distinctions are affective, mobilizing good intentions that produce their own impossibilities. *Efforts to create equality are produced through a reasoning of inequality.* The categories to differentiate "all" children from "others" are cultural inscriptions that simultaneously recognize differences as the need to include. That recognition, however, is instantiated within a continuum of value that differentiates the normal and the pathological. The latter are pathologies that threaten the unspoken normalcy given in the determinant category of "all"—those who are not "all" and classified as different—"disadvantaged," and the child left behind.

## What Is "Really" Taught? Alchemy, Making Kinds of People, and Practical Research

I began this chapter with thinking about school subjects as an alchemy. The alchemy is the translation practices that operate as the a priori school subject knowledge that the codifications and standardizations of measurement are developed to form the objects of change in practical research. While the names of school subjects are given as the substance of research, the principles generated as the objects of change are something different. The principles generated as the curriculum models intersect with pedagogical practices are about the different potentialities of people. These principles about differences become the origin of research and the unexamined object of practical and useful knowledge about children's achievement in science, music, art, and mathematics education.

The alchemy entailed the connection of two different translation principles assembled in research. One is that translations into the objects of research entail the grid of practices that form the modern curriculum at the intersection of a Cartesian logic about the representations and identities of the objects of the world. The curriculum practices objectify science as particular forms of knowledge separate from methods and cultures of science. The analytical separation of knowledge/content from methods in the curriculum ignores how "facts" and "data" are produced through the intersection of the measurement systems applied, the theories or style of reasoning possible, and the cultural fields that make certain modes of thought (im)possible. Analytical reifications in the sciences act to orient experience and the objects of change as the potentialities that inscribe differences in making of kinds of people. The making of people and differences is, paradoxically, the object of practical, useful knowledge.

The second principle is the connection of Cartesian logic with psychologies of the child as the social technology through which practical knowledge is ordered. Psychology is the magisterial knowledge of the curriculum. Psychology as the arbiter of what counts in American research is evident when one looks at US national and state curriculum standards in music and mathematics. When compared, what would seem to be differences melt away (Popkewitz and Gustafson 2002). The curriculum standards are psychological: they are about the child's ability to think (as in informed decision making or problem solving), to develop skills in communication (as in defending an argument, working effectively in groups), to produce quality work (as in acquiring and using information), and to link individuality with collective belonging or "community" (as in recognizing and acting on responsibilities as a citizen). Differences are thus in the degree of psychological distinctions.

The rules and standards of children's modes of reflection and action are calculation of the "soul." It is the psychological distinctions and differentiations that connect with sociologies of the child and family that are continually explored in the book.

I turn finally to the commitment of research embodied in the pursuit of practical knowledge—that is, the hope of the social and psychological sciences as a knowledge that enables a more progressive, just, and equitable world, and, with that hope, are salvation themes about the agency of the individual that has historical homologies with Enlightenment anticipation of creating freedom and liberty.[6] The twin purposes of social change and human agency move across ideological spectrums in the sciences of liberal societies; yet, as this book interrogates, the concrete enactments of good intentions to generate possibilities for transformation create their own impossibilities.

The salvific and redemptive discourses (re)vision the American Jeremiad. The Social Question of inequality in schools is brought into the objectifications of social theories of differences as the object of change. The objectifications appear as the political struggle of the teacher to regain the voices of those disenfranchised. That loss regained and given legitimates the teacher's participatory presence. Equity is defined through inequality, giving an authentic voice to those children, parents, and community members who have been excluded from the decision-making processes of schools.

But the recognition of differences reinscribes differences. A phrase such as "to recover their own voices" assumes something natural to a group's expression and thus as outside of the history in which the distinctions of its objectifications are formed. Yet the naturalizing of the voice of "others" is a policing of the boundaries that produce the partitions of difference. The good intentions of participation and problem solving (even when the word "democracy" is tacked on) inscribe particular dispositions and sensitivities whose naturalness and normalcy is produced through the objectifications and comparativeness inscribed in "reasonable" actions. This normalization is not necessarily spoken about but is silently positioned through the grid of distinctions and divisions deployed, such as those which differentiate the children of rural and urban education from "others" (Popkewitz 2017b).

Paying attention to the paradoxes of the reason of practical research and the alchemy does not mean foregoing the social commitments expressed. It means tracing the connections that form the enactments through social epistemology. The historicizing is to examine the particular assemblages as they historically activate and articulate the objects of change. The notion of agency, central from the Enlightenment to contemporary research, is today given expression through "seeing" people as problem solvers and lifelong learners and correcting social wrongs through concepts that articulate notions of voice, indigeneity, and empowerment. These distinctions bring forth an affect related to the contours of the cosmopolitism of the European (and North American) Enlightenments[7] in which human reason is the site for guiding change and bringing intentionality and purpose into actuality.

Yet ignored in this notion of agency performed in the research is the historical grid that interns and encloses their enactments. These grids are not merely about describing and explaining. They produce intentions and purpose through connecting the notion of human agency to principles of representations and identities, "the arrow of time," and desires as potentialities of differences. The reason of research paradoxically interns and encloses agency as the production of differences.

The following section gives greater depth and nuance to the connections and erasures of the alchemy as historical lines in the forming of the object of practical and useful knowledge of research. The section explores particular historical events in which the social and psychological sciences have generated principles about changing the everyday modes of living in American Progressivism, post–World II educational sciences mobilized to change schools, and contemporary international assessments of student performance and teacher effectiveness and teacher education research. Explored in each of these historical events are the relation of the alchemy to salvific and redemptive themes, desires about the potentialities of what children are to be, and also what is excluded as different and abject from those cultural spaces. Practical and useful knowledge, I will argue, is embodied in these objects of desires and exclusions.

I can only suggest at this point but I will explore in the last chapter that different approach to human agency and change in research might be possible without erasing its social commitments. But there are no guarantees.

# Section 3 • Coming to the Present

## Alchemies, Desires, and the Production of Differences in American Practical Research

The previous section examined the *uneven* historical lines or flows that rendered the object of science as changing everyday life and people. The prior discussion concerned different historical lines in generating the principles of reason related to sciences about change. These principles related to the idea of human agency, and the ordering of time (history) into sequences of development and desires about human potentialities as comparative practices of differences and divisions. These principles are explored in this section through the specific analyses of different historical moments in the social and education sciences.

The four chapters give attention to specific and shifting terrains of research oriented to changing everyday life and people that is rearticulated and assembled to evoke today a knowledge that is practical and useful for change. The four chapters examine turn-of-the-20th-century American Progressivism; the 1960s War on Poverty school research, where science was defined as "problem solving" that combined program development (R&D); the OECD's recent Programme for International Student Assessment (PISA); and contemporary teacher education research. Each is treated as singular events that produce new surfaces in the working of reason in the making of people.

Of importance are epistemic shifts from the turn-of-the-20th-century sciences to the inscription of theories of systems analysis and cybernetics brought into postwar educational research. Systems analysis combines with other principles to shape and fashion the borders that define objects to know and act on. Examined as well are how principles of systems theory and cybernetics are (re)visioned in the cultural spaces generated at the turn of the 21st century in the macrostatistical analyses of international assessments and the micro-classroom observations of teacher education research.

In particular, the chapters explore historically the different grids of principles that form in the sciences to instantiate cultural theses about the responsibilities, modes of living, and dispositions of kinds of people. The chapters examine how these principles about people are not merely about governing the present, but embody desires about potentialities to be enacted through the practical knowledge of research. Further explored are the affective qualities generated as new technologies of science work to mobilize change. These technologies entail shifts from expressing moral agendas through theories about society and people to the inscription of numbers and algorithms that increasingly functions as political theology. Finally, the chapters continue the exploration of the manner in which practical research instantiates a comparative style of reason. Double gestures are generated to differentiate kinds of people whose potentialities are placed outside and abjected to unlivable spaces—a style of reasoning whose epistemic forms make possible eugenics and racializing.

# 6 ♦ American Progressivism

## Practical Sciences as Desires to Actualize the Future

This chapter brings the prior historical discussions about science, change, and desires into a conversation with the sciences related to American Progressive education at the turn of the 20th century. American Progressivism is not used normatively but as a reference to diverse social movements that formed the American welfare state. Progressivism, at one level of analysis, is an icon used by historians to focus on the new social, economic, and the state arrangements—arrangements that included the emergence of the common American Progressive school. The new social and psychological sciences were given institutional "homes" in the new scientific universities concerned with production of knowledge.

The chapter, however, is less interested in the institutional qualities of Progressivism than it is in Progressivism as a historical event that explores the social epistemology inscribed in the sciences organized in the new common Progressive school. My concern is with the particular rules and standards of reason that shaped and fashioned the conflict and debates around which the school and other social movements were formed (Popkewitz 2008). The first section turns to the salvific and redemptive narratives that (re)vision particular religious narratives in the sciences in forming the teaching and curriculum of Progressive education. The second section connects salvific and redemptive narratives of reform and science with the Social Question. The common school for all populations (or almost "all") gave attention to the Social Question of what was perceived as the moral disorder of urban conditions and the dangers of what was normalized as collective, national belonging. The American psychological and sociological sciences related to education intersects with The Social Question as a cognitive and affective infrastructure explored in sections 3 and 4. The writings of the University of Chicago's community sociology, and the psychologies of G. Stanley Hall, Edward L. Thorndike, and John Dewey, are discussed. The different writings congeal in the sense of embodying particular conceptual apparatuses or "frameworks" that enunciate ways of thinking about people and change that related to the Social Question and American cultural narratives of belonging.[1] The final section examines the comparative reasoning of the sciences directed to the Social Question; urban populations were recognized for inclusion but as different from the cosmopolitan narratives and images of "the citizen." The grid that connects the historical lines pursued in this chapter form the rules and standards of the knowledge "useful" for effecting change.

The chapter is indebted to curriculum studies of American Progressive education. The seminal works by Herbert Kliebard (1986) and Barry Franklin (1986) discuss the American common or mass school as brought into existence through the ideas of the school curriculum formed through educational committees, programs, and sciences (also see Labaree 1988; Franklin 2008).[2] American Progressive education is viewed as a normative project of American exceptionalism; that is, the nation and its people embody a unique political and social experiment that was an inheritor of the Enlightenment.[3] These historical analyses give emphasis to different social interests, social movements, and dilemmas represented in the school's curricular and instructional practices, what Kliebard (1986) called the "black box" of schooling.

The chapter's attention to Progressivism and Progressive education (re)focuses on the "black box" of schooling, going against the grain by considering the reason of the sciences that was central to the formation of social and political Progressivism and the schools. While formal departments developed in sociology and psychology at that time, there were no institutional separations between the education sciences and those of psychology and sociology as exist today. The sciences gave attention to educational concerns in relation to broader concerns about social change. The object of the sciences was to change social conditions and rescue particular "urban" populations from moral disorders that simultaneously would redeem "souls."

The discussion recognizes that Progressivism and the sciences were not merely American phenomena. The international New Education Fellowship and American Progressive education were historically homologous in developing scientifically organized schools (see, e.g., Popkewitz 2005; Hultqvist 1998; Popkewitz 2013a, 2013b). The importance of science and the making of the "new" child were also connected across the Americas (see Buenfil Burgos 2005; Caride 2015; Dussel 2013), and with different cultural theses and activations in China and Japan (see, e.g., Qi 2005; Ohkura 2005).[4]

## Sciences as Revelation and Calculating Desires

Often lost in discussions of American Progressive education is its construction and link with the formation of the welfare state (e.g., Skowronek 1982). The welfare state has the double qualities of the state assuming the obligation for providing for the health and well-being of its populations and producing freedom and liberty. The historical lines governing the sciences related to the formation of Progressive education enable an exploration of these double qualities and what are constituted as the objects of change.

American Progressivism, at one level, signaled the end of 19th-century laissez-faire. Laissez-faire is a view that the government should not interfere in economic and social conditions as their development was best served through unconstrained markets (see, e.g., Fine 1956). The institutions formed in Progressivism worked to end the idea that the free market would provide security as the state assumed a role in the care of people.[5] New institutions of security emerged such as regulating industrial work, urban environments, and the zoning of development. These institutions were made possible through theories and distinctions about urban life that were not available previously. Categories of workers and working classes, for example, were invented as classifications that defined discrete populations for mapping poverty, urban environments, social planning, and state legislation.

The making of the welfare state embodied new technologies through which the internalization of notions of civic virtue and the common good could be produced. The founders of the French and American republics recognized, for example, that the citizen was made and not born and thus the "necessity" of education in making kinds of people. The school curriculum and psychologies of the child in American Progressivism and the New Education Fellowship gave order, classifications, and methods for finding the proper restraint and moral behavior necessary for individual self-fulfillment. That individualization was given as universalized for the benefit of society as a whole.

The educative processes incorporated a generalized philosophy of science about the processes of rational thinking for the qualities of mind that ordered children's learning (Rudolph 2005). The sciences of childhood and pedagogy instantiated notions of rational thought and action that gave expression to cultural principles about the desired responsibilities, obligations, and sensitivities of the child as a social subject. The thinking, feelings, and actions generated principles of the civic obligations of participation of the "citizen" that were not universal but historically particular (see, e.g., Tröhler, Popkewitz, and Labaree 2011).

American Progressivism embodied changes that were interconnected transnationally (see, e.g., Popkewitz 2005). Most of the first generation of social and psychological researchers studied in Europe, where many received their PhDs. On both sides of the Atlantic, the theories, sciences, and programs of schools installed variations on notions of rationality, self-determination, freedom, and the idea of growth, development, and change (Siljander, Kivelä, and Sutinen 2012). What is considered as the uniquely American philosophy of pragmatism, articulated in the writing of John Dewey, for example, intersected with European thought and particularly with the German theory of *Bildung* (Retter 2012; Oelkers1995, 2005). In much of Europe and the Americas, the theories of social change in the sciences connected the Enlightenment's cosmopolitan idea of the universality of reason and rationality with the pedagogical actions of schooling (Popkewitz 2015; Popkewitz, Diaz, and Kirchgasler 2017; Sobe 2008).[6]

### National Exceptionalism and Forming "the Mind and Spirit" of the Child

Science was to provide the practical knowledge to attain social rectification and individual redemption (Wagner et al. 1991, 2).[7] American social and psychological sciences joined narratives of salvation and redemption with other historical lines to express the nation's exceptionalism, which told an epic tale of the nation's unique political and social system and people. When Alexis de Tocqueville, the French historian and political philosopher, wrote *Democracy in America* (1835–40), the phrase American exceptionalism was used in describing what was thought as the distinctive character of the nation, its institutions, and its people. That distinctiveness was expressed in American literature as the particular frontier character of the individual who had to persevere in harsh environments in settling the middle and western parts of the nation, expressed by early 20th century historian Frederick Jackson Turner (Faragher 1994; Jehlen 1986). The character of the nation and its people were seen as ingenuity and "grit."

The cultural narratives of American exceptionalism were drawn and revised Puritan narratives of the 1600s of reclaiming what God gave in the Garden of Eden in the finding of the New World. This founding narrative was reassembled as the cultural and social promise of scientific and technological progress by the turn of the 20th century (Nye 1999). The new epic tale of the nation was told through the *technological sublime* —cultural narratives of the triumphs of science as the liberating human spirit of the young republic. The technological narratives portrayed the story of the nation and its people as the inevitable and harmonious process of development and the fulfillment of progress through human intervention. The natural power of Niagara Falls, the physical awe of the Grand Canyon, and the technologies of industrialization represented in the railroad, bridge, and city skyscrapers were defined as the apotheosis of nature and human wisdom embodied in the nation.

The cultural narratives of American exceptionalism were inscribed in the theories of society and the school. Charles Horton Cooley (1909), a founding member of the American Sociological Society,[8] wrote about education in relation to the larger corporate body. The United States was placed as "nearer, perhaps, to the spirit of the coming order" that would be totally different from anything before it, "and so perhaps more likely, in due time, to give it adequate utterance in art" (Cooley 1909, 167). Evoking the narrative of American exceptionalism, Cooley wrote that "the new industrial modernity of America is close to being the first real democracy" in its "emphasis on individuality and innovation" and which "does not inherit the class culture of Europe" (cited in Ross 1972, 245).

The narratives of the eternal promise of the nation through scientific knowledge were woven into psychological theories of child development and learning. Psychologies prior to American Progressive education focused on the mental disciplining of the child. The psychologies emphasized character training through mental exercise. Faculty psychology in pedagogical practices was to produce "higher emotions and [the] giving [of] mental pleasure" (Stanic [1987] 2018, 155). The new scientific psychologies, in contrast, mapped the spirituality of the educated subject ("the human soul") as attached to the ethical techniques of individual self-monitoring and control—consciousness and self-consciousness—developed through the disciplining of the child.

The potentialities of the child were given attention in research as the progressive realization of universal ideals. G. Stanley Hall's ([1904] 1928) child studies, for example, discussed education in the context of the nation beginning as "the only complete history [which] is the story of the influences that have advanced or retarded development of man toward his completion, always ideal and forever in the future" (ix). Edward L. Thorndike's Connectionism, or stimulus-response psychology, provided practical and useful knowledge for schools to build intelligence in the society. Scientific knowledge posited a universality to the "nature" of that intelligence. Science functioned to discover the laws that would enable the forming of "the mind and the spirit of man" so the child can be "responsible for his/her progress, or trustful of his/her future" (Thorndike [1909] 1962, 37–47). Science discovery of the laws of the given "nature" of the child was to govern the range of human abilities and differences in achievement—notions that carried with them principles of eugenics, given as scientific laws that differentiated populations.

### Democracy as Revelation: Prophetic Visions and Faith in Science

By the end of the 19th century, the sciences articulated democracy as the prophetic vision that linked the ethics of a generalized Christianity (Calvinism) to the progressive revelation of truth. Research was concerned with mapping the spirituality of the educated subject ("the human soul"). The Christian Democracy, as Dewey spoke about in his early writing, emphasizes the triumph of reason and science in the calling of democracy (Dewey [1893] 1975). Dewey saw no difference between the reasoning that made possible the democracy of the nation and a universalized notion of Christian values concerning the good works of the individual. Analogous to Christ's teaching, democracy's spiritual meaning was in its notions of freedom as the continuous search for truth through the loosening of the bonds of tradition, the wearing away of restrictions on individual growth and development, and the breaking down of barriers and partitions that limited the possibilities of people. Both Christianity (Calvinist reformism) and democracy were processes through which individuals sought the "continuously unfolding, never ceasing discovery of the meaning of life" (Dewey [1893] 1975, 4).

This relationship of religion to democracy, Dewey argued, defined the political process as a mode of life rather than as a machinery of government.

> I assume that democracy is a spiritual fact and not a mere piece of governmental machinery. . . . If God is, as Christ taught, at the root of life, incarnate in man, then democracy has a spiritual meaning which it behooves us not to pass by. Democracy is freedom. If truth is at the bottom of things, freedom means giving this truth a chance to show itself, a chance to well up from the depths. Democracy, as freedom, means the loosing of bonds, the wearing away of restrictions, the breaking down of barriers, of middle walls, of partitions. (Dewey [1893] 1975, 8)

Dewey's pragmatism articulated the prophetic language of Protestant reformism and assembled with historical lines joining science, pedagogy, and the political forms of democracy as a practice of "revelation." Enunciated were principles of change connecting, for example, nineteenth-century English moderate Calvinism with science (see Sorkin 2008). Revelation in religious debates replaced Calvinist rigidness with the coordination of doctrines of reason and natural religion among the proliferation of religious groups during the Great Awakenings of 19th century America, with evangelical ministries reacting to the orthodoxy of Calvinism that included the embrace of Christianity by large numbers of African Americans.[9] The Great Awakening encourages personal spiritual introspection and commitment to morality. Revelation as a religious notion rested on an awareness of God's accommodation or condescension, depending on sectarian views, to time, place, and mentalities in creating the moral good.

Democracy took on these articulations but in a different register. Revelation linked notions of civic virtue to a mode of living ordered by what Dewey called an open-mindedness (Westbrook 1991). Dewey's "habits of the mind," notions of problem solving, experimentation, community, and action were concepts that formed as a general method of sciences in pragmatism. Science as a mode of reflection was meant to free individuals from unreflective habits and subjection to instinct, appetite, and routines. These concepts of action and problem solving were directed to the future and human potentialities.

The folding of prophetic visions connecting ideas of progress, potentiality, and revelation was expressed in George Herbert Mead's *Mind, Self, and Society*. Mead, a colleague of Dewey at the University of Chicago, discussed Christianity as having

> paved the way for the social progress—political, economic, scientific—of the modern world, the social progress which is so dominantly characteristic

of that world. For the Christian notion of a rational or abstract universal human society or social order, though originating as a primarily religious and ethical doctrine, gradually lost its purely religious and ethical associations, and expanded to include all the other main aspects of concrete human social life as well; and so became the larger, more complex notion of that many-sided, rationally universal human society to which all the social reconstructions constituting modern social progress involve intellectual reference by the individuals carrying them out. (Mead [1934] 1967, 293)

Change was giving an order to change and its administration as a rational pursuit through which society gradually improved to achieve the grand destiny of perfection for all mankind. That perfection was expressed in the principles organizing children's learning. The latter had particular contours and inscriptions in which particular Protestant ethical doctrines were part of the "traveling library" as different sets of ideas and states connected to constitute order and classifications of the rational individual.

### Calculating Desires as the "Eternal Promise" of Childhood

Theories of children's learning, development and growth, and problem solving embodied desires to be calculated and ordered in research as children's learning. Children's development or problem-solving skills, for example, was the progressive path that provided the optimism of the "eternal promise" of childhood (Monaghan and Saul 1987). That optimism was not only about the child as the future citizen in the Promised Land. The hope, the American historian Darrin McMahon (2006) suggested, was the translation of the Reformation's ultimate question of "How can I be saved?" into the American Enlightenment's pragmatic question of "How can I be happy?" (209). Pleasure was no longer seen as a distraction in the pursuit of virtue but as the affective infrastructure of virtue itself.

Pleasure and happiness are commonly understood as nurtured through the "experiences" of the child; however, both need to be historicized. They are not phenomena of nature. Pleasure and happiness were linked to freedom.[10] This linkage was formed within the social and cultural spaces in which desires were generated about what might be. Edward L. Thorndike's Connectionist psychology, for example, was thought as enabling happiness in governing the soul. The psychology brought "the mind and the spirit of man [sic]" as a mode of living where individuals "could be responsible for their progress or entrusted with their future" (Thorndike [1912] 1962, 142–43).

Thorndike's psychology narrated science as both a social project and a mode of living. The school was likened to building a house foundation. The teacher was the builder who had to know "how to erect a frame, how to lay a floor and the like with reference to what is to be built; the teacher should often study how to utilize inborn tendencies, how to form habits, how to develop interests and the like with reference to what changes in intellect and character are to be made" (Thorndike [1909] 1962, 57).

The science of psychology identified the nature of the individual, which pedagogy developed to bring greater happiness. Thorndike accepted Jeremy Bentham's notion of seeking the greatest pleasure for the greatest numbers (Joncich 1968). Happiness was expressed in Thorndike's educational psychology as preparing children for "the serious business of life as well as for the refined enjoyment of its leisure" (Thorndike and Woodworth [1901] 1962, 5). Science was to identify the correlations between those actions that gave pleasure and those that promoted survival.

The preparation for life entailed Herbert Spencer's (1884) question of "What Knowledge Is of Most Worth?" as the problem of the curriculum (Thorndike [1909] 1962). The curriculum of the school was assembled and ordered within a social Darwinian conception that transformed the criterion of *happiness* into a psychological one that calculates individual wants: "We judge the relative value of different sorts of knowledge by the extent to which each helps toward the ultimate end of education—the improvement and satisfaction of wants" (Thorndike [1912] 1962c, 144–45). The idea of worth was "worth more to most people" (ibid.). The cultural premise of happiness was expressed as the psychological concern with producing the self-motivated and self-responsible individual believed to be necessary for the working of the republic.

The "happiness" that the scientific methods of psychology pursued were social conventions. The conventions differentiated "democratic" ways of thinking that protected society from the abuse of power and the evils of wrong development. With the rules and standards of reason were fears of unreflective habits. The differentiation functioned as cultural theses that instantiated a continuum of value that inscribed the normal and the pathological.

The psychological paths to happiness evoked the American Jeremiad. Optimism was formed through fear of the fall of the nation if action was not taken. Connectionist psychology was a cure for the nation's ills through education preventing "each new generation from stagnating in brutish ignorance, folly and pain." Better education was "needed to reduce the still appalling sum of error, injustice, misery and stupidity" (Thorndike [1912] 1962, 72). Education was the hope to make "human beings wish each other well, should increase the sum of human energy and happiness and decrease the sum of discomfort of the human beings that are or will be, and should foster the higher, impersonal pleasures" (Thorndike [1909] 1962, 46–47).

## The Social Question: Science and the Double Gestures of the "Eternal Promise" of Childhood

Progressive education and its sciences of pedagogy were embedded in social and political cross-Atlantic social movements related to Northern European and North American Protestant reformism. Central to the reform movements was the Social Question (Rodgers 1998; also see Castel 2017). The Social Question, what German social theorists called "Die Soziale Frage," was discussed briefly in previous chapters. It entailed different Protestant political and social reform movements concerned with the economic dislocations and the amelioration of the conditions of the city through planned intervention that formed the welfare state.

The Social Question directed attention to hopes embodied in American exceptionalism and fears of moral disorder and deviancy. Progressive reforms created institutional organizations important to changing the conditions of urban living. Reforms, for example, made possible poor relief, public ownership and development of urban transportation, planning of city streets and zoning, wage labor protection, the development of public housing, ordinances that regulated building construction, and mass schooling. Reforms were also directed to civic life and its deviances, such as identifying the causes of alcoholism, delinquency, and prostitution, among other practices, that violated the presumed norms of civility.

The institutional reforms need to be placed with the Social Question and the cultural anxieties that articulated the twin themes of the American Jeremiad of rescue and redemption. The optimistic hopes of American exceptionalism were activated in the research concerned with the urban child and family. The hope of the Jeremiad joined fears of the debilitating effects of modern conditions and dangerous populations of the urban poor, workers, and racial and ethnic groups.

The double gestures of hope and fear were embodied in the sciences of childhood, which were expressed in the different psychologies brought into schooling. The fears were that if the development of the family and childhood was not controlled, the child would potentially be dangerous to the future of the republic (Krug 1972).

Science was an actor in producing distinctions and methods to cognitively and affectively order and bring into existences principles that reference the hopes and fears acted on in the school pedagogy. Science was a mode of reasoning that circulated in two distinct forms. The first was the theories and methods of sociology and psychology that identified and ordered the distinctions and classifications about schools and its processes. The second was that science is a model of the way the mind should operate to actualize the potentialities of society and the child.

This second science, the "scientific method" represented and identified in the psychologies of learning, embodied a generalized philosophical ideal of ordering and planning life. The methods of science were not drawn from any inquiry into how science is done. Science as a method of thought, as earlier discussed, was a form of revelation imprinted in the mode of democratic living. In Dewey's pragmatism, it undid the slavish, harmful powers that were produced in the Gilded Age of unrestrained capitalism:

> The existence of scientific method protects us also from a danger that attends the operation of men of unusual power; dangers of slavish imitation partisanship, and such jealous devotion to them and their work as to get in the way of further progress. (Dewey 1929b, 11)

The language of rescue and redemption in science brought into existence the inscriptions of human potentialities that were comparative. It divided the qualities and characteristics of those who were or had the possibilities of being enlightened and civilized from those qualities and characteristics that threatened the potentiality-to-be. The comparative reason was evident in the alchemy of the formation of the school subjects discussed previously in chapter 5. At the turn of the 20th century, those who threatened the moral unity of the whole were classified as the backward, the savage, the barbarian, and feebleminded. The social and psychological sciences embodied concerns about social differences, cultural differentiations, and deviance associated with urban conditions—a concern today in urban education about the disparities among racialized, ethnic, and poor populations that is expressed as eliminating "the achievement gap." By the

1920s, the sources of danger were located in the motivation of the child and today are recognized as the child "left behind."

## Progressive Urban Reforms and the "Great Awakenings"

The principles inscribed in Progressive urban reforms and its sciences were marked at the interstices of changes in different Protestant denominations' notions of poverty and sin (see, e.g., Clark 1995; Hatch 1980).[11] The American religious revivals of the Second and Third Great Awakenings of the 19th century no longer considered poverty as solely the moral failure of the individual but as the result of the social conditions of industrialization and urbanization in which poverty existed.[12] Charity, previously the church's mission for helping the poor, was no longer sufficient for dealing with the effects of capitalism and its dislocations (Fink 2015; Nichols and Unger 2017).[13] Social reform was taken as an awakening of the social mission of the various churches.

The changing notion of the nature of sin and salvation was expressed in a wide range of public critiques that responded to the Social Question. American Progressivism entailed, for example, newspapers and literature that focused on the conditions of urban life and the poor. The popular literature of the penny newspapers and ten cent magazines captured the religious shifts as political and social obligations in writing about the conditions of the poor. Journalism and popular literature developed a particular "muckraking" genre that gave expression to exposés, such as child labor, industrial conditions, and governmental corruption as in New York's Tammany Hall. The ostentatious displays of wealth and political corruption were given the name of the Gilded Age, a term drawn from a novel by Mark Twain and Charles Dudley Warner. The settlement house movement of the middle class was formed to help improve and better understand the lives of the poor and immigrants; the knowledge gained was useful for creating programs to alleviate poverty.

The historical lines folded the religious mission of rescue and redemption with social, literary, and political principles into a grid that formed as the practices of the social and psychological sciences. The Social Gospel movement, to which many of the early social scientists belonged, gave expression to Christian ethics as guiding principles in the particular mission of science as a project of social change.[14] The social theology of the Social Gospel movement saw American democracy and the nation as "blessed by God, sacralizing the new republic's political system" (Greek 1992, 45).

The purpose of science was seen as identifying the laws that liberated urban populations from these existing barbaric or irrational conditions that were sinful and morally wrong. While Darwinism challenged New Testament views of revelation and design, the Social Gospel refocused social Darwinism as the redemptive effort to produce human perfectibility and social progress. "If God's design could be seen in the laws of nature, laws subject to verification, social gospelers intended to look for that design in scientifically measurable terms" (Greek 1992, 64). Science explained the human origins and paths for social change, with God as a driving force behind evolution.

The new American university that was formed in the 19th and early 20th centuries connected social affairs and evangelical Protestantism with science. University extension programs were created; initially associated with rural agricultural development, they gave attention to the conditions and lives of workers and the poor. One of the early, if not first expressions of this relation of society, state, science, and reform occurred at the University of Wisconsin–Madison. Called the Wisconsin Idea (McCarthy 1912), it called for the university to apply its scientific expertise to find solutions to public problems, "extending the work of the University, through its personnel and facilities, to the boundaries of the state" (Hoeverler 1976, 282). The extension of science to state and civic life entailed elements of the Social Gospel Movement, of which many of the university's leaders were members. The idea of university extension, along with broader social and political reforms of Progressivism in which the university provided its expertise, connected religious and social objectives of evangelical Protestantism with science as "the logical and critical vehicle of their ideals: the perfection of the Christian state" (Hoeverler 1976, 283).

## Psychology and the Liberation of Urban Populations

The sciences of psychology were central for the design of saving and redeeming "the soul." The new scientific psychologies of the child engaged in the redemptive projects of correcting urban populations that posed dangers to the moral order. One critic of the teaching of algebra worried about the high failure rate and pressures on children that injured "the mind, destroyed the health, and wrecked the lives of thousands of children," and that the child would "lose her soul" (cited in Krug 1972, 347).

New distinctions and categories were produced to study deviance. The opening up of American schooling for children of immigrants and racial groups in the early decades of the 20th century, for example, produced distinctions of the "backward" urban child who did not succeed or left school. The classification of difference was soon given finer sets of categories that moved into the interiority of the child by the first decades of the 20th century. It was possible to "see" the child through concepts of motivation, IQ, and academic achievement that, as discussed below, directed attention to the populations placed in the Social Question (Franklin 1994). Youth was cast as a particular kind of person who represented the moral panic about the future degeneration with specific attention on teenagers who may fail to act in civilized and responsible ways (Lesko and Talburt 2011). The temporalization of experience built into the representation of youth inscribed principles to differentiate and distinguish the desirable/undesirable inner qualities and modes of living in children and teachers.

The double qualities of redemption and abjection ordered G. Stanley Hall's ([1904] 1928) child study. Child study was to replace moral philosophy as the arbiter of the good and righteous. The child psychology of adolescence was a fabrication about the nature of the child's place in the arrow of time as stages of development. The psychological instantiated Protestant salvific themes, political theories of order and participation, and Enlightenment desires of sciences that would enable human perfection. Psychology was an intervention to enable the child to assume the true nature of development.[15]

The hope of development was continually juxtaposed in psychology to correct the impediments to growth, development, and morality among these changing populations of immigrants and racialized groups in the new common school. Child studies was a design strategy "meant to contribute to the amelioration of social evils and provide a basis for the rational and enlightened ordering of societal affairs." "The momentum of heredity often seems insufficient to enable the child to achieve this great revolution and come to complete maturity, so that every step is strewn with wreckage of body, mind, and morals" (Hall [1904] 1928, xiv). That intervention was to challenge the moral disorder and social deviance through science and education, captured in the title of Hall's book on adolescence: *Adolescence: Its Psychology and Its Relations to Physiology, Anthropology, Sociology, Sex, Crime, Religion and Education* ([1904] 1928).

The gestures of civilizing coupled with the fears of the uncivilized were woven, albeit differently, in the Connectionist psychology of Edward L. Thorndike. Connectionist psychology was to provide the redemptive path from ignorance and moral disorder. It would provide children with means by "which they may get health, escape poverty, enjoy their leisure hours, and otherwise have more of what a decent, but not very idealist, person wants" (Thorndike [1912] 1962c, 142–43). Education about desires as potentialities-to-be simultaneously expressed its opposite, what should not be. The creation and intensification of the good will of people, Thorndike ([1909] 1962b) argued, occurs through psychological studies that identify what is natural to people in "the facts and laws." Identifying differences that are based on "nature" enables the "treatment of subject races, in legislation for criminals and dependents, in the care for public health, and in the new view of the family, we may see the influence of Darwinism beginning to spread to statesmanship and social control" (46–47). He maintains that

> to change men's wants for the better, we must heed what conditions originally satisfy and annoy them since the only way to create an interest is by grafting it onto one of the original satisfiers. To enable men to satisfy their wants more fully, the crude curiosity, manipulation, experimentation and irrational interplay of fear, anger, rivalry, mastery, submission, cruelty and kindliness must be modified into useful, verified thought and equitable acts. (Thorndike [1912] 1962, 76)

Studies of the classroom were to make visible the laws and facts of the nature of children. These rules gave teachers the scientific basis of teaching "to produce and to prevent changes in human beings; to preserve and increase the desirable qualities of body, intellect and character, . . . to get rid of the undesirable" and "to control human nature—hence the teacher had to know it" (Thorndike [1906] 1962, 60).

> The laws of plants that the gardener needed to know to grow plants, the mechanics the engineer needed to understand to plan for the stresses and strains of bridges, and the physician's knowledge of disease to treat patients, were similar with the sciences that the teacher had to know to discover the laws of nature for children's development: "the teacher must act in accordance with the laws of the sciences of human nature." (Thorndike [1906] 1962, 60)

Education, in Thorndike's psychology, for example, was the "only cure" for the nation's ills and the foundation of progress directed "toward the good will of men." "Worth," "responsibility," and "happiness" gave expression to liberal theories regarding individual freedom and self-actualization through the teacher's discovery of "where the child stands and lead him [*sic*] from there" (Joncich 1968, 21).

Dewey's anthropological psychology, Hall's child studies, and Thorndike's Connectionist psychology generated a particular affect related to their particular distinctions and social agendas in the conduct of schooling.[16] The sciences congealed, arranged, and rearranged "things" to articulate redemptive themes. The themes embodied particular cosmopolitan notions connected to the comparativeness of kinds of people and differences enunciated in the Social Question and the principles of collective belonging embodied in American exceptionalism.

The redemptive practices were paradoxical—differentiating, dividing, and abjecting in its inclusionary gestures. The social Darwinism in Thorndike and Hall evoked divisions between the qualities of urban immigrants, Catholics, and racialized populations, and the rural pastoral cultural thesis of reform Protestantism. The redemptive form was given as the freedom and self-actualization of the child.

### Community Sociology, the Pastoral Image, and Designing "Agency"

The Social Question in American Progressivism is the tale of two "cities" and the trilogy of one of the two cities. One "city" was of the urbane, the knowledge that I have been discussing of a grid formed through Protestant notions of redemption and salvations connected and revisioned within themes of collective belonging and particular Enlightenment cosmopolitan desires of science in the search for the perfection of human conditions.

The images and narratives of the urbane were the reflective mode that was brought to bear on the other city of urban populations that did not embody cosmopolitanism. The nostalgic image was brought as a cultural thesis in changing urban life and people in the trilogies of immigrants and racialized children, families, and communities. Change lay in transforming the urban "home" into a purified, cleansed, and moralized domestic space.

This transformation was embodied in urban community sociology, which was to domesticate the dangerous passions of adults and children. The research was to move families and children away from public vice in their communities, which was symbolized as drinking "gin" and the gambling halls. The potentialities to-be were in the duty of responsibility and the revision of the home. The autonomy of the family was enhanced through articulating the public ethic of social order and public hygiene with the private ethic of good health and morality.

The sociology that emerged in Progressivism inscribed a nostalgic image of a past rural community and collective belonging. The inscription of civic virtue and its dangers related to the urban family and childhood were instantiated in *The Dynamics of Sociology* by Lester Frank Ward, a founding member of the Chicago school of sociology and a colleague of John Dewey. The sociology expressed a social Darwinism that gave attention to "civilizing" the ethnic habits and traditions of the immigrant family. The sciences would find the practical pathways to change "the savage person whose actions springs from emotions and not the intellect." Methods in socialization in education took "the lesser of a civilization, the savage and . . . stagnant people" and were "to raise the *uncivilized* classes up toward its level" (Ward 1883, 159–60; emphasis in the original).

The hopes of change and the fears of urban populations were brought into the problem of the common school. Another early founder of American sociology, Edward Alsworth Ross ([1920] 1930), argued that the school replaced the Medieval church in providing the cohesion, "concord and obedience" necessary for modern societies (524). Education was "the social institution to produce a like-mindedness among diverse populations through stressing the *present* and the *future* rather than the *past*" (259, italics in original). Reminiscent of the earlier Enlightenment's debates of who could possess cosmopolitan reason, the school was for the child to learn to be productive within his or her assigned role as a future citizen.

The pedagogical theories and research expressed the threat of the growing diversity of the American population. Education was a mode of reflection and action that disseminated the collective ideas and ideals by which immigrants unlearned their past traditions. The moral disorder was placed into questions of class. Well before the Cold War of the mid-20th century, Russia was the Antichrist (Boyer 1992). Change was to prevent the "disruptive ideas" that had emerged with "pseudo-Darwinism as of the competitive struggle for life, conflict of classes represented in the Bolshevik revolution or the idea of employers as exploiters" (Ross [1920] 1930, 410). Schooling was presented as preventing deviance. It was a cultural enterprise to create a "comprehension and sympathy through different social strata that previously shared little in the life of society" (Ross [1920] 1930, 410).

Ross continued:

> Thoroughly to nationalize a multitudinous people calls for institutions to disseminate certain ideas and ideals. The Tsars relied on the blue-domed Orthodox Church in every peasant village to Russify their heterogeneous subjects, while we Americans rely for unity on the "little red school house." (Ross [1920] 1930, 409)

The notion of a community as a social theory about cultural belonging performed as a strategy for the nationalizing of different peoples. The Chicago school of sociology that emerged in the early 20th century drew from and altered German social theories about communities to (re)vision the city. Sociology recaptured the rhetorical form of the American Jeremiad. The Social Question articulated the fall and the resurrection of the city as a center of culture, belonging, and home. Sociology drew on the work of the German sociologist Ferdinand Tönnies. The Lutheran pastoral image of community was revisioned in the concept of *Gemeinschaft* as a method to organize truth and honor in the new abstract relations of society. This notion of the abstract social relations found in urbanizations was captured in the concept of *Gesellschaft*. The notion of community embodied the pastoral notion where neighbors come closest to nature (*gemeinschaft*) that counteracts modernity's abstract relations symbolized in the concept of modern *society* (*gesellschaft*) without the moral or ethical grounding of the memorialized pastoral images of Christianity.

Tönnies's work about society and community was translated to articulate a romantic liberalism and the urbanization of its pastoral image. Charles Horton Cooley, a founding member of the American Sociological Society, argued that "the American spirit is peculiarly 'at one with the general spirit of human nature,' and this [Cooley] attributed to America's exceptional history" (D. Ross 1991, 245). The sociology of communities (re)visioned ideas of face-to-face interactions into symbolic interaction theories concerned with the design of urban spaces.

Community was a sociological concept that expressed cultural theses to link urban relations and the family with norms of social unity. Theories of primary groups and symbolic interactions, for example, rendered Tönnies's cultural thesis into the American sociology of community. The sociology and social psychologies urbanized its pastoral image within a context of organizing face-to-face interaction in the abstract relations of society. The sociological concepts rethought the pastoral image in the abstract, anonymous conditions and qualities associated with industrial and urban societies. The theories of communication and interaction in education were "habits of thinking" to "create attitudes favorable to effective thought" (Boyer 1978, 73, 79). "Effective" and practical knowledge instantiated by the patterns of small community interactions was an "urban" technology in which intimate, face-to-face communication among people would eliminate the alienating qualities of modernity.

In the concept of "primary group" of Charles Horton Cooley (1909) and the theorizing of symbolic interactionism of George Herbert Mead ([1934] 1967), it is possible to focus on how human agency is inscribed within theories about individuality, collective belonging, and differences, all articulated through the Social Question of urban conditions. Symbolic interactionism gave expression to communication patterns as processes of mediation between individuality to collective belonging and a "home." Mead ([1934] 1967) and his colleague John Dewey at Chicago, for example, pursued the relation of individual and social belonging through theories about the processes of mediation and self-realization in the domains of community. Notions of "intelligent action," problem solving, and community in Dewey's pragmatism embodied the *urbanized* notion of *gemeinschaft*'s pastoral and rural face-to-face relations, which together produced a way to reason about a mode of life in the industrial conditions of *gesellschaft*. Mead's social interactionism revisioned the imagined *gemeinschaft* as an urban idea of community "without doing violence to liberal democratic values" (Franklin 1986, 8).

The concept of community and "primary group" in the work of sociologist Charles Cooley (1909) served as a regulatory principle to think about stability and change in American society. Community provides a way to organize principles of change in the family that links individuality to collective belonging and "home." The image of the family as the most immediate place for the paradigm of self-abridgement of culture was not new. In the conditions of the long 19th century, the family was conceptualized as the site that brought love and sympathy into the industrial world. The family as *a primary group* created a space where a child learned about civilization. The family and the community was to enable the child to lose the greed, lust, and pride of power, and thus for the child to become fit for a civilized society.

The importance given to face-to-face, primary groups and social interaction embodied potentialities ordered through principles of the moral imperatives of life and self-sacrifice for the good of the group, shaping and fashioning principles of the agency of the individual. The notion of community reterritorializes the practical objects of change in designing reforms and programs as the encounters and experiences (see Popkewitz 2008).[17] The social and the prior psychological theories were "actors" in ordering what is but also what should be—the double qualities of potentialities that order research.

## Practical and Useful Knowledge of What?

Obscured in histories of the American Progressive education and its sciences at the turn of the 20th century are conditions as forming new patterns of governing. The unspoken object of knowledge to change social conditions in the Progressive sciences were salvation and redemption themes generated about the potentialities in changing people. This chapter explored the formation of American sciences as part of and responding to conditions given expression as Progressivism and the Social Question connected with the new school's curriculum and pedagogy. The theories focused on the trilogy—the child, family, and community—as the inscription of desires of standardized public virtues in governing life. Change was directed to the interiority of the person, concerned with responsibilities for self-development and growth that brought into existence double gestures of normalcy and pathology—differences and divisions.

The inscription of desires is what Rose (1999) refers to as technologies of *responsibilisation*, where the schools, like the family, "link public objectives for good health and good order of the social body" with the aspiration of "individuals for personal health and well-being" (Rose 1999, 74). The idea of planning organized the processes of everyday life. Science was

> to domesticate and familiarize the dangerous passions of adults, tearing them away from public vice, the gin palace and the gambling hall, imposing a duty of responsibility to each other, to home, and to children, and a wish to better their own condition. The family, from then on, has a key role in strategies for the government of freedom. It links public objectives for good health and good order of the social body with the desire of individuals for personal health and well-being. A "private" ethic of good health

and morality can thus be articulated on to a "public" ethic of social order and public hygiene, yet without destroying the autonomy of the family—indeed by promising to enhance it. (Rose 1999, 74)

Practical, useful knowledge travels along with the objects of change. The urban sociologies of the turn of the century instantiated a comparative style of thought that differentiated and divided. The hope and fear in the Social Question, however, were not produced by conscious intent. In fact, just the opposite! The double gestures were instantiated between a continuum of values about the child in the reason of the different sciences, although there were substantial differences between the eugenics of Hall and Thorndike and Dewey's pragmatism. Inscribed in the rules and standards for reasoning were distinctions, differentiations, and divisions about kinds of people.

# 7 ◆ The Reason of "Systems" and Practical Knowledge

Post–World War II Educational Research and Development

Turn of the 20th-century education sciences in American Progressivism intricately connected with the art of governing in the formation of the modern welfare state. The governing entails the making of social identities and collective belonging. That desire was about the potentialities of people that generated double gestures in the Social Question to correct urban moral disorder. American post–World War II sciences can be thought of, at one level, as a continuity of the object of science as changing people that produce differences. But that historical continuity, by itself, elides the different assemblages in the theories and methods of research. The post–World War II decades mobilize a particular expertise and institutional practices linked with the expansion and redefining of the governing of the welfare state. The War on Poverty and the Great Society initiatives as well as the calls for national security in relation to "Others" external to the US, often framed as the Cold War,[1] embodied different assemblies, connections, and technologies than those of the turn of the century.

This chapter explores those rules and standards of the reason ordering the social and psychological sciences related to education and its objects of change. The first section examines the mobilization and (re)visioning of science as cultural practices linked to policy; (re)visioning the American Jeremiad as the hopes and fears in social and individual change. The second section explores how the postwar humanities and social sciences were epistemologically shaped and fashioned through systems theory and cybernetics. The Wisconsin Center for Research and Development for Learning and Reeducation (hereafter Wisconsin R&D Center), one of the national centers established in the 1960s, is studied to understand how systems/cybernetic theories connect with other principles about children and schools to order what was called "research and development" (R&D). Examined in sections 3, 4, and 5 is the research and development (R&D) of the Center. The Center viewed its research an experimental, pragmatic, and organized as "problem solving" for changing elementary schools and teacher education.[2] The sixth section examines the (re)visioning of the redemptive themes and comparative qualities of the principles ordering the mid-20th-century Social Question, (re)visioning the double gestures.

The epistemological principles that form in the R&D, I argue, are naturalized in the contemporary international assessments and teacher education research discussed in subsequent chapters. What is in question in these chapters is how the research produces new objects in the making of people and differences, objects that order practical and "useful" knowledge of the research.

## Science as "the Beacon" for Social Change: The American Jeremiad (Re)Visioned

Post–World War II welfare states across the Atlantic and Pacific mobilized science for problems of recovery, reconstruction, and the reimagining of societies and education (Popkewitz forthcoming b). The end of World War II was portrayed as the triumph of the scientific superiority of goodness over evil that had a transnational resonance. In the United States, the defeat of fascism generated an optimism about the future defined through narratives of American exceptionalism and science in the rebuilding of a progressive society.

### The End of Ideology: Finding Wise Policies and Good Science

Science had the aura of theology (Boyer 1992). Science was synonymous with reason. It was given the practical power to shape life and bring order to things that associated it with the progress of the nation and the world (Gilman 2003). The atomic bomb and technologies of splitting the atom were given cultural narratives of utopic promises in transportation, energy, and agriculture as the anodyne to their destructive fears and as "a way of avoiding unsettling immediate realities" (Boyer 1985, 122).

Harold Lasswell (1951), a prominent political scientist, argued that the sciences should focus on the fundamental problems of society to assist in finding solutions to social problems rather focusing than on the topical issues of the moment.[3]

The nation was optimistically portrayed as a mature and great power dedicated to ushering in a new age in its own image of freedom and democracy (Fousek 2000; Hartman 2008). Although American optimism was continually put to the test with the Vietnam War and the civil rights movement, popular and social science literature asserted that there was a social consensus and that the societal challenge was creating wise policies and good science to find solutions to social problems. Change was portrayed as "the end of ideology" as political conflict was no longer important for social development because a consensus had been achieved (Bell 1962).[4] The problem of change was finding the correct paths to enable "democratic" institutions to grow and the economy to prosper.

The social sciences to mobilize change folded in the utopic promises into particular cultural principles as desires about the potentialities of what society and people are to-be. Prior theoretical assumptions of people operating rationally out of their own interest were challenged by the horrors of Nazism and Fascism. Theories that circulated in sociology, anthropology, and psychology revisioned people as "naturally irrational" (Heyck 2012).

The new unit of analysis was the processes and communication patterns that governed how people made choices and decisions. Analyses gave attention to the processes used to control and manage irrationality, fallibility, and authoritarianism. Studies about family and personality, for example, delineated a hierarchy of liberal/authoritarian political attitudes, the norms of family interactions, and children's development (Vicedo 2012). Research was to detect the antithetic qualities of a democratic kind of person, for example, who was defined as marginalized, closed-minded, rigid, conformist, intolerant, ideological, and prejudiced. Social anthropologist studies of adults gave focus to the fears and anxieties about authoritarian personalities and uncontrollable "emotional childishness." These dangerous qualities were placed in the new cognitive psychology as a contrast to the characteristics of the "nature" of the liberal, democratic mind as "open-minded," creative, autonomous, tolerant, flexible, unprejudiced and capable of using "reason" (Cohen-Cole 2014). The cognitive psychology was important to the New Curriculum Movement between 1965 and 1975, performing as the alchemic tools that translated the complex edifices of disciplinary fields into models of curriculum (Cohen-Cole 2014, chap. 7).

The concern with communication and processes evolved, as well, in the notion of "community." Community emerges in response to social movements and as a concept of the social and psychological sciences. At the turn of the 20th century, it had different sets of coordinates than those in Chicago urban sociology. Community in the postwar sciences was, at one level, a method to open spaces of participation and decision making to control human irrationality. It was attached to political strategies for mobilizing efforts to decentralize social institutions to be more responsive to the particular social groups that faced social and economic inequalities, particularly in the wake of the civil rights movement. For example, calls for "community control," became important for providing greater autonomy to parents and social organizations that clustered around urban schools in the 1960s and 1970s (Grant 1978). Political agendas to enlarge participation to foster social and cultural counternarratives, however, were quickly transformed in the social and educational sciences and social policy as an administrative category for organizing relations of government and social movements (see Popkewitz 1976, 1978).

## Mobilizing the Expertise of Science

The desire for reform, reconstruction, and change joined policy with science. This is expressed by Solovey (2013) in funding of research considered as having practical implication in what was called "development":

> Whereas federal research and development (R&D) expenditures had amounted to less than $100 million in 1940, a dozen years later the federal contribution was nearly twenty times greater, almost $1.9 billion. (56)

The mobilization of research produced what Savage (2010) argues was "the creeping rise of the social science apparatus" (10).[5] This institutionalization of reform-oriented research was formed through federal legislation for programs such as the War of Poverty as well as social, economic, and military programs. Expanded authority for federally sponsored social research was provided by the Cooperative Research Program of the National Defense Act (1957). Four federal agencies that supported research were established in the 1950s and 1960s: the US Office of Education, the National Science Foundation, the National Institute of Mental Health, and the Office of Economic Opportunity.

Educational research was given specific authorization in the Congressional Cooperative Research Act (1954). It called for new national centers for educational research and development to be placed in universities. Between 1964 and 1965, congressional legislation created five national educational R&D centers, enlarged to ten after a decade. The hope was that research would transform the education system by "bringing order out of educational chaos" through taking on the findings of research to produce the "institutional character as a new kind of schooling" (Chase 1977, xiii).[6]

The research agenda of the legislation gave focus to expanding "a well-developed, university-based social science system that was already distinctly empirical and applied in orientation" (Wagner et al. 1991, 10). The legislation authorized the United States Office of Education "to enter into a cooperative arrangement with universities, colleges, and state education agencies to conduct educational research, surveys, and demonstrations" (Klausmeier and Wisconsin Associates 1990, xiii; Dershimer 1976, 47). Educational research was to generate "theoretical and empirical knowledge to assist governmental policies that were seen as presently lacking" (Dershimer 1976, 38).

The president of the University of Wisconsin–Madison, Fred Harvey Harrington, asserted that this mobilization of the university's expertise responded to "the urgent national needs and the public interest" that could "help solve pressing problems and improve the quality of life in the United States and abroad" (Harrington 1990, ix–x). Harrington drew on the earlier discussed proposal of *The Wisconsin Idea* (McCarthy 1912) that emerged during American Progressivism to express the university's obligation to extend its expertise to civil society to improve people's lives "in service of the democratic ideal." The Wisconsin Idea involved the university's sponsorship of science as the regeneration of a long-standing tradition of "the union of basic and applied research" of American land grant universities (Harrington 1990, ix–x).

The mobilization of scientific expertise would assess and guide reform through translating research to address problems of "development" in a manner that was previously unavailable. The educational R&D centers were not only the sites in generating knowledge useful for school reform; they produced the necessary expertise in what was thought of as an "acute shortage" of researchers for directing large-scale social research (National Center for Educational Research and Development 1969). The Wisconsin R&D Center, for example, had researchers from a dozen faculties on the campus. More than 500 PhD students were trained in the research projects during the ten-year period from 1965 to 1975.

The scope of the expansion of scientific know-how can be seen nationally as well. The American Educational Research Association (AERA), initially a department within the National Educational Association from 1909 to 1964, became an independent organization and reflected the growing cadre of research expertise. AERA grew from 3,156 members in 1964 to 12,000 members by 1974. The scope of the AERA annual meetings expanded from 43 papers read and 105 persons participating in the 1956 annual meeting to 240 papers and 542 participants in 1966.[7]

## Changing Technologies of Science

Social science in the service of social reforms entailed a number of different historical lines that come together in the postwar years. The impetus for legislation overlapped with changes in the technologies of science. Techniques of mass observations, and greater formalism and empiricism, created possibilities for new kinds of questions and methods for linking research to policy questions of reform. These included new techniques of sampling and "natural experiments," the latter where social scientists engage in field studies of ongoing interactions and communication in everyday life. The algorisms to study people enabled the invention of "the average American" as statistical categories in American social science (Igo 2007).

Large-scale data became more commonplace as technology to arrange phenomena for their typicality or generality (Isaac 2009, 424). The research efforts drew on the development of mass data that emerged from military research as well as prior research (see, e.g., Bruner 1983). Mass surveys and interviews techniques established in Columbia University's Bureau of Applied Social Research's quantitative analyses directed by Paul Lazarsfeld, an Austrian émigré (Sterne 2005), for example, were developed in the 1930s and connected with the reform-oriented research (Fine 1995).[8]

The inscription of algorithms and technologies of statistical analysis of large data made it technically possible to study large populations, such as the national assessments of school achievement. The creation and expansion of measurement bases, for example, were collected in federal publications about "the conditions of education" as a comparative tool of national "modernization." The measures entailed creating categories of equivalence related to achievement and resources (see, e.g., Normand 2016).

The methodological and theoretical changes gave expression to new approaches to studies of the social and cultural dimensions of schools. "Field study" research drew on approaches found earlier in sociology and anthropology that were drawn into educational research (see, e.g., Popkewitz and Tabachnick 1981; Campbell and Stanley 1963; Glaser and Strauss 1967; Homans 1950). The research designs of "qualitative naturalistic observation" emphasized participant observations and ethnography that worked with positivist, anthropological, and communication studies of classroom principles (Smith 1981; Becker et al. 1961; Bellack et al. 1966).

The research stressed a methodological sophistication concerned with "knowledge utilization," a technical sounding phrase that gave focus to how the knowledge generated would be practical and useful for organizing change. Emphasis was given to the methodological development of the instruments for ordering and representing statistical data placed in charts, tables, and models, which is examined further in the discussion of educational research.

## Systems Analysis and Cybernetics as Potentialities

The methodological concern with research as problem solving was not merely a phrase about research having a direct practicality. The phrase was assembled and folded into a range of epistemological principles to generate the objects of change as potentialities that research actualizes. That future articulated the arrow of time in words like "development" and "growth" and the appearance of "benchmarks" as the standards to achieve. The future, for example, was incorporated into new institutional agencies such as the Organization of Economic Co-operation and Development (OECD). The OECD sought to create developmental indicators as *forecasting tools* in the 1960s (Bürgi and Tröhler 2018).[9]

The problem solving, the arrow of time, and the idea of "benchmarks" in research had a particular historical specificity in connecting systems theories and cybernetics to the social and psychological sciences. Systems becomes an abstraction of a hypothesized set of relations that are codified and standardized components about how "things" work and change machines, social life, and people.

The principles of systems theory were brought into multiple human sciences. Systems theory was thought of as an "unprecedented synthesis" during the 1950s and 1960s (see, e.g., Easton 1965; Simon 1969; also see Halpern 2014). Principles of systems analysis were embodied in organizational and institutional theories, Saussurian linguistics, and Claude Lévi-

Strauss's anthropology, all of which were important in the American social sciences.[10] The research of social psychologist Kurt Lewin, influential in teacher education reform movements of "action research," bore the imprint of cybernetics (see Ivens 2018; Lee 2019). The "Tyler Rationale" (Tyler 1949),[11] enunciated as a model for national and international curriculum development and assessment, drew on cybernetics to identify any "cultural lag" between the school's promise and what was thought of as an outdated social order (Ivens 2018). The National Science Foundation funded New Curriculum programs that deployed systems theory, such as in the evolutionary anthropology that organized the social studies program Man: A Course of Study (Ivens 2013).

Thinking of the development of human life and change as a system gave emphasis to thinking about societies, culture, and individuality as ordered patterns of information, control, and communication that operated jointly (Hayles 1999). The principles of systems theory brought into existence particular principles about social life, people, and change that travel in the research discussed later. These following seven principles travel in the research.

(1) Systems theory is a symbolic model for organizing the problem of change with the biological metaphors of an organism to think about how human organizations grew, developed, and changed (see, Easton 1965; Simon 1969). The biological thinking of life as an organism was, in one sense, not new. The notion of organism was used in 19th-century theories of biological communities, such as in the work of Karl Möbius (Nyhart 2009). What was different from the 19th century was combining the biological analogy of system with cybernetics. Cybernetics enabled theory to work through the analogy of the relation between the mind and the machine for the study of social affairs—the machine as the computer and its analogy to the mind as artificial intelligence (Halpern 2014).[12] The joining of the two seemingly reconciled the dichotomy of mind and body, as well as the world of meaning with the world of physical laws, to think about the sciences of control, mastery, and governance (Dupuy [1994] 2009). Change entailed the link between human behaviors and machines (for example, computers, photocells, and radar) as directed by processes and communication networks for achieving system's goals.

(2) Principles of certainty and uncertainty were joined in managing change. As discussed later in the Wisconsin Research and Development Center, the alchemic structures of disciplinary knowledge fields were taken

as true, certain statements. The psychology of mastery learning provided the foundation to identify the most efficient strategies for learning. The qualities of people as openness, flexibility, and the uncertainty of the classroom were "to provide frames of reference for reconciling the claims of the learner, the society, the disciplines, and scientific modes of inquiry" (Chase 1977, xiii). The measure of change was given expression in policy and research through the phrase *knowledge utilization* to maximize the efficiency of social processes.

(3) Change was the ordering of the constellation of system's components to achieve the optimal relations. *The operational definition of change was measures of feedback loops.* Change was in organizing and monitoring the processes and communication expressed as inputs and outputs, networks, flows, and circuits. These processes and communication networks contained the triggers for system growth and development. The notion of feedback loops as used in teacher research to explore classroom communication, discussed in chapter 9, connecting system theory with the development of the professional teacher.

(4) The optimal system was theorized as one where the components are in harmony and consensus—that is, where there is an equilibrium. The principles of harmony and consensus connect with the theoretical supposition that optimal efficiency lies in the system's state of equilibrium. Kurt Lewin's "Frontiers in Group Dynamics: Concept, Method and Reality in Social Science; Social Equilibria and Social Change" (1947) defined change as social feedback processes and social management in a "quasi-stationary social equilibria." Optimization is the school system's harmony in the dynamics of the system's components where all girls learn mathematical knowledge equally with boys, there is no achievement gap, *all* children read, all are mathematically able, and consensual professional knowledge brings into being the potentialities of teacher "effectiveness."

(5) The equilibrium of the system is about potentialities rather than descriptions. The notion of potentialities is expressed in systems analysis as "benchmarks," hypothesized as the desired optimized system performance. Benchmarks become a commonplace in public administration, economy, and education as desires about potentialities to actualize. Algorithms became important to managing the equilibrium of the system. Although not essential earlier in turn-of-the-century social thought or mathematics, algorithms grew as significant for thinking about the set of rules that provided solutions to the given problems, or for delineating the most efficient

means to achieve certain given goals. The inscription of algorithms shifts focus onto networks and communications that elide the ontological objects (kinds of people) organized in organizing processes.

(6) The system's harmony and stability (its equilibrium) presupposes its disequilibrium—that is, the factors that diminish, hinder, or prevent the optimization of goals. *Change is functionally what eliminates the factors that produce disequilibrium in the system and allow harmony and consensus.* The social and psychological research connected principles of equilibrium/disequilibrium through expressions of the achievement gap in American educational reforms, with the "gap" registering the disturbance of the system's consensus and harmony between the system's external components (population differences) and internal components (differences in children's school achievement).

(7) *The inscriptions of equilibrium/disequilibrium in research about change are no longer a purely theoretical proposition when brought into the social and psychological sciences. They embody particular cultural theses of normality and pathology.* OECD's PISA, for example, organizes systems principles to measure "well-being" (discussed in chapter 8). The measure correlates the personal, family, and social characteristics of the child to identify which system components contribute to the harmony. That harmony is what is theoretically defined as fostering high student performance (i.e., the normal), while simultaneously identifying those qualities that interfere and restrain the achievement of optimized efficiency. The distinctions and categories are expressed through aggregates presented as national statistics; but the aggregates are formed through differentiating people along a continuum of the normal and the pathological, such as differences in family and community experiences as well as the personality traits of lacking motivation and engagement.

Systems theory appears as directed to organization processes and communication patterns, but it intersects and assembles with other historical lines. This assemblage produces an ordering and classification of kinds of people and differentiates who they are and should be. When systems analysis is examined in various research programs in this chapter and subsequently in international assessments and teacher research, the research is directed to the very interior or soul of the child. The new mathematics curriculum of the 1960s, for example, focused on the processes and communication patterns that could be "theorized and its components identified through a particular set of behaviors and traits thought to make up that kind of person (and thereby a rational and democratic collective)" (Diaz 2017, 31). The research embodied liberal values about who the child was and should be, expressed as useful and practical knowledge for the making of the citizen. "The soul" is the object of the professional organization for mathematics teachers when it is argued that learning mathematics is "contributing to effective living, otherwise it does not have worth and usefulness" (National Council of Teachers of Mathematics 1945, 200).

The agency of the child is given shape within the principles of systems theory. The learning of mathematics, the report continued, links social norms with the interiority of the child, expressed as the "applications of mathematics to problems of industry, physical science, aviation and business should be used for purposes of motivation, illustration and transfer" (National Council of Teachers of Mathematics 1945, 201).

There was debate about the role of certainty in research and development. In computer sciences during these years, for example, the question was whether to create programs that eliminated all error or to create programs that reduced errors as much as possible, knowing that the perfect system was not possible. The latter approach to reduce error in programing won; it is talked about as optimizing achievement or teacher effectiveness today.

The object of the practical knowledge of research forms through the inscription of these principles of social life, normalcy, pathology, and change. What follows explores how the elements of systems thought are connected in educational research.

## Wisconsin R&D: Educational Systems and the Practical Research of Reform

The Wisconsin R&D Center connected systems theory and cybernetics with organizational theories and learning psychologies in the structuring of school reform and change.[13] Reform was expressed in psychological distinctions to identify the proper processes and instructional strategies for the optimal level of learning. The research provided "theory and practical help on what to do and how to do it" (Gage 1976, ix; also see Berliner and Gage 1976, 4).

The research and development assumed the consensus of system goals and harmony as the object of change. The Center's mission was about processes and feedback mechanisms expressed as synthesizing, developing, and demonstrating paths for school improvement. It did so by

- conducting and synthesizing research to clarify the processes of school-age children's learning and development;
- conducting and synthesizing research to clarify effective approaches to teaching students basic skills and concepts;
- developing and demonstrating improved instructional strategies, processes, and materials for students, teachers, and school administrators;
- aiding educators, which helps transfer the outcomes of research and development to improved practice in local schools and teacher education institutions. (Klausmeier et al. 1973, n.p.)

In formulating the R&D tasks, the Center planners adopted systems analysis to identify and correlate the various organizational components of schools. Romberg (1968), a national leader in the mathematics education reform movements,[14] articulated the importance of systems in research about instructional improvement. Romberg studied with people who had returned from the war and brought systems analysis into the study of education.[15] In the context of the Wisconsin R&D Center, he argued that "the word 'system' . . . refers to a man-made controlled functional structure" (15). The "man-made" control function gave attention to "the interdependent components which can be changed or manipulated" through "the feedback or monitoring procedure" used to manage the system as a functional means to orient the processes toward the goals of the system. The system had four components: "input, mechanism, feedback and output."

School improvement expressed in a grant proposal for elementary school teacher education was called "Cybernetics Model for Teacher Education" (DeVault, McCarthy, and Van Ess 1967). The general components for interventions were categories such as school administration, the organization of teaching, teacher education, and district coordination of programs. The different system elements were connected with "input components" (e.g., admissions), the teaching-learning component (e.g., professional foundations and classroom laboratory experience), the output components (e.g., clinical experiences), and elementary school components (e.g., placement for experience). The system elements were called the "intrasystem of feedback for assessment and evaluation of operations."

The operation and feedback mechanisms and research were directed by the psychology of mastery learning. Mastery learning connected systems theory with behavioral principles of the psychology of the child. It entailed breaking down and sequencing specified outcomes of knowledge and skills into hierarchies of learning outcomes. These outcomes were referred to as "behavioral objectives" and "the specific teacher skills, knowledge and attitudes" that were developed through "a systems model of essential components and their interrelations" (DeVault, McCarthy, and Van Ess 1967, 1).

The behavioral objectives enabled a standardization and codification of "outcomes" that could be universalized and replicated across different schools. Behavioral objectives were devices to organize, develop, and demonstrate processes about how certain activities could be maximized by school leaders, teacher practices, and children's learning. The objectives were standards to detect points of disequilibrium, discussed as a "screening mechanism for admission, a diagnosis of students' needs, and a predictor of performances" in a continuous feedback loop (DeVault, McCarthy, and Van Ess 1967, 1).

The principles of cybernetics ordered the model of change as a "rational loop of synthesizing research designed around behavioral objectives" and as "a set of standards." The clinical experiences of teacher education, for example, were structured "in a continuous assessment and [with] evaluation procedures to fulfill the feedback requirements of the system" (DeVault, McCarthy, and Van Ess 1967, 1).

The objective of the R&D was "to expedite educational improvement" (Kreitlow and MacNeil 1969, 1). The Center's curriculum research focused on processes and communications measured as learning in the reading, writing, and mathematics curricula. Research concerned with school administration, for example, considered school district offices to have, "in one form or another, the social machinery necessary for institutional adjustment." The adjustments occurred "within the system which translates purposes, problems, and needs into solutions and action, and that it is possible for ideas to be stalled or permanently lost in the system" (Kreitlow 1972, 1). Processes and communication in research enabled the "meaningful individualization of instruction via media-oriented and computer-facilitated technology."

In the language of the reform movements, the teacher was the *change agent*. The "force" and agency of the teacher was not any absolute concept of freedom; it was bound within the categorical distinctions through which

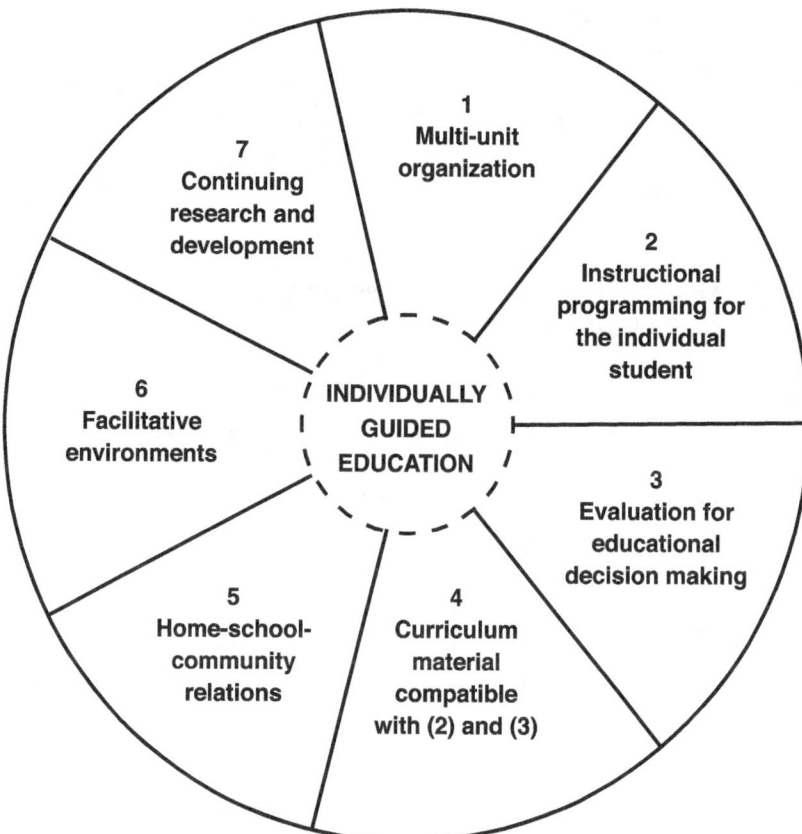

Fig. 4. Major components of Individually Guided Education. Reprinted from *Individually Guided Elementary Education: Concepts and Practices* (Klausmeier 1977b, 11).

the psychology, sociology, and organizational principles defined "nature" as the *system* of ecology relating the social, individuality, and change. The teacher participated in "change agent teams" in the schools as a 'system' of people who were "aware of their authority to act as a force to stimulate their responsibilities to coordinate various effects to initiate and influence change" (Kreitlow 1972, 1).

The research and development of the Center was organized into a reform program, Individually Guided Education (IGE), created as a system for the "meaningful individualization of instruction." Individually Guided Education was an elementary school reform program used in 2,000 schools by the end of the 1970s (Popkewitz, Tabachnick, and Wehlage 1982). The program entailed seven major components and their interrelations to identify "the desirable conditions" for attaining "quality education" (see fig. 4). The program used research as the developing and testing mechanism for organizing school instruction and the curriculum designs generated by the Center (Kreitlow 1972, n.p.).

## The Working of an Abstraction: The System as the Practical Knowledge to Actualize

The research was problem solving that gave a particular epistemic focus to what was to be known. The school was conceptualized as an ideal of harmonious and consensual relations: a social system of "clearly defined roles and responsibilities, shared decision making, continuous pupil progress, personalized instruction, active learning, evaluation related to instructional objectives, involvement of parents and support from the community, and support by responsible education agencies" (Klausmeier 1977b, 6).[16] Research and development of the program integrated instructional planning, school leadership, district policies, school architecture, and school/family/community relations into a feedback mechanism that was to achieve optimal outputs (see fig. 5).

Behavioral objectives were the application of the principles of mastery learning to the school curriculum. The objectives subdivided skills and knowledge to be learned into components. The components provided the necessary prescribed sequence to enable the systemic organizing of teaching and learning. That sequence was ordered as the arrow of time, with each step measurable to ensure the "mastery" of individual learning. The subtasks of learning mathematics, reading, and prereading skills, for example, were divided into subunits that could be codified, standardized, and ordered into a sequence of behavioral objectives (Romberg 1977; Otto 1977; Venezky and Pittelman 1977). As indicated in figure 5, the behavioral objectives were considered as providing a clear and universal cycle of activities related to maximizing system performance, such as the progression of different levels of skill development for learning to read.

The notion of cycle of activities and the arrow of time seem to be oxymorons, but they are not. The attainment of reading skills was considered invariant and contributing to the optimal performance of the system. The

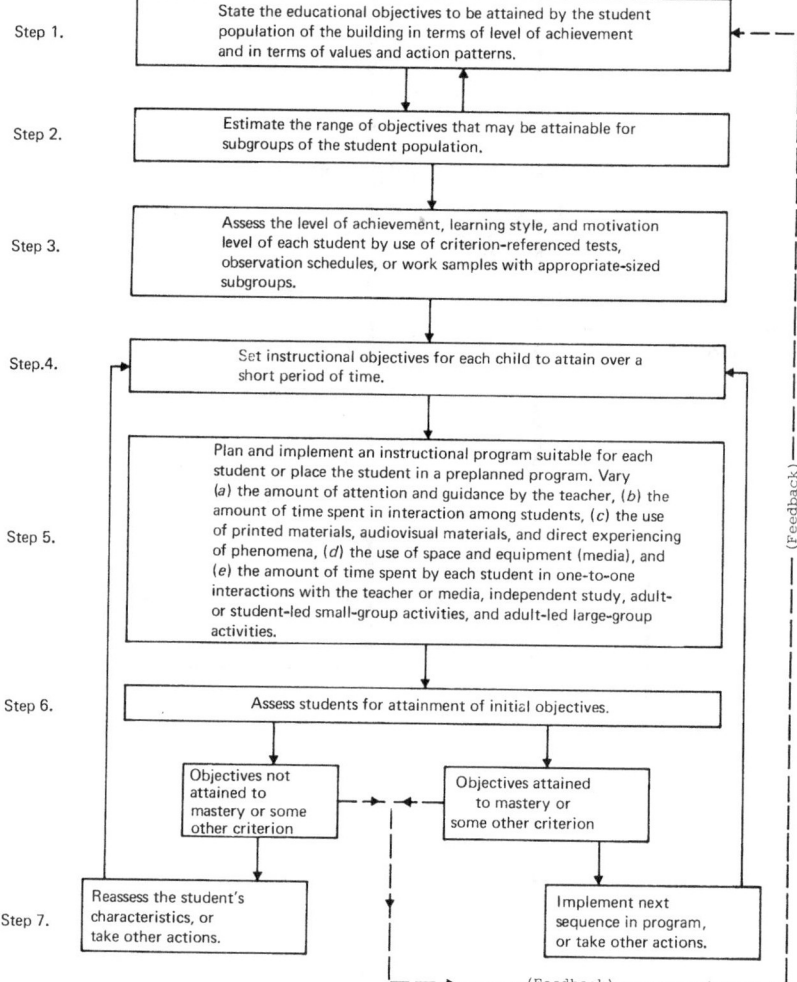

Fig. 5. Instructional programming model in IGE. Reprinted from *Individually Guided Elementary Education: Concepts and Practices* (Klausmeier 1977b, 16).

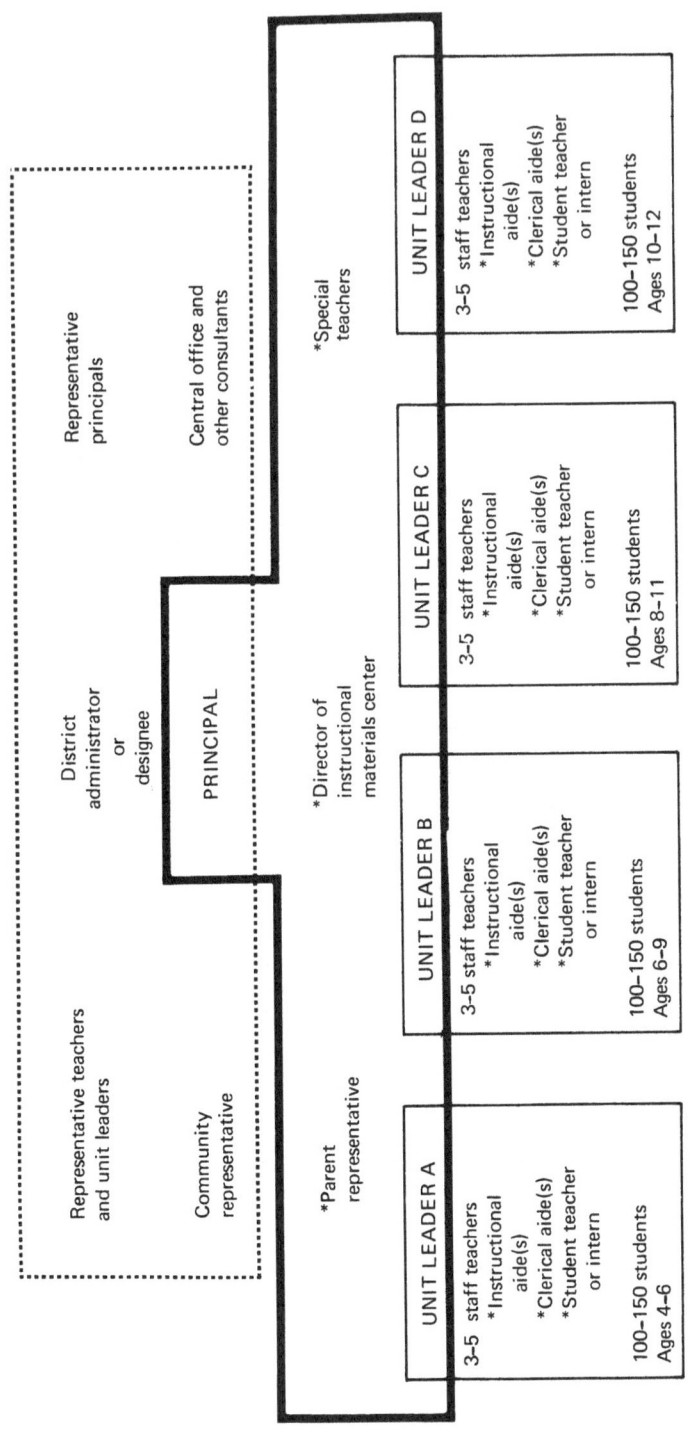

Fig. 5. Multiunit organization of an IGE school of 400–600 students. Reprinted from *Individually Guided Elementary Education: Concepts and Practices* (Klausmeier 1977b, 12).

invariant quality of the objects codified and the standardized processes, "proceed through the same sequence of units and attain the same objects to the same criterion of full mastery" (Klausmeir 1977a, 63).

Classroom instruction organized students into *units* that varied in size depending on learning goals. The instructional units provided flexibility in the implementation of behavioral objectives. The unit's instructional flexibility to organize children was thought to supersede the idea of children in fixed age-graded and self-contained "classrooms." The unit grouping of children responded to the learning objectives of the different subject areas of learning (music versus mathematics, for example), where the learning progression could be measured through the standardizations of the mastery learning (fig. 6). The flexible grouping was an idea dictated by the sampling norms of randomization of the methods of educational psychology ("the unit" was also called I&R—Instruction and Research) (Popkewitz, Tabachnick, and Wehlage 1982).

The organization of the students, teachers' planning, and assessments were functionally linked to the other components of the school "system." "Each I&R Unit carries out [its] functions in accordance with school and school district policies" as related to the school "instructional improvement committee and the Systemwide Program Committee" (Klausmeier 1977b, 13).

Individually Guided Education and behavioral objectives conceived the school as an ordered system whose processes embodied means-end sequences called "individualized learning" (fig. 6). Research was to provide more efficient understandings of the particular relation of instruction, psychology, curriculum, and school leadership as interrelated components of the system whose outcomes were "mastery learning" that gave expression to hierarchies of behavioral objectives. The instruction of children organized into *units* provided an order that could be measured in the mastery learning schema. The sampling norms of the methods of educational psychology dictated the flexible grouping.

### Mastery Learning as Feedback Loops and Levels of Performance

The Wisconsin R&D Center's director argued that cognitive psychology replaced earlier studies of school learning organized through classical and operant conditioning following B. F. Skinner with an empirically substantiated and scientific approach to change (Klausmeier and Wisconsin Associates 1990). In fact, children's cognitive development was formed through an assembly of different psychologies. It interrelated the "environmental" conditions of the classroom with the operant conditioning principles of behavioral notions. It also connected systems thought and cybernetics with the structuralism of the Swiss psychology of Jean Piaget and the processual approach and functionalism of the Russian Lev Vygotsky (see, e.g., Bruner 1983).

Systems theory emphasized ongoing instructional processes and communication practice that omitted any reference to ontological objects. Of course, these objects were there in the presumed notions of childhood and ability, for example, to define what was (im)possible for the child and teacher, but they were obscured in the attention to processes. The creativity and problem-solving skills of the child were treated as independent of any specific subject matter; they were linked to characteristics of the child, such as intelligence and gender, and to accomplishing broader performance measures of "productive thinking" and intelligence (Wardrop et al. 1969, 67).

Cognitive psychology joined with mastery learning to establish levels of performance (behavioral objectives) that all students would master before moving on to the next unit (Klausmeier and Wisconsin Associates 1990). Behavioral objectives were related to a more general instructional reform movement of Allan Bloom's taxonomies drawn from educational psychology (Bloom 1968).[17] Instruction was designing the processes and communications practices, expressed as "an environment in which individual students learn at rates appropriate to each student and in a manner suitable to each student's learning style and other and personal characteristics" (Klausmeier 1977a, 7).

The model of learning combined the organic (mind) and machine in the open system that entailed both principles of certainty and uncertainty. Certainty entered through the ontological givenness of the world. The processual approach was called a modeling-process method in the mathematics curriculum, capturing the strategies of the learning generalizations emphasized in the New Curriculum Reform Movement (Bruner 1960). The learning processes were a fabrication that took the modeling procedures of the curriculum as the structuring principles for children's access to what was given as real. The Developmental Mathematics Program incorporated into IGE defined learning as the "functions and relations which reflect[ed] underlying properties as the unifying theme" in mathematical knowledge (Romberg 1976, 6).[18] The learning of mathematics was considered as "heavily dependent on the acquisition of specific concepts and skills, because in using any process efficiently children must acquire concepts and skills," such as learning common names for geometric figures and how to add three-digit numbers (ibid.).

The psychology performed to universalize and give a commonality across curriculum fields. The focus on processes and communication assumed the alchemy discussed previously. Literacy, science, and mathematics were treated as concepts to learn. Learning mathematics was about an anticipated mode of living, to be "used, or may profitably be used, in the lives of children and of adults alike" (National Council of Teachers of Mathematics 1945, 202).

The uncertainty was expressed in different ways. Learning was "purposeful and problem based to accomplish outcomes that are uncertain" (Romberg 1977, 80). The Developmental Mathematics Program stressed children's "openness" in discovering mathematical ideas, "rather than simply assimilating the record of other people's activities."

*Mastery and its hierarchy of scales and performance levels were anticipatory about potentialities to be actualized.* The outcomes described as the objectives of mastery learning were desires that were directed in the psychological language about helping children learn to participate. The learning to participate embodied notions of potentialities of what the child is to become. Instruction was for children to take "mathematical terms, sentences, and phrases as 'models' of situations" that can then be used in constructing activities that "children like to do and can perform" (Romberg 1976, 6). Mathematics education was about making kinds of people and "the soul": "A desire to learn and active participation are required . . . [to produce children's] sensing, manipulating, and direct participation in learning" (Klausmeier 1977b, 7).

### Research as Experimentalism, Empiricism, and Pragmatism

Research contributed to and monitored the ongoing processes in a developmental, experimental, and pragmatic fashion that deployed different technologies and inscriptions from the previously discussed Progressivism. The R&D knowledge was directed toward "output-optimizing," toward improving policy delivery and advocating for the expansion of policy measures over time (Haveman 1987). The empiricism was rooted in the "'relativist theory of democracy that was a stripped-down version of John Dewey's pragmatism . . . made normative. . . . [D]emocracy was a process of empirically-driven experimentation instead of an ideology, and in a post-ideological age, Americans had perfected this process" (Hartman 2008, 55).

The empirical evidence in the research standardized and calculated the theoretical entity of mastery learning as though it did exist. The "nature" of learning in mastery learning was tied to systems theory. The empirical evidence was a historical agent to name and measure the effects of the abstractions of systems theory. The Wisconsin Design of Reading, a reading acquisition program in the IGE schools, was defined in a figure as the "Framework For Organizing Skill Instruction," with the system components of "management, assessment, instruction, skills and objectives, with the circle fed by evaluation" (Otto and Askov 1974, 13).

The learning of reading was linked to Thorndike's turn-of-the-century research on "reading as reasoning" (Otto 1971). The emphasis was on the particular empirical needs for data, linking the discrete components that produced the ability to read. The research, for example, assessed the "effects of pictures on the reading comprehension" of elementary and secondary school pupils (Koenke 1968, 2). Students were asked, for example, to state the main idea in the three paragraphs or the accompanying photographs to assess effective reading strategies.

The statistics embodied none of the visual culture found in today's international assessment (discussed in chapter 8). The statistics and survey research of the Wisconsin R&D Center were concerned with causal laws and variance. Initial research entailed experimental designs. Differences were identified as variations correlated with the physical and mental achievement of "children of low, average and high intelligence" (table 1).

This notion of difference was brought into the study of mathematics education. In one study, differences defined as the effects of three kinds of information conceptualized as facilitating the acquisition and retention of mathematics content were studied (Romberg and Wilson 1973). The interest of the research was how prior information influences children's learning. The research defined the prior information operationally as advanced organizers—such as the information given to students prior to instruction, the cognitive set as the information to inform students of anticipated associations expected to acquire in instruction, and advanced organizers that bring past learning to help understand the content to be learned. The results were statistically analyzed through a 2x2x2 fixed effect analysis of variance on learning and retention tests (Romberg and Wilson 1973, 74).

Table 1. Summary of acceptance and rejection of hypotheses 3, 4, and 5 dealing with development and within-child variability and concerning relationships among physical and mental achievement measures in children of low, average, and high intelligence

| Hypothesis | 1956<br>101 months old | 1957<br>113 months old | 1958<br>125 months old |
|---|---|---|---|
| (3) Uneven physical development with the child (split growth) accompanies low achievement in arithmetic and reading. | Rejected, but all correlations are negative, the hypothesized direction. | Rejected, but all correlations are negative, the hypothesized direction. | Rejected, but all correlations are negative, the hypothesized direction. |
| (4) A low level of physical development within the child accompanies low achievement in arithmetic and reading. | Upheld for boys. Rejected for girls. | Rejected for both sexes. | Rejected for both sexes. |
| (5) The within-child variability in grip, IQ, reading, arithmetic, and language achievement is the same among children of low, average, and high intelligence. | Rejected on the basis of comparison of means. | Rejected | Rejected |
| (5$_1$) The within-child variability in the three achievement measures is the same among children of low, average, and high intelligence. | Upheld | Upheld | Upheld |

*Source:* Reprinted from *An Analysis of Learning Efficiency in Arithmetic of Mentally Retarded Children in Comparison with Children of Average and High Intelligence* (Klausmeier, Feldhusen, and Check 1959, 110).

*Note:* With hypothesis 4, except with children at the youngest age and only for boys, no significant relationship was found between the levels of physical development in four measures—height, weight, strength of grip, and carpal age—and achievement in either reading or arithmetic. With hypothesis 5, the within-child variability in these measures is not the same. In the low and high IQ children, the levels at which the average IQ children were performing in the five functioning areas were most consistent (Klausmeier, Feldhusen, and Check 1959, 109–10).

The Center's technical reports registered the measures as the mapping related to the mastering of the curriculum's content knowledge as correlated with other elements associated with learning. "Cognitive style," for example, was a concept created to show differences in performance on concept-learning and information-processing tasks in classrooms correlated by sex, age, and IQ. The empirical data and their magnitudes were ordered as regulated components governing the optimization of the system. Statistically driven research examined, for example, the effects of a content-relevant picture on the comprehension of the main idea of a paragraph (Koenke 1968) or the development of lesson plans, tests of knowledge, comprehension, and their application related to instruction in the physical concept of force for grades 2–6 (Helgeson 1968).

## Science as a Redemptive Theme against Dangers and Dangerous Populations

While the recognition of differences and deviances was generated in the interstices that constituted the Social Question of Progressive research at the turn of the 20th century, there were no prior scientifically oriented definitions of poverty to standardize and calculate poverty to guide policy and research until the 1950s (Cruikshank 1999).[19] Title I of the Elementary and Secondary Education Act of 1965 was, among other efforts, to direct attention to organizing classifications to rectify the conditions for the poor and "Others" classified as socially and economically marginalized populations (Haveman 1987, 16). Governmental definitions were used to operationalize research to identify the causes of failure and to consider what policy instruments were available and cost-effective (Haveman 1987, 32).

The research articulated redemptive themes in addressing social divisions. The rhetoric of the American Jeremiad's hope was expressed in the statistics that iterated the hopes and fears inscribed in the theories and programs to reform education. The statistical narratives were affective. The affect was spoken of as the breakdown and possibilities of "the demographic restructuring of the American metropolis, technological and commercial expansions" and the "economic agreements about how segregation wasted the potential utility of Black children" (Hartman 2008, 158). The Wisconsin R&D Center's reports, for example, expressed social commitments to equality through statistics that objectified particular populations as different and targeted for special programs. Existing research and development was taken optimistically, part of processes that had already increased high school graduation rates: 75 percent of pupils entering the fifth grade in the fall of 1964 had graduated from high school in 1972 and 23 percent of the high school graduates were expected to complete college (Klausmeier 1977b, 3–4). With the hope was the fear that "one out of four students has a significant reading deficiency, half of our unemployed youth are functionally illiterate, and approximately 2.5% of our nation's youth drop-out" (4).

The emergence of issues of inequality and school practices was related to the more general research literature, social legislation, and social movements whose historical lines crossed with the social and psychological sciences. Studies focused on the social and cultural dimensions of urban life, education, and unequal schools of urban education and participant observations that opened up the "black box" of classroom life (Smith and Geoffrey 1968).

The initial research reports of the Wisconsin R&D Center, however, had no differentiations of populations. The psychological distinctions were tied to psychometrics: the stages of concept mastery included classification of "the reluctant learner" and the disabilities of different kinds of children. Differences were spoken about as individual capacities generalized in universal categories related to learning, motivation, sensation and perception, thinking and communication, emotions, and intelligence. Differences were defined as sex discrimination that had to do with X and Y genes. Referencing the relation of psychology to particular aptitudes in music, for example, differences were defined as the abilities to discriminate pitch, loudness, rhythm, time, timbre, and tonal memory. The characteristics of music ability draw on the revisions of the test about populational differences in music ability produced in the 1920.

The differences were described as the natural aptitudes of children that better teaching will enable those potentials through remediation (Ringness, Klausmeier, and Singer 1959, 281). The distinctions were between children with low, average, and high IQ, and with occupations classified as semiskilled and unskilled, professional and semiprofessional. One of the few uses of populational distinctions to define differences were in measures of learning efficiency in arithmetic that differentiated "mentally retarded children in comparison with children of average and high intelligence" (Klausmeier, Feldhusen, and Check 1959).

By the late 1960s, the social distinctions became finer and more elaborate, and they were combined with psychological categories that were explicitly related to race and poverty. Studies of differences compared the amount and scope of vocabulary and grammatical structuring in parent/child interactions among social classes. The differences were to think about inclusion and how educational practices could extend their capabilities to respond to the diverse society they served (Glaser 1977, v).

The research designed interventions to change social conditions that influenced the disparities facing children and families in poverty. The Wisconsin R&D Center reports, for example, increasingly produced new sets of distinctions and divisions that articulated notions of what was healthy, normal, and desired, and at the same time instantiated that certain children did not have these qualities. Categories of the socially disadvantaged, for example, appeared as psychological distinctions of difference. They concerned children of the poor and racial populations that "lacked" efficacy and self-esteem, "at-risk," and, at one point, as "the reluctant learner." The classifications were given as the differentiation of the effects of poverty on the school or political participation (see Cruikshank 1999). Psychological taxonomies created distinctions to differentiate middle-class youth as "self-directed," "adaptive," and having traits of intelligence from the adolescents of poorer families who were more likely to be "submissive," "defiant," "unadjusted," and academic "failures" (Hartman 2008, 66).

Research brought into existence the double qualities of potentialities-to-be and the potentialities-not-to-be as the object of changing the school system. Potentiality appears in the conceptualization of differences spoken about as acquiring higher-level conceptualizing skills and other abilities linked to the idea that children "should have *developed healthy self-concepts*" (Klausmeier 1977b, 7, my italics). Health was a cultural quality, but it was expressed as principles of a system's functions, structures, and developmental processes. The methodological references for obtaining "robust" data for educational improvement brought into play notions of equilibrium and disequilibrium (Kreitlow and MacNeil 1969).

The developmentalism of the problem-solving research directed what was the practical object of change. Research located points for planned interventions to change those elements that disturbed the system's equilibrium, whether they were organizations related to teacher training or psychological categories about disadvantaged children, and children's motivation and family structures. The ordering and classifying generated a comparative system of reason articulated in programs of remediation that would reduce social and psychological pathologies.

The teacher, again, was the agent of change: the making of the teacher was entangled with classifications that expressed desires of who the child should be. The teacher brought cultural understandings of differences to enable the child to learn. The teacher was to understand "the culturally disadvantaged child and his background, but they [teachers] must also believe that he is teachable" (Otto 1969, vii). The problem of change was in the processes that enabled the early remediation and the enrichment of a language-experience approach to reading and the provision of effective and varied materials. The emphasis was on practical knowledge for the processes and communication patterns that embodied a comparative reasoning. Eliminating the system's disequilibrium was providing remediation and enrichment to change the child, family, and community abjected into spaces outside of the normal.

It is important to recognize that this abjection was not the intent of researchers, but was embodied in the epistemic rules and standards that ordered change. The statistics connected distinctions that objectified, racialized, classified, and gendered classifications of the limits of conversational skills. The language spoke of environmental and physical consequences of poverty that simultaneously overlapped bodily and medical distinctions with cultural pathologies—the "handicap" of children with malnutrition, disease, inadequate medical attention, or with parents' child rearing working against the goals of the school (Harris 1966).

## Practical Research as Materializing Potentialities in the Present

The mobilizations of the R&D resonated with but also disconnected from earlier images and narratives of American Progressivism. The "abstract spaces" of the school system demarcated the child's success and failures through particular epistemological principles for defining differences and fabricated human kinds. American exceptionalism, the double qualities of the Jeremiad, and science in making kinds of people and differences were the objects of change. The rationality and "democratic" dispositions desired, however, were rendered in a constellation of reflexivity ordered through systems thought and cybernetics. The assemblage formed a grid to authenticate and generate potentialities. The temporality was operating as anticipatory of the future, but without necessarily defined endpoints or contexts.

If I return to one set of principles pursued about the actor and agency, these principles are enunciated in the research as correlated with the mechanisms at work within the systems and cybernetics theories to design change. Agency in the R&D was bound to the epistemic ordering of problem solving, actualized through the self-authorizing qualities of the school "system." The teacher as agent of change and the child as master of learning provided the coordinates for determining the reason of action itself.

It is important to return to the abstraction of the school systems as not empirically deduced but a priori, self-referential, and self-authorizing. The idea of a system as an organism to replace earlier mechanical notions with more seemingly dynamic models of change did not make the determinism of the machine disappear. The school conceptualized as a social organism having stages of growth and processes of development that change over time congealed with determinism. That determinism was present in the ontological objects given in the alchemy of the curriculum and the modeling as learning. Learning was organized for the child to access "reality" embedded in inscriptions of the codifications and standardizations.

The emphasis on processes and communication elided the objectifications of social life in schooling embedded in the classifications and desires generated. The problem solving of the system engendered desires that research was to produce. These desires were embedded in principles that organized R&D to produce social and educational improvement. The notion of system linked theories about the child as a universal claim about producing rational processes of representations that "described what could be as if this potential was simply waiting to materialize" (Poovey 1998, 248). The inscriptions of systems were acted upon as techniques of social life to be "utilized as the basis of organization architecture and divisions of managerial responsibility, and utilized as a grid to realize the real in the form in which it may be thought" (Rose 1999, 213).

The erasure of the ontological objects in favor of processes and communication, however, did not eliminate the objectifications but only made them sightless in the "eye" of seeing. The distinctions and differentiations, I argued, revisioned the fabrication of kinds of people through a comparative reasoning embedded in the research. The abstraction generated standards about who the child was, should be, and how she/he did not "fit" into the spaces of normality.

In the next chapters, the problem solving is explored as embodied in the abstraction of the school as a system through the macrostatistical studies of the international assessments of student performances and the micro, qualitative studies of teacher effectiveness and teacher education reform. These research programs both connect and disconnect with the postwar epistemological principles discussed in the research of this chapter.

# 8 • Numbers, Desires, and International Student Assessments

## Benchmarks and Empirical Evidence

The postwar sciences, I argued in chapter 7, brought into view a particular kind of applied research defined as "problem solving." Problem solving was explored not merely as a phrase orienting research to find useful or practical knowledge for change. Problem solving was embedded in a complex grid of social, cultural, and political lines that brought into existence new epistemological principles for managing change. The principles of systems theory and cybernetics folded into the sciences embodied particular abstractions about people and change. Benchmarks exemplified those principles, with their construction ordered through the principles of equilibrium or harmony and consensus of the system that projected desires in the objects of change. Change is to reduce or eliminate disturbances (disequilibrium) to achieve harmony. The assumption of equilibrium/disequilibrium embodies a continuum of value between normalcy and pathology when brought into social analysis.

By the turn of the 21st century, the reasoning of social life and change through systems theory is so naturalized that it is assumed in practical research. Systems as an organizing principle is never mentioned but performs to order important international assessments of education systems: the Organization for Economic Co-operation and Development's Programme for International Student Assessment (PISA)[1] surveys student skills and knowledge in science, mathematics, and literacy and McKinsey & Company's educational reports, which draw on PISA results to "help educational systems and providers to improve outcomes for millions of students globally."[2] The abstraction of the school "system," connecting with social, cultural, and pedagogical lines, provides a style of reasoning about what matters, how problems are articulated, what notions of methods are reasonable, and what counts as solutions or practical knowledge for the problems identified. The criteria of systems theory become self-referential in constituting what counts as context and the empirical evidence that testifies about what works to secure change.

This chapter approaches the idea of "benchmarks" and having "empirical evidence" as not merely policy instruments for educational improvement.[3] The Programme for International Student Assessment and the McKinsey reports are explored as generating particular desires about the organization of society and kinds of people embodied in their rules and standards of reason. The international assessments connect national policy, research, and the organization of social life to create new social spaces of action through its codifications and standardizations (Carvalho 2012; Gorur 2011; Grek 2016; Lindblad, Pettersson, and Popkewitz 2018).

The first section turns to benchmarks and empirical evidence in the international assessments as enclosed within a particular historical space of action. That space entails visual technologies in which numbers and statistical correlations articulate comparisons assembled through cultural and social theories ordered through systems/cybernetics. The second section focuses on desires and potentialities instantiated in the models of change generated, constituting the boundaries of "context" and the practical knowledge of change. The third section examines how the numbers generated in PISA perform as technologies for telling the truth about nations, society, and people in "the arrow of time." Attention in the fourth section is given to numbers as embodying cultural distinctions, generating the double gestures of the normal and pathological. The final section explores how social and cultural principles are erased through concerns with change as "highways" and "pathways" to follow for success.

The International Large-Scale Assessments (ILSA) are affective as well as cognitive. This affective element about change forms as a particular horizon for what today is called "post-truth," the populism that challenges the scientific expertise of modern governing by emphasizing emotion and affect. While not arguing a causal relation, this chapter illustrates how the affective elements of post-truth are instantiated and given intelligibility, ironically, through the visual culture by which the reports redefine how truth is told at the intersection of science and society.

## International Assessments and the Chimera of What Is Named: The PISA and McKinsey Educational Reports

While the OECD is officially defined as an organization that promotes economic development, that relation is spurious at best when its studies of education are considered. The economic language is less about the economy and more about cultural and social categories of differences. This section explores three cultural sets of principles within OECD's Program for International Student Assessment (PISA). The section initially examines the international assessment as a particular theoretical space that seems denuded of theory in connecting national policy, research, and schooling. This is followed with a discussion of how the assessments embody an alchemy that produces measures as other than what is named—science, mathematics, and literacy. The final part examines how systems theory connects with distinctions and classifications of schooling to shape and fashion what is seen and done.

### PISA as a Theoretical Space Denuded of Theory

OECD's Program for International Student Assessment has its roots in the late 1950s and the International Association for the Evaluation of Educational Achievement, which was established in Paris in 1963 by UNESCO with financial support from the World Bank and the Ford Foundation (Husén Postlethwaite 1996; Keeves 1995; Mølstad and Pettersson 2018). The methodological focus was on large-scale systems of management and processes. Comparisons were made through the development of large quantitative descriptions of educational achievement within and across systems of education. The focus was on the assessments of school subjects relating to mathematics, science, reading, and civic and citizenship education, among others.

The Program for International Student Assessment was initiated in 1997, following the pattern of the OECD indicators that began to be developed in the 1960s (Bürgi and Tröhler 2018). The first triennial international survey was administered in 2000. Its purpose was a worldwide evaluation of national education systems of the skills and knowledge of 15-year-old students. According to its website, "over half a million students, representing 28 million 15-year-olds in 72 countries and economies, took the internationally agreed two-hour test in 2015."[4]

The measurements rank nations but function within a model of change

## The OECD Education Policy Review Process: Sweden

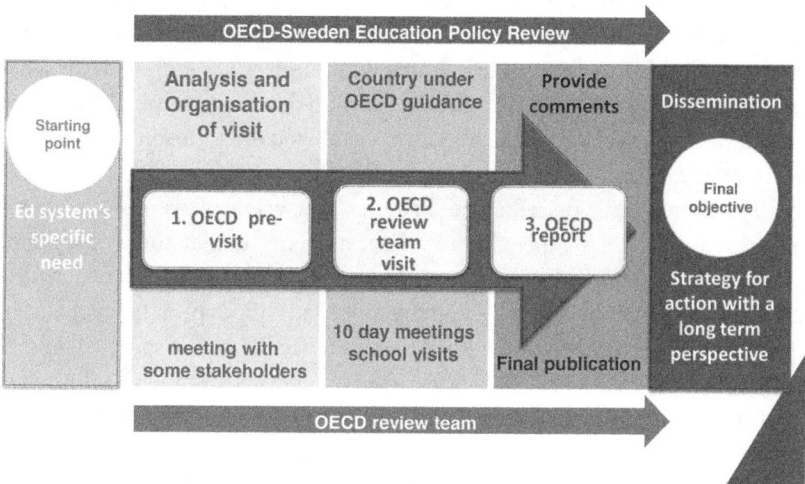

Fig. 7. The OECD-Sweden Education Policy Review. Reprinted from *The OECD-Sweden Education Policy Review: Main Issues and Next Steps* (Pont et al. 2014, 2). Reprinted by permission of the OECD.

by which nations can achieve the philosophical ideals of the successful student and society that are embodied in its abstraction of the school as a system (see fig. 7). The OECD model of change correlates the universal international measures of students' performances with universal measures of social and psychological factors. The statistical relations perform as indicators by which prescriptions are "tailored" for each nation. The "tailoring" is described as the "contextualization of [a] country's needs," with contextualization defined within the self-referential categories and distinctions of the systems analysis, something I return to later in this chapter. The process of change assumes there is a consensus, harmony, and "the arrow of time" in designing "pathways" or "highways" for educational improvement. Deviations from the optimum scores, indicating disequilibrium in the system, provide the basis of "recommendations, specific considerations and specific proposals" to steer the nation's improvement of its performance (Pont et al. 2014).

The PISA assessments and its national rankings are about the potentialities of societies that the research authorizes: the "readiness" of nations' schools for what are thought as the imperatives of the 21st-century knowledge economies and knowledge societies (Popkewitz 2011c). The comparative measures are expressed through benchmarks. The benchmarks are philosophical ideals that act epistemically as desires generated about what schooling, people, and society should be. The desires are embedded in the distinctions of the statistical measures established as those of science or mathematics educational skills and knowledge.

These measures inscribe the alchemy that was explored in chapter 5 and discussed later in this chapter. That alchemy is that the measures of assessment are about kinds of people and a particular moral order, discussed in PISA as modes of living of future kinds of people's "participation, economic preparedness and global competence." The alchemy of school subjects in the measured categories and distinctions are not about science as a disciplinary field of knowledge production and understanding. The statistical measures are calculations about kinds of people fashioned as equivalences from which differences in nations are established.

Providing indicators on the effectiveness, equity, and efficiency of education systems, setting benchmarks for international comparison, and monitoring trends over time are goals of the Programme for International Student Assessment. In addition, it is stated that PISA builds a sustainable database that allows researchers worldwide to study basic and policy-oriented questions on education, including its relation to society and the economy (OECD 2016, 102).

The standardizations and calculations are statistically elaborated as correlations and comparative ranking of national school systems in a developmental sequence. The benchmarks perform to articulate the philosophical ideals of society and people as the standards to achieve. Assessment is of the nation's "readiness" for the anticipated future. The statistical correlations compare what is defined as the necessary future student's "practical knowledge" in literacy, science and mathematics, collaborative problem solving, and literacy, and more recently measures of student "well-being."

Within the field of measurement, the statistical procedures are thought of as innovative, relating school performance and benchmarks rather than school inputs, such as school leadership qualities, teacher credentials, or resource allocation (Hopmann 2008).[5] The statistical techniques deployed in the algorithms of the international assessments are sophisticated and often extend previous research in the field of measurement (see, e.g., Kuger et al. 2016). The statistics create a common content through standardizing the categories for examining similarities and differences in educational systems. Kuger and Klieme (2016) argue, for example, that issues of assessment previously have been fractured through localizing the analysis. PISA, in contrast, has been important for the development of technologies "to increase generalizability or results by actually including different school systems, teaching traditions and cultural settings in research studies, so as to empirically compare effects across countries. The exceptions are international large-scale assessments (ILSAs), which are best known for their use in system-wide educational monitoring" (5).

The methodological sophistication of the statistics, however, is an important but not a sufficient criterion for considering the research and it promise for educational change. What is important are the conditions in which the numbers are connected and assembled through different historical lines to create the objects of reflection and change measured. The application of the statistical methods does not merely describe and explain the data but "acts" within a grid of different historical principles that give intelligibility to OECD's assessments.

### The Chimera That What Is Named Is Measured

The benchmarks are standards to represent the theoretical points of the school system's optimal performance, or its points of equilibrium. Its categories, which are tied to concepts about knowledge and skills, are given as learning about, for example, science, mathematics, and literacy. However, the alchemy comes back into view. What is named is not what is measured. If the notion of "scientific literacy" is examined, the alchemy becomes quickly visible. The diverse and complex conditions of the spaces that form as the enunciation of the sciences are deterritorialized, and reterritorialized through the translations into school "content." In PISA, concepts from multiple fields of science are a translated, unified, global set of principles that are no longer about the practices of science but are now activated and articulated in the spaces of pedagogy and the psychologies of learning.

The chimera of this de/reterritorializing is exemplified in the PISA assessment in the science question asked about acid rain. The rhetorical form of the question creates the appearance of merely assessing children's knowledge of science.

QUESTION 1

Normal rain is slightly acidic because it has absorbed some carbon dioxide from the air. Acid rain is more acidic than normal rain because it has absorbed gases like sulfur oxides and nitrogen oxides as well.

Where do these sulfur oxides and nitrogen oxides in the air come from? (OECD 2013, 103–4)

The question inscribes the alchemic practices in which the knowledge of "acid rain" performs as part of a grid of principles about the potentialities of children. Differences of fields are made into a universal logic of science itself, as the acid rain question is posed about a unified quality of knowledge "developed into analytically different fields of competences, knowledge, and attitudes" (OECD 2013, 12). The classifications about the child's ability to answer the assessment question express particular analytical distinctions about the concept of acid rain. The logic is Cartesian that has a different trajectory than the reasoning of the sciences from which the curriculum borrows. That Cartesian logic expresses the concepts, generalizations, and propositions of the sciences as objectified representations about human and natural conditions. The representations are the object to be known and learned. The concepts are cognitive entities that are phenomena external to the mind but which the mind can apprehend and act on as knowledge about the world.[6]

This cognitive distinction defining acid rain is placed in the assessment performatively as the moral claim that learning the content of science creates the responsible citizen: "What is important for citizens to value about science and technology? An answer should include the role and contributions to society of science and of science-based technology, and their importance in many personal, social, and global contexts" (OECD 2013, 99). The competencies of the person is not about "doing science" as a form of knowledge, reflection, and interpretation but in recognizing "the role and contributions to society of science and of science-based technology, and their importance in many personal, social, and global contexts" (99).

The "competencies" are expressed as the rules and standards of the reason of "science" that are external to the child but whose principles organize conduct. The functional use of knowledge requires the application of those processes defined through learning psychology as the characteristics of science and scientific enquiry (here termed the scientific competencies), to regulate an individual's appreciation, interest, values, and action.

The objectifications given as science constitute the child's "scientific literacy." A student's ability to carry out the scientific competencies involves stabilizing the knowledge of science to understand the objectifications of characteristics of science, reterritorialized as a way of acquiring knowledge (i.e., knowledge about science). The definition reverts to psychology in governing the child: the object of change and the dispositions to carry out these competencies depend upon an individual's attitudes toward science and a willingness to engage in science-related issues (OECD 2013, 100). The representations to learn are taken as the realities to be internalized in the making of kinds of people.

## "Systems" as Self-Referential and Self-Authorizing

The epistemic framing of the benchmarks in OECD's assessment is shaped through the self-referential and self-authorizing qualities of "system theory"; that is, systems theory generates rules and standards for the classification and ordering of what is recognized as understandable, manageable empirical evidence and the valid "solutions" in the comparisons and ranking of nations.

The self-referential and self-authorizing qualities travel within both the OECD and McKinsey models of change. The alchemy of school subjects intersects with what count as measurable, calculable objects of teacher professionalism and student engagement. They are correlated to map the system's "structure, resource, or process, and in terms of which agent the intervention acted upon (e.g. principal, teacher, student)" (Mourshed et al. 2010, 10). The rationality of change expressed in the OECD and McKinsey reports is to maximize people making "rational" or the "right" choices for students' higher achievement, and to design paths for student employment through better, harmonious communication between schools and employers (Barton, Farrell, and Mourshed 2013).

The self-referential and self-authorizing qualities generate the notion of context that appears in the OECD and McKinsey reports. Context, a concept used to explain the factors influencing the assessment, is an abstraction about what matters and is not something *naturally "there"* to explain the influences on what happens and should happen. The categories and distinctions of context are generated through historical lines that activate what is noticed and thought about as objects under scrutiny.

In the international assessments, context is a word whose meanings are enclosed and interned through the systems classifications and the application of the statistics deployed. "Context" reflects the theoretical concerns of system equilibrium hypothesized as enabling nations to achieve success and the factors of disequilibrium that disturb and prevent the optimal outcomes or achievement of benchmarks. Context is the adjustment and coordination of teacher practices, leadership, and community factors hypothesized to bring about system equilibrium. The report on unemployment (Barton, Farrell, and Mourshed 2013), for example, is about correcting the system's failures to achieve harmony and consensus so all students have jobs.

Context is defined textually in the McKinsey's unemployment report as where there is harmony between the interactions and communications of educators and employers. The search for harmony makes sense of the conclusion that unemployment is the result of the lack of coordination between the educator and employer. That coordination, however, is not merely about nations and the institutional organization of schools, but about statistical correlations about the psychological qualities of the child and the social qualities of family and community.

The self-referential and self-authorizing qualities of theory in methods are not unique to systems theory. The paradigmatic or seemingly circulatory qualities are conditions of different styles of reasoning about the sciences (Popkewitz 2013d, 2014b). Attention is directed here to the particularities of the system principles "acting" in the international assessments to form the context through which practical, useful knowledge is generated to orient and assess change. The epistemological principles at work concerning development, consensus, harmony, stability, and equilibrium/disequilibrium are theoretical, and not empirically derived.

## Utopic Promises and the Empirical Evidence of Desires in the Arrow of Time

The self-referentially and self-authorizing qualities of the systems reason bring the principles organizing benchmarks and context into a relation of the arrow of time and desires. The intersections "act" to create the object of practical knowledge in the problem of change.

Fig. 8. The OECD Education Policy Review Process: Sweden. Reprinted from *The OECD-Sweden Education Policy Review. Main Issues and Next Steps* (Pont et al. 2014, 3). Reprinted by permission of the OECD.

### Utopic Promises as Empirical Evidence

The models of change applied have the effect of the promised future that each nation can achieve. That achievement seems within reach if there is the proper planning and coordination of educational systems. The OECD Education Policy Review for Sweden (2014), for example, suggests a three-part process (see fig. 7). The process remains universal but seemingly localized. Change is expressed as the recommendations "tailored" to the specific education system's "needs." Change is a planned, orderly, and linear process that ensures progress, articulated as better policies for improving learning outcomes (fig. 8).

The models of change hold a utopic promise of providing the technologies for nations to reach the future. The promise is a democratic world.

The promise is bringing into existence prosperity, happiness, and well-being to societies and people if they work hard and follow the identified highways of change.

The technologies of change are affective. Benchmarks articulate salvation themes about future student participation, economic preparedness, and global competence. The initial OECD language of *forecasting* in the 1960s has been transformed into a language about the future by present management schemes of planning that link words like "development" and "growth" to "benchmarks." Recent PISA measures of student "well-being" announce they are the "world's premier yardstick for evaluating the quality, equity and efficiency of school systems" (OECD 2017, 3). The yardsticks are "universal scale[s] of calibration" created as equivalences (see, e.g., Mourshed et al. 2010, 7). The benchmarks are the desired qualities and characteristics of achievement for nations (Mourshed et al. 2010, 14). The promise of the models of change is that if nations properly apply the abstraction whose categories and correlations that organize the assessments, then nations, schools, and economies will function at the high level of efficiency and productivity necessary to achieve prosperity.

Numbers are given as the indicator of what needs to be ordered for nation's development, growth, and equity. The measures codify the distinctions that indicate the "needs" of better-performing and low-performing students in relation to the system's criteria of functionality. Change is identifying processes of "feedback" loops organized through categories about autonomy, respect, parent involvement, and interactions with the school and other parents, and as psychological characteristics of motivation versus disruptive behaviors (OECD 2015).

The measurements embody an experimentalist view of changing people and society. Experimentalism is the collection of data whose numbers are correlated as if it is the magnitudes and differences that explain successful schools and people. The experimentalism appears devoid of theory and the alchemy. The numbers appear as measuring only, recouping what is naturally there.

The OECD statistical categories, classifications, and expression of differences constitute the criteria of change. Change is maximizing the system components that appear as organizational. The components are, in fact, about a desired people and society. The OECD asserts, for example, that it measures what children will need for their economic success and well-being. The future is spoken through the tests that are "to assess to what extent students at the end of compulsory education can apply their knowledge to real-life situations and be equipped for full participation in society" (OECD 2017, 306; also see Gurria 2016, 3). The knowledge assessed as mathematics is about conduct and potentialities: "More than ever, students need to engage with mathematics concepts, think quantitatively and analytically, and communicate using mathematics. All these skills are central to a young person's preparedness to tackle problems that arise at work and in life beyond the classroom" (Piacentini and Monticone 2016, np). Global competence is, as well, the potentialities of the world-to-be, "to prepare young people for an interconnected world where they will live and work with people from different backgrounds and cultures."[7]

*The future of success and well-being that the assessments are to guide toward a national fulfillment are, paradoxically, not derived from any causal laws or empirical evidence. They cannot be! Benchmarks and the criteria of "successful" performance are about the potentialities of a future that has not yet arrived.*

## GPS about People in the Arrow of Differentiated Time

The numbers and comparative listings of nations affectively work as a GPS (global positioning system) to express hopes and fears (fig. 8). The ranking and visualization of the graphs are to enable people and governments to immediately locate themselves and identify differences of kinds of societies and people. The inscription of differences is ironic. The complexities of the differences among nations and cultures disappear, only to reappear in reading the charts and graphs as standardized and comparative descriptions of singular, universal norms about national populations from which differences are calculated. Mosaics of numbers are assembled as truth-bearing statements about the effective functioning of schools that appear as a unified abstraction of "nation" and its potentialities (see, e.g., Popkewitz 2018a).

Change is placed in the arrow of time (figures 7 and 8). The models of change give a directionality to signal that pathways are available and "tailored" for educational improvement (fig. 8). The processes of change are visualized through categories that appear as what everyone "knows" is important for school improvement: teacher professional preparation, student psychological characteristics, and school leadership qualities. The change models appear to provide orderly linear processes that instantiate clear and logical procedures. The procedures are available to all if they are wise enough to follow the "highways"—a word used, for instance, by the OECD and the McKinsey reports (see, e.g., Mourshed et al. 2010).

The graphs, statistics, and charts can be thought of as a particular way of "telling the truth" about people, societies, and change. The visual culture of the representations in the reports performs as "immutable mobiles" (Latour 1986). The visualization technologies fold complexities into standardized categories and calculations in which phenomena seem well arranged, easily accessible, and monitored to steer what is seen and acted on. The charts function as visual techniques to map the flow of information into stable objects that are fixed but can move among different social spaces to "tell" of the routes to innovation.[8]

The numbers and charts perform as the "empirical" evidence that has an optical consistency in the ranking and differentiations of "the needs" of nations. The domain of quantified knowledge creates an abstraction of uniformity among different qualities of things (Porter 1995). Numbers in the assessments are perceived as descriptive and outside of time except as descriptions of the present. The statistical distinctions appear as information having a "communicative objectivity"[9] that entails a particular calculative rationality in which process and method are made into the material objects of change. The empirical evidence is represented as the true, efficient, and effective pathways for charting national change. Models of change correlate and compare statistically qualities and characteristics of people and organizations that collapse different measures into universal lists of ranking for people to "see" where they are in a global world (see figures 9 and 10).

Visual information about the comparison and ranking of nations is placed into models of change that bring the universal qualities into the immediate and local conditions. The policy reviews provide "tailored advice" (see fig. 7) that is contextualized as responding to the "country's needs." The tailoring is, in fact, the inscription of desires formed through the self-referential and self-authorizing qualities of systems theory.

The arrow of time expresses the hope and dangers of nations and their populations if not taking precautionary or preemptive actions. There are continual refrains that unless a nation makes "sufficient investments to develop capabilities in the present, students are unlikely to enjoy well-being as adults" (OECD 2017, 62).

| Education system | Below level 2 | Levels 5 and above | Education system | Below level 2 | Levels 5 and above |
|---|---|---|---|---|---|
| OECD average | 23 * | 13 * | Sweden | 27 | 8 |
| Shanghai-China | 4 * | 55 * | Spain | 24 | 8 |
| Singapore | 8 * | 40 * | Latvia | 20 * | 8 |
| Chinese Taipei | 13 * | 37 * | Russian Federation | 24 | 8 |
| Hong Kong-China | 9 * | 34 * | Croatia | 30 * | 7 |
| Korea, Republic of | 9 * | 31 * | Turkey | 42 * | 6 * |
| Liechtenstein | 14 * | 25 * | Serbia, Republic of | 39 * | 5 * |
| Macao-China | 11 * | 24 * | Bulgaria | 44 * | 4 * |
| Japan | 11 * | 24 * | Greece | 36 * | 4 * |
| Switzerland | 12 * | 21 * | Cyprus | 42 * | 4 * |
| Belgium | 19 * | 20 * | United Arab Emirates | 46 * | 3 * |
| Netherlands | 15 * | 19 * | Romania | 41 * | 3 * |
| Germany | 18 * | 17 * | Thailand | 50 * | 3 * |
| Poland | 14 * | 17 * | Qatar | 70 * | 2 * |
| Canada | 14 * | 16 * | Chile | 52 * | 2 * |
| Finland | 12 * | 15 * | Uruguay | 56 * | 1 * |
| New Zealand | 23 * | 15 * | Malaysia | 52 * | 1 * |
| Australia | 20 * | 15 * | Montenegro, Republic of | 57 * | 1 * |
| Estonia | 11 * | 15 * | Kazakhstan | 45 * | 1 !* |
| Austria | 19 * | 14 * | Albania | 61 * | 1 * |
| Slovenia | 20 * | 14 * | Tunisia | 68 * | 1 !* |
| Vietnam | 14 * | 13 * | Brazil | 67 * | 1 * |
| France | 22 * | 13 * | Mexico | 55 * | 1 * |
| Czech Republic | 21 * | 13 * | Peru | 75 * | 1 !* |
| United Kingdom | 22 * | 12 * | Costa Rica | 60 * | 1 !* |
| Luxembourg | 24 | 11 * | Jordan | 69 * | ‡ |
| Iceland | 21 * | 11 * | Colombia | 74 * | # !* |
| Slovak Republic | 27 | 11 | Indonesia | 76 * | ‡ |
| Ireland | 17 * | 11 * | Argentina | 66 * | # !* |
| Portugal | 25 | 11 | | | |
| Denmark | 17 * | 10 | | | |
| Italy | 25 | 10 | | | |
| Norway | 22 * | 9 | **U.S. state education systems** | | |
| Israel | 34 * | 9 | Massachusetts | 18 * | 19 * |
| Hungary | 28 | 9 | Connecticut | 21 * | 16 * |
| **United States** | 26 | 9 | Florida | 30 | 6 * |
| Lithuania | 26 | 8 | | | |

■ Below level 2
□ Levels 5 and above
# Rounds to zero.
! Interpret with caution. Estimate is unstable due to high coefficient of variation.
‡ Reporting standards not met.
* p < .05. Significantly different from the U.S. percentage at the .05 level of significance.
NOTE: Education systems are ordered by 2012 percentages of 15-year-olds in levels 5 and above. To reach a particular proficiency level, a student must correctly answer a majority of items at that level. Students were classified into mathematics proficiency levels according to their scores. Cut scores for each proficiency level can be found in table A-1 in appendix A. The OECD average is the average of the national percentages of the OECD member countries, with each country weighted equally. Italics indicate non-OECD countries and education systems. Results for Connecticut, Florida, and Massachusetts are for public school students only. The standard errors of the estimates are shown in table M1b available at http://nces.ed.gov/pubsearch/pubsinfo.asp?pubid=2014024.
SOURCE: Organization for Economic Cooperation and Development (OECD), Program for International Student Assessment (PISA), 2012.

Fig. 9. Percentage of 15-year-old students performing at PISA mathematics literacy proficiency levels 5 and above and below level 2. Reprinted from *Performance of U.S. 15-Year-Old Students in Mathematics, Science, and Reading Literacy in an International Context—First Look at PISA 2012* (Kelly et al. 2013, 14). Reprinted by permission of the National Center for Education Statistics.

## Erasing Differences to Create Differences: Double Gestures

The indicators of national performance given as universal distinctions about future students' performances, I argued, bring into existence a utopic vision as desire of the present. This section explores this utopic vision in which the arrow of time is no arrow but multiple temporal dimensions that erase differences through comparing and ranking the statistics.

### The Transcendent Character of Differences

The reduction of complexities to those of the rational management of the system makes it seem that "all" national systems can anticipate equality through the application of categories that recognize difference (fig. 10). The magnitude of differences in the statistical correlations "tells" of a continuum of values that appears ostensibly to be about the nation. The ordering as ranking is conceptually about desired interactions, communication, and outcomes among system's actors. These actors are given symbolic value as organizational components, but the measures are produced through organizing qualities of the communications and processes of parents, teachers, administrators, children, and their social world or communities.

The universalized qualities of nations and people seem transcendental and national, as standing outside of history and culture. The measures of the well-being of students, for example, speak about a generalized and globalized student: "The evidence base . . . [of PISA] goes well beyond statistical benchmarking" to examine children's "enjoyment of life," asking

> are students basically happy? Do they feel that they belong to a community at school? Do they enjoy supportive relations with their peers, their teachers and their parents? Is there any association between the quality of students' relationships in and outside of school and their academic performance? Together they can attend to students' psychological and social needs and help them develop a sense of control over their future and the resilience they need to be successful in life. (OECD 2017, 3)

The visualization technologies of measures of student "well-being" appears as national characteristics in need of development (see, e.g., Borgonovi and Przemyslaw 2016, 132), but the standardization of qualities and characteristics of people represented in the numbers are produced through

| | Systems | Reform start date[1] | Time period of student assessment data[2] | Sustained improvers | Promising starts |
|---|---|---|---|---|---|
| **Sustained improvers:** Systems that have sustained improvement with 3 or more data points over 5 or more years | 1. Singapore | 1979 | 1983 – 2007 | ✓ | |
| | 2. Hong Kong | 1980 | 1983 – 2007 | ✓ | |
| | 3. South Korea | 1998 | 1983 – 2007 | ✓ | |
| | 4. Ontario, Canada | 2003 | 2003 – 2009 | ✓ | |
| | 5. Saxony, Germany | 1992 | 2000 – 2006 | ✓ | |
| | 6. England | 1997 | 1995 – 2007 | ✓ | |
| | 7. Latvia | 1990 | 1995 – 2007 | ✓ | |
| | 8. Lithuania | 1990 | 1995 – 2007 | ✓ | |
| | 9. Slovenia | 1992 | 1995 – 2007 | ✓ | |
| | 10. Poland | 1998 | 2000 – 2006 | ✓ | |
| **Promising starts:** Systems that have started improving as represented by ongoing improvement with just 2 data points or less than five years of improvement | 11. Aspire Public Schools, USA | 1999 | 2002 – 2008 | ✓ | |
| | 12. Long Beach, CA, USA | 1992 | 2002 – 2009 | ✓ | |
| | 13. Boston/Massachusetts, USA[3] | 1995 | 2003 – 2009 | ✓ | |
| | 14. Armenia | 1995 | 2003 – 2007 | | ✓ |
| | 15. Western Cape, South Africa | 2001 | 2003 – 2007 | | ✓ |
| | 16. Chile | 1994 | 2001 – 2006 | | ✓ |
| | 17. Minas Gerais, Brazil | 2003 | 2006 – 2008 | | ✓ |
| | 18. Madhya Pradesh, India | 2005 | 2006 – 2010 | | ✓ |
| | 19. Ghana | 2003 | 2003 – 2007 | | ✓ |
| | 20. Jordan | 2000 | 1999 – 2007 | | ✓ |

1 Reform start date based on dates identified by system leaders interviewed. These mark the start of interventions catalogues in the Interventions Database.
2 Refers to dates for which relevant student assessment data available, during the identified reform time period
3 Primary focus was on Boston, within the context of Massachusetts State Reforms. Start date of 1993 refer to Massachusetts (Mass State Education Reform Act of 1993) and 1995 refers to Boston (*Focus on Children* / development)
SOURCE: McKinsey & Company interventions database

Fig. 10. Sustained improvers and promising starts. Exhibit from "How the World's Most Improved School Systems Keep Getting Better." November 2010, McKinsey & Company, www.mckinsey.com. Copyright © 2019 McKinsey & Company. Reprinted by permission.

microstudies ordered by psychological and social theories whose data are correlated with the assessments. The microstudies disappear in the reports and reappear as statistical measures in the models of change narrated as having universal relevance for the progressive future. The PISA data are expressed as providing global explanations about where there are "significant, sustained, and widespread student outcome gains and as examining why what they have done has succeeded where so many others failed" (Mourshed et al. 2010, 10).

The connections to psychological categories of children's social and communicative patterns in the microstudies are erased and visualized as the ranking and comparing through graphs and charts. The visual ordering of numerical data is correlated with variations of performance that measure, for example, "endurance" and motivation as comparative qualities of collective and national differences. The differences in psychological and social skills and competencies of the child are connected to organizational qualities (e.g., teacher professional development and school leadership) and desired sociological and psychological characteristics of children.

The comparison of people is explicit in the 2015 PISA assessment about the characteristics of children's "well-being," a measure defined as those qualities and characteristics that contribute to successful school performance. The social/political outcomes are coupled with psychological outcomes to bring salvation themes to fruition: students' happiness, well-being, and life satisfaction. The numbers generated in the statistical measures are inscription devices that assemble pedagogical, psychological, and social/cultural principles. The numbers embody "a comprehensive set of well-being indicators for adolescents that covers both negative outcomes (e.g. anxiety, low performance) and the positive impulses that promote healthy development (e.g. interest, engagement, motivation to achieve)."[10]

The social and individual characteristics are placed in a continuum of value defined through the theoretical principles about the system's harmony and consensus. McKinsey, for example, performs secondary statistical analyses that are arranged as a spectrum to form comparisons that

> rests, in turn, on a universal scale of calibration that we developed by normalizing several different international assessment scales of student outcomes discussed in the education literature. Our findings are not, however, the result of an abstract, statistical exercise. In addition to assessment and other quantitative data, they are based on interviews with more than 200 system leaders and their staff, supplemented by visits to view all 20 systems in action. (Mourshed et al. 2010, 12–13)

The success and failure (equilibrium/disequilibrium) are visualized as scales that map the development and changes of populations in the arrow of time. The qualities as distinctions and differentiations are recalibrated into national tables in which the submeasures and statistical distinctions about people disappear and reappear as macrostatistical categories about society and nation. The scales appear initially as institutional trajectories that identify different characteristics of the developmental patterns of nations and cities to achieve success. The differences are not merely statistical but comparative about the social and kinds of people.

## The Comparative Logic of Research

The rankings of the macrostatistics are a comparative logic of nations. The comparativeness projects desires about potentialities as distinctions about society and individual connected in the statistical equivalences. The systems principles of harmony and consensus become cultural practices of normalcy and pathology of prefigured divisions. The differentiations are formed through a number of prior studies that fold into the macrostatistical measures; those studies are about populations that generate distinctions in which the hope of following system's pathways entails fears of dangerous populations if they are not followed.

The statistical knowledge provides the grounds that require precautionary and preemptive actions against the imagined dangers. The OECD country report, *The OECD-Sweden Education Policy Review* (2014), for example, was initially submitted without any text. The story of Sweden's educational system and society were visualized through graphs and charts. Sweden's position in the world was highlighted in yellow that placed the nation as ill-prepared in the GPS (illustrated in figure 11 with dark gray). The graphs and charts were titled, for example, "High performing systems combine equity with quality," "Change in mathematics performance throughout participation in PISA, 2003–2012 annualised," and "Percentage of top performers in mathematics in 2003 and 2012." If we think of the graphs and charts as embodying a visual culture about how to tell the truth about people and collective "being," the highlighting, listing, and ranking generate a continuum of value in which Sweden appears as outside of the normal.

The highlighting (shown in dark gray) is affective. It generates national fears and requires actions to rescue and redeem. This affect of the report is not to dismiss challenges that the Swedish schools face in relation to social changes, such as the large populations brought into the country in the face of wars elsewhere, for example. But these changes are not addressed through the PISA models; in fact, they are erased.

What is important to this discussion is how the lists and rankings in the international assessments produce a scaling that is never merely about the abstraction of "nation" but about differences and divisions of people (see, e.g., Hansen and Vestergaard 2018). Scaling in the international assessments is produced through correlations of the data to project, for example, "integrated set of actions" within a hierarchy that forms "intervention

## Student truancy reported by 15 year old students and principals 2012, PISA

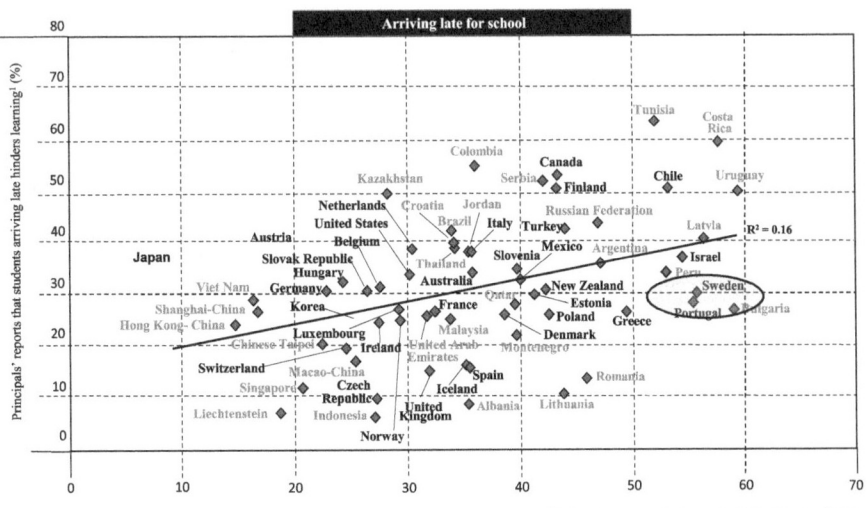

Fig. 11. Student truancy reported by 15-year-old students and principals 2012, PISA. From *The OECD-Sweden Education Policy Review. Main Issues and Next Steps* (Pont et al. 2014, 3). Reprinted by permission of the OECD.

clusters" for improving the performance levels of the system (Mourshed et al. 2010, 14). The scales combine institutional and organizational qualities with personal qualities in a seamless movement that gives the system measures of "accountability, performance, and professionalism" (14).

The scaling through universalized standards are, as in the case below, without overt ontological objects or content. The scales appear as a clear and linear progression of discrete markers about "stage dependent interventions" that produce school improvement. Variations are registered as scales that produce continua of values about the normal and pathological. A continuum of values appear, however, merely as processes to improve the system:

- Fair to good: consolidating system foundations, high quality performance data, teacher and school *accountability*, appropriate financing, organization structure, *pedagogical models*;

- Good to great: teaching and school *leadership* as a full-fledged profession, necessary practice and career paths as in medicine and law;
- Great to excellent: more locus of improvement from center to school, *peer-based learning*, support of system-sponsored *innovation and experimentation*. (Mourshed et al. 2010, 20; my italics)

When looked at closely, the scales are about kinds of people. The scales embody standardization of the qualities and characteristics of kinds of people who are "fair," "good," and "great" at "fitting" into the system's "desires." The characteristics of the desired person are represented in what seem to be organization words, like supporting *system-sponsored innovation, experimentation,* and collaboration (*peer-sponsored learning*). Each term instantiates particular cultural principles about modes of living that are embodied in the concepts. The scales measuring student "endurances" in PISA, for example, are correlated with psychological research on differences in motivation and perseverance in order to solve "real problems and situations . . . [as] important attributes that will help students successfully transition into adulthood" (Borgonovi and Przemyslaw 2016, 128).

The generalized social and psychological characteristics are desires about social attributes of kinds of people. The desires are the potentiality-to-be of the child. For example, it is stated that "the findings from PISA show how teachers, schools and parents can . . . attend to students' psychological and social needs and help them develop a sense of control over their future and the resilience they need to be successful in life"; that is, to obtain "well-being" (OECD 2017, 9). The psychological attributes such as the measure of "endurance" are bound to abstractions that have particular historical and cultural trajectories, projecting the desire of becoming. The measures elide their historicity in the canopies that universalize potentialities, defined as children "successfully transition[ing] to adulthood."

The scales are double gestures. The potentialities-to-be include the potentialities not-to-be and to be abjected. The social and psychological characteristics are simultaneously about the child who "develops" and controls the future that stands in opposition to the characteristics and qualities of others, objectified, for example, as produced through the "socioeconomic background of underperformance and disengagement of boys in schools." The macro and statistical data presented in charts produce differences that exclude in their inclusionary thrusts; differences as "population subgroups" of children who are not only different but are hoped to "successfully perform at designated levels" (Borgonovi and Przemyslaw 2016, 128–29). The research is "to target policies and practices attempting to address boys' educational disadvantage and poor outcomes" (Borgonovi and Przemyslaw 2016, 136). The latter children challenge the hope of the future child; they are feared as lacking "motivation," not "hard working" and collaborative; and having "fragile families" and lacking "social status" (e.g., immigrants and poor populations), among others.

The quantifications become "social facts" that enable comparisons of differences. The comparisons are formed through objectification about people embedded in universal calibrations. The comparisons, paradoxically, erase variations, as differences are inscribed as the possibilities of change in relation to what is given as universal. The distinctions are based on objectifications of the normative qualities that differentiate the qualities that are classified as family influence on children's achievement and the well-being of the child. The McKinsey report on youth unemployment, for example, begins by viewing unemployment as a problem of all youth, including the college-educated child. The report's discussion, however, quickly moves to examine the youth not attending higher education, identified as the "struggling youth." Unemployment is considered as being produced through qualities that connect the dysfunctional modes of living produced in the trilogy of "struggling" child, family, and community.

At this point, it is possible to "see" how systems theory is assembled and connected with the cultural principles that involve not merely systems theory but an assemblage about kinds of people and differences. As the principles of equilibrium/disequilibrium are worked into a social and institutional theory of change, the theoretical propositions generate double gestures about "the nature" of social life, differences, inclusion, and exclusion. The principles of equilibrium/disequilibrium are translated into abstractions about cultural principles that differentiate people and society as the problem of change.

## Practical Knowledge: "Follow Me!" on Highways to the Future

The abstraction of systems is articulated in a grid of historical lines and connected in the assessments as models of change. The assemblage "acts" to produce abstractions whose relations become devices to identify and find the pathways that produce success and to correct the deviations (disequilibrium) that disturb the hypothesized harmony, for example, embedded as benchmarks. Practical and useful knowledge is functionally what contributes to actualizing the models of change in the school system. The McKinsey report's language of highways, for example, posits that the models of change are the paths to increase the school's ability to provide for sustainable skills. The OECD posits a similar claim. The problem of change is to get on "the route" so all "can get there" (Barber and Mourshad 2007, preface, n.p.).

Change is the application of the universal "to navigate the challenges in their context and to use their context to their advantage" (Mourshed et al. 2010, 26). Practical and useful knowledge is the "scientific" and empirical evidence that leads the highways to the "benchmarks." The future, the OECD states, is embodied in PISA actualizing the measured skills, the knowledge, and the well-being that enables satisfaction and competence for future participation. Innovation relates to how well the pathways are delineated to access the highways to success.

Differences are only in how well one travels on the highways, what is referred to as being "tailored" to individual national systems. No matter where in the world, the scriptures of the GPS system provide the navigational tools to follow. In the report on education-to-employment, for example, the highway has three drivers—educators, employers, and young people. Tailoring the pathways enables the harmony of all actors going to the same destination (Barton, Farrell, and Mourshed 2013). The proper alignment of these drives inaugurates the pathways to optimize system goals. The aim of interventions is both coordination and consensus "to gain requisite support of the various stakeholders" for the interventions being made (Mourshed et al. 2010, 27).

The language of reports suggests some ambiguity about change, expressed in a language of "suggesting," "merely reporting," and "tailoring" to local contexts. The uncertainty is short lived. The ambiguity is accompanied with declarative statements about certainty and the machine side of the cybernetic relation. For instance, a McKinsey report argues that identifying "the best practices" is a schema that exists "irrespective of the culture in which they are applied" (Barber and Mourshed 2007, n.p.). The statistical methods are "getting at what lies behind the numbers and are thus generating key insights and questions . . . [with this report] portraying the inner workings of successful pathways of reform given different beginning points" (Fuller, preface to Mourshed et al. 2010, 11). It is asserted that "educational attainment can be achieved within as little as six years"

(Mourshed et al. 2010, 14). And as figures 9 and 10 suggest, change is encapsulated in the certainty of the arrow of time.

Finding the right highways means recognizing that there are dangers and dangerous people. For instance, a McKinsey report expresses the dangers of not getting rid of potholes and the hope of "patching the pavement" for educators and employers to solve the future problem of unemployment (Barton, Farrell, and Mourshed 2013, 54). The language seems descriptive and prescriptive through scientific evidence about processes and communication.

> In all nine of the countries we studied, the road from education to employment is under constant repair. Signs are missing and the traffic is heavy. Drivers tend to concentrate on the patch of pavement ahead, not on the long haul. The result ... only a small fraction of young people and employers reach their destination in a reasonably efficient manner. The situation is not hopeless. Not only do many educators and employers accept that they need to be part of the solution, but many also have proved distinctly ingenious in filling in some of the potholes. (Barton, Farrell, and Mourshed 2013, 54)

The promise is the possibility of coming out on top. Certainty is in the pathways and highways to achieve the optimum state of harmony and consensus. The pathway's differentiation and divisions of the qualities and characteristics of nations erase the distinctions that make possible the differences—the double gestures that positioned differences in the qualities and characteristics of children's home environments and society. The ranking and comparative calculations appear as universals; the universals are in fact about cultural principles about potentialities.

## The Cultural Practices of Numbers and Practical Research

No surprises are indeed imagined in the assessment narratives. Why should there be? The salvation theme beckons with benchmarks and "scientific evidence" that tell of finding the future. The only issue of importance is whether school systems can actualize potentialities captured in what is calculated and measured. The assessments are desires about potentialities scaled as the continuum of development that simultaneously performs as the boundaries within which solutions are expressed.

The certitude of the assessments is culturally inscribed through the numbers that provide a mechanical objectivity and visual consistency to the problem of change. But the numbers are never merely about statistical calculations or a pure logic of mathematics. They perform in the social world as cultural inscriptions that assemble distinctions about people and differences in the numbers. The numbers do not act directly and immediately on others, but presuppose freedom within the principles generated in the classifications and ordering about individuals as populations. The calculations are not merely about the present but about an anticipated future that can be realized. The desired future is about a universalized society and people to be actualized through the research and models of change.

The narratives and images of the OECD and McKinsey reports (re)present what Medieval alchemists thought of as the philosopher's stone: the ultimate or foundational knowledge for all of humankind. The models are elixirs of change. The charts and graphs perform visually as a way to tell the truth that has no laws or ontological objects. The ontological objects are present, formed through the classifications and ordering of alchemy, but sightless in the research. Time as if in the arrow of time orders change, with the focus on process and communication as its objects. "Seeing" like a system translates differences as the potentialities of people that are indistinguishable from the system's organizational and institutional properties.

The charts and graphs are affective as truth-telling devises. Governments and people read the charts as ways of telling the truth about nations, society, and people: the ranking delineates the nation's quality of life and preparedness for the future!

The statistical measures abandon ontological concerns and memory except within the system's notions of the past as what secures the future. The self-referential measures seem to emanate only from within the system's networks and flows that define context. The past and the future have no historicity. The epistemology is a pragmatic behaviorism in which data form the design problem of change. The documentation, indexicality, and archiving that appear prior to the visualization disappear and historical lines are erased through the data visualizations of networks that form pathways and highways.

The future is told as a truism and not from any significant general laws that research identifies. Using advanced visualization technologies, truth is projected in the international assessments about what is as are the options available for the immediate operationalization of the pathways for change (Anderson 2010a, 777; Hansen 2015, 213). The system's modeling deploys numbers as the way to tell the truth about nations and people: the development of the system is visualized as sequences and stages for nations to achieve efficiency, perfection, and equality as seemingly mechanistic qualities in the arrow of time. The fabrications, however, have a materiality. The counting, standardizing, and codifying of populations perform as desires and as potentialities. The potentialities are expectations generated about universal characteristics of societies and people to be actualized as a common and harmonious world.

The "seeing" numbers, as assembled in a system of reason, bring back a continual methodological theme that *what is noticed and selected entails prior historically formed rules and standards that are partially assembled and activated in the present to see the objects that matter.* The objects of practical and useful knowledge are governed within the categories and distinctions that define the configuration of the system seen as what is but also as desires. *The assessments are not assessing but generating cultural theses about society and populations given in the statistical variances that order the spaces called "context."* Context is the site where the consensus and harmony exist for maximizing school system performance. The pathologies are given as the system's context or environment that hinder optimizing efficiency as criteria of the successful school system. The common world becomes accessible as highways to rectify the dangers that are disruptive of the equilibrium.

The numbers are anticipatory. The future is calculated as desires that have similar algorithmic formats as Google, Amazon, or Netflix search engines that anticipate what you want and want to be. The difference between the international assessments and the web searches is that in the case of the former, our preferences have not been registered prior to the algorithms' work on us. The preferences are prefigured in the abstraction of the school as a system.

A relation of policy, society, and research generated through the statistical knowledge is, as argued earlier, grounds for precautionary or preemptive actions provided by the models of change. Precautionary or preemptive actions are taken as an affective and anticipated threat that is not fully articulated (Massumi 2007). That threat provides the grounds for finding solutions to the problems that are imagined to arise if an action is not taken. The precautionary and preemptive programs are engendered, on the one hand, as fears of the qualities and characteristics of particular populations, and on the other, as rescuing and redeeming those populations as the desires about a universalized potentiality for "humanity." The precautionary and preemptive actions were evident in the assessment reports, which differentiated nations as economies linked to the most successful schools identified in the PISA results, and as "telling" of the dangers faced in not adequately responding, such as in the country report on Sweden (fig. 11 above). While the overt reference was continually made to economies, the actual categories and classifications were to differences in kinds of people registered in a continuum of value of psychological, organizational, and sociological characteristics.

The argument should not be construed as being against statistical analysis. Rather, the argument is concerned with the grid in which such practices of practical research are substantiated. The intelligibility given to research is not merely ordered in the macrostatistical studies of the international assessments. In the following chapter, microstudies of classroom interaction and communication to improve teacher education are examined as having similar sets of system principles. This is indeed ironic as these microstudies on teacher education seek to offer a counter and an alternative to the hyper-reliance on statistical measures as ways of telling the truth about schools, teachers, and children.

# 9 • Teacher and Teacher Education Research

## The Practical Knowledge of Change That Conserves and Divides

The field of research on teacher "practices" and teacher education reform would seem at first glance far away from the international assessments' macro analyses and big data. The teacher research generally entails qualitative approaches to study classroom processes, interactions, and communications that connect teachers with students. Gone mostly are the statistical analyses, algorithms, and assertions of benchmarks. They are replaced with qualitative research viewed as more synchronized with what teachers actually do in classrooms. The microstudies identify the knowledge and practices that enable the development of what are called, alternatively, the expert, the ambitious, the authentic, and the professional teacher. Yet the differences in the research techniques (quantitative versus qualitative) may not be as that different when the rules and standards of reason are examined. The practical and useful knowledge to be generated about pedagogical knowledge connect systems theories, the alchemy of school subjects, and psychologies. The assemblage generates the double qualities of potentialities as the objects of change.

Contemporary research to change teacher education is examined to explore these connections. "Core practice" research related to teacher and teacher education reform is given significant attention, having high public and professional visibility. The purpose of the research is to identify the expert-professional knowledge that will make for the successful development of novice teachers. I also explore the making of the teacher in Teach For America, a national program that uses systems theory to organize teacher development, as well as "value-added" research that claims to identify the factors in classroom teaching that account for children's success beyond external factors of social class and parental educational level. The latter two are discussed, although to a lesser extent.

These research efforts can be viewed in relation to the prior discussions of post–World War II efforts to change teacher education. The Holmes Group (1986), for example, formed by American research-oriented schools of education and the Carnegie Forum on Education and the Economy (1986), brought together major universities to build research interest in teacher education and classroom teaching. The research and related reform programs drew on principles of systems analysis and cybernetics systems articulated as an ecological view of classroom studies. The studies pronounced "the teacher as a researcher" who engaged in, for example, "action-research," "research-based decision making," or "research-oriented teacher education reform" (Lee 2019). Professional development drew on the notion of "communities of practice" to promote teacher reflection. That reflection was placed in a liberal political theory as democratizing teacher education through directly engaging the teacher as an active participant (Shimoni 2012). The philosophical ideal is of the teacher as a professional whose expert knowledge enables system effectiveness in achieving the goals of student achievement (see Popkewitz [1987] 2018a, 1991, 1993).[1]

Contemporary teacher research works with the ghosts of these earlier research and reform efforts. The first section examines the invocation of teacher practice as an abstraction in the research about what teachers do, but that abstraction acts as a theory about who the teacher is and should be. Then research about teacher practices is explored as embodying desires in the second section. The inscription of desire is about the potentialities of kinds of people as the object of change. The desire of the potentialities is not only about the teacher but also the trilogy of the child, family, and community.[2] The theory of practice (and practical knowledge) is discussed as generating desires, discussed in the third section. The research is explored not as empirically derived qualities but as philosophical ideals about the modes of being as the professional teacher, characteristics that are shaped through systems analysis. The fourth and fifth sections pay attention to the paradoxes of teacher research as naturalizing the objectifications of schooling and the curriculum alchemies, producing double gestures that normalize and pathologize.

As previously, research reports are examined as cultural artifacts. The notion of practice picks up on the earlier discussions to explore its different set of meaning in this research. Practice signals the research programs that seek direct (practical) knowledge for changing teachers (and children). Second, practice is also posed as the origin of what is done and real in the school that is understood and changed. The third notion of practice directs the study of this book. It gives attention to the historical conditions that give intelligibility to the activities of research signified as "practice."

## Teacher Practices as Theories of Change and Desires to Actualize

In contemporary teacher education research, practice is given as an activity to describe educational change. Yet practice is neither a transhistorical concept that describes what people do nor is it merely the origin of research to collect empirical "data" about how to improve the school system (see, e.g., the critique of this naturalizing in Biesta, Allan, and Edwards 2011). What is taken as the "real," authentic, and professional teacher are fabrications that require theoretical concepts to order what is "seen" and done that includes the alchemy spoken about in chapter 5. The principles generated in research are cultural theses about people and society engendered through the philosophical abstraction of the teacher as a professional, and about desires about kinds of people that embody the double potentialities of children as the object of change.

### Practice as Theories of Desires of the Teacher to Be Actualized

Teachers' "practice" is stated as the origin of research to create more effective teaching and schools. The research concerns "learning the work of teaching" (Lampert 2010). It appears *as if* the research is merely descriptive of the real activities and events of schooling. The research is taken as providing more concrete understanding of "what *teachers really need to know and be able to do*" (Grossman et al. 2008, 247, italics added). This doing and learning of the work of teachers becomes the goal of teacher education: "Initial teacher preparation must help novices learn how to *do* instruction, not just hear and talk about it" (Ball et al. 2009, 459). Research is what generates the practical knowledge "to fill the gaps between desired teacher education practices and what novices see in the school setting" (Grossman and McDonald 2008, 190).

Practice has a duality in organizing research. Practice is given as what is real, with an autonomous and authoritative status. It serves as the source of change, asserting that the starting point is practice as descriptive of what teachers "really do." At the same time, and seemingly rooted in the reality of teachers' practices, are its potentialities. Research is thought of as providing the knowledge directed to the future about processes, communication patterns, and the habits of the mind that teachers need for effective and authentic instruction.

*The reality known as "practice" instantiates a paradox of a theory/not a theory* in the study of the teacher. The conceptualizing of teaching is meant to explain "what it means to demonstrate and articulate expertise, of and in practice" (Loughran 2013, 19). "The reflective teacher," a phrase in contemporary reforms, has teachers develop ways of thinking and ordering everyday experiences that are conceptualized as "the birthplace of new theories" (Shimoni 2012, 46).

Theory, in this strand of practical research, is thought of as providing descriptions that make visible relevant, useful, and meaningful knowledge. This replication of reality "link[s] theory and practice more closely" (Loughran 2013, 17). The process of reflection exists as simply giving a language to an unfiltered, nontheorized element of teaching. Theory, in this usage, is merely a device to clarify the intentionality of teachers and make the outcomes of the classroom more productive.

The idea of this grounded theory as describing what is real travels with another use of a theory of practices to articulate desires about what teachers should be. The "core practice research," in its more sophisticated encounters, speaks about research as enabling the desired teacher, expressed as eliminating "the gap between the practices that teachers do and what is *being advocated*" (Grossman and McDonald 2008, 190; italics added). The "doing" is linked to "what is being advocated," which embodies a theory and a desire. The teacher is fabricated as a kind of person who enacts "particular practices, practices that embody theoretical principles of instruction, learning, development, culture, and practices that can be developed and refined" (Grossman et al. 2008, 247). Research conceptualizes, standardizes, and calculates in order to realize the abstraction about the teacher whose expertise of knowledge and skills is enclosed in a theory of "practice."

The first use of "practice" in which the idea of theory is "born" in classrooms—teachers' practices—relies on the inscription of theory to order, categorize, and describe the experiences that are noticed and acted on (Scott 1991). Advocacy of what is described as actual, genuine, and authentic teaching is formed in a grid, as were the international assessments, that connects with social and psychological theories and methods that place some things under categories of description. In the practical teacher research, its categories are about motivation, higher-order learning, identity beliefs, and interactive performance that connect with cybernetics languages about feedback mechanisms.

Research that is practical formulates salvation and redemptive themes as desires of change. The National Council for Research, for example, issued a report about changing practices as the standard of relevance and rigor in education research (Gutiérrez and Penuel 2014). The report articulates that the research on practice can "open up new pathways and social futures for youth, particularly youth from non-dominant communities" (Gutiérrez and Penuel 2014, 20). That focus is to actualize social commitments to produce a more equitable society by identifying and mastering variations that teachers can use for productive adaptations (Gutiérrez and Penuel 2014, 22). Inequality is addressed by calling for more effective learning, fostering better (ambitious) teaching, and creating professionals necessary to enable children "to master their own future."

As in prior chapters, the analysis of research is not about good intentions and social commitments. Rather, it is about the concrete sets of principles enacted to order and classify what is done and acted on as the objects of change.

### The Melting of Differences in Heterogeneous Research "Systems"

The core problems of teacher practice are ordered through sets of distinctions and classifications that connect to systems theory, although assembled differently from that of the international assessments. Expert knowledge links learning theories and teachers' classroom communications and activities. In "value added" research, the practical knowledge is a theory that is given as "a more robust" relation between the capabilities of the teacher and the children's achievement results.

Teacher education research is designed "to expose and analyze a set of core problems involved in building a useful and usable knowledge base on teacher education and to propose features of such a knowledge base crucial for addressing those problems of teacher education" (Ball et al. 2009, 459). The desired teacher in core practice research is someone whose actions have "high-leverage" or "high-impact" qualities. These "high-leverage" qualities are about the communicative activities of the teacher that are specified as standardized rules. The novice teacher is to (1) identify the representations of practice in teaching school subjects, (2) decompose those representations through analytically parsing the elements of the existing practice, and (3) engage novices in the approximations of practice that "are more or less proximal to the practices of a profession" (Grossman et al. 2009, 2,058).

The research stresses an experimental, pragmatic, and empirical approach to teacher education. The research problem is puzzle solving: research fills in the map for the optimization of the system. The goal of teacher education research is "to expose and analyze a set of core problems involved in building a useful and usable knowledge based on teacher education and to propose features of such a knowledge base crucial for addressing those problems of teacher education" (Ball et al. 2009, 459).

Finer distinctions are created to codify and standardize the processes and communications that perform in a theory about "the practice" of pedagogy. Distinctions are created as representations of practice that include the teacher "noticing," teacher "rehearsals," procedures for eliciting student ideas, the decision-making processes of the teacher, the levels and hierarchy of kinds of explanations and degree in which evidence is used in children's answers, and what constitutes sources of evidence in children's responses. Teaching is broken down into subsets of categories, having a similar logic to mastery learning (chapter 7) ordered through the relation of systems and communication theories. "Rehearsal," for example, is a concept used to talk about how novice teachers can collaboratively deliberate about the appropriate skills and knowledge required for "rigorous" and "ambitious" teaching (Lampert et al. 2013, 227).

As with the international assessments, a continuum of value and hierarchy is produced. The hierarchy is about an ideal called the professional teacher. A scale is produced about teacher development that provides the "opportunities for novices to engage in practices that are more or less proximal to the practices of a profession" (Grossman et al. 2009, 2,058).

The value-added research follows similar epistemic principles of systems theory but through the inscription of statistical measures. The language is the new public management that appears in multiple social and governmental institutions to regulate change (Normand et al. 2018). That language rationalizes the social system by identifying the actors and connections in which decisions are made, similar to what was discussed with the OECD's international assessments. The use of "value-added" engages what seems as an economic language related to controlling external variables to measure the impact of the individual teacher on children's achievement (see, e.g., Day, Sammons, and Gu 2008). The organizational qualities, as with the previous core practice research, are not about the economy but are connected with social, psychological, and organizational qualities whose identification constitutes a "holist, nuanced understanding of teachers' work and lives" (Day, Sammons, and Gu 2008, 330).

The economic language is transfigured into cultural distinctions, as with core practice research, in the performance standards related to systems theory. In the "value added" research, the statistical categories are not merely describing "empirically" teachers' practices but embody cultural theses about what is done, said, and thought. The standards are philosophical ideals about the teacher (and child) as kinds of people. The optimal points that define the expert teacher as a state of static balance or equilibrium expressed as the capacities of the teacher who enables "all" children's success in school achievement (see, e.g., Day, Sammons, and Gu 2008). The "all" signifies the unity and harmony that is presupposed in defining achievement as the outcome of an integrated system.

The Teach For America program, the third program examined, exists in a similar epistemic framing about schools, people, and change. Central to its program is the Teaching as Leadership Comprehensive Rubric (TALCR). The TALCR is a management device that identifies six qualities and characteristics of teacher's actions that are said to correlate with student achievement.[3] The rubric, originally a liturgical tool, is an abstraction applied to manage changes in the teacher (Popkewitz and Kirchgasler 2014). The TALC rubric is organized into a grid of teacher actions, organized in developmental sequences and stages. Six principles define the exemplary teacher: Set Big Goals; Invest in Students and Those Who Influence Them in Working Hard to Achieve Big Goals; Plan Purposefully; Execute Effectively; Continuously Increase Effectiveness; and Work Relentlessly (Teach for America 2013a).

The space of action is "the arrow of time," with the rubric oriented to actualizing the philosophical ideal of the teacher as potentialities generated within the self-referential qualities of the system. The practices or actions are ordered in a hierarchy of behaviors that progress as stages of development from the novice to the expert teacher. The six principles are divided into subactions, such as the six subcategories under Setting Big

Goals, such as "B-1 Develop standards-aligned measurable, ambitious and feasible goals that will dramatically increase students' opportunities in life." The vertical axis of the TALCR, for example, has five types of actions that indicate linear movement broken into five stages leading from actions of the Pre-Novice to that of Beginning and Advanced Proficiency to Exemplary. The Pre-novice shows "a lack of attempt or action" in setting Big Goals; whereas the Exemplary classroom actions "design feasible, highly ambitious goals."

The "practices" (and "actions") are in the arrow of time as a developmental or stage theory used for self-assessment and program assessment for the making of the expert teacher. The principles make "sense" as they capture certain aspects of American culture about working hard, commitment, and "grit" as what enables success, which are brought into the idea of the actions of the expert-professional teacher. The organizing of this space for action erases the ontological objects of teaching.

The research programs are not merely what the teacher does but are intertwined with making the trilogy of the child, family, and community. If I return to "core practices," the syntax in the research is about the "*real* setting of practice with actual clients*"* (Grossman et al. 2009, 2,093; italics added). The objects of reflection are ordered through social, psychological, and communication theories. Communities, learners, instruction, and meaningful experiences, among other distinctions about practice, are abstractions that instantiate theories. If I return to the first section, the theories of "practice" are cultural theses about "human nature," change, and the moral individual (Biesta, Allan, and Edwards 2011).

## Salvific and Redemptive Practices of the Professional Teacher

The overt purpose of the research is to create the professional teacher. The accounting of teaching and the teacher as the professional is not merely a description of what teachers do or should do. The word "profession" is not just there to describe people, their actions, and the psychological interiority as having certain dispositions in acting. The professional teacher is an abstraction about a kind of person that has no historical instantiation.[4] The classifications about the professional teacher are the philosophical ideal of a kind of person whose activities, if properly executed, enact the conceptually defined expertise inscribed in the research. The professional teacher is a desire that acts in research to generate the potentialities of teachers. The expert professional teacher is articulated as what knowledge and skills are "in practice" identified as the useful and meaningful knowledge that research explicates in the novice learning what to become and *to do*.

The inscriptions of the teacher as the professional functions as a salvation and redemptive theme. It articulates and (re)visions Enlightenment ideals about reason and science, revisioned in the 19th century as a particular expertise discussed in chapter 3, and (re)visioned today as the promise of an unspecified and universal mission of "social improvement" (see Cohen 2005; Grossman et al. 2009). The profession gives wisdom to the teacher in transforming people and their social conditions in the name of "improvement." The professionalization of the teacher is "like psychotherapists, social workers, pastors, and organization developers" who work directly on other humans "to transform minds, enrich human capacities and change behavior" (Cohen 2005, 280).

The professional mission of the "authentic," "ambitious," and "effective" teacher is bound and visualized through systems theory. The imperative of systems is the imagined equilibrium produced by the "hard-won consensus" that enables the unity of common instruments, a common research agenda, a shared language, and more precise methodological and theoretical tools in the preparation of teachers (Grossman and McDonald 2008, 188). The professional consensus of knowledge in the common instructional syllabi directs attention to the teacher's collective responsibilities and shared commitments to system goals, most often stated as student academic performance. The effective teacher is one whose personal motivation and feelings "fit" into a comprehensive and "organic whole" (a phrase about the school systems that continually appears).

Professional expertise expresses theoretical principles of harmony, consensus, and equilibrium formed through the inscriptions of system principles for designing teachers. Harmony and consensus is expressed as professions with specific universal knowledge and skills that utilize and maximize the organizational elements of the system. The common language and syllabus directs attention to optimizing school efficiency. The task for making the new teacher is working with standardized processes. For teaching to be a profession is to identify the representations of the curriculum, build capacity, maximize problem solving, and parse analytically what is done in the classroom.

The professional curriculum for teacher education is one that is defined as universally applicable, usable by people with varying experience. The "core practice" research uses standard points of reference that enable reaching *"down to the details of how many minutes a student should use for enacting one of the practices"* (Ball et al. 2009, 465; my emphasis).

> Our approach discourages individuals from improvising in their own sections of a course; instead, the goal is to offer a common curriculum to the prospective teachers in our program. Moreover, asking instructors to work on and use the collective materials is at the heart of our approach to collective study and continuous improvement. (473)

The focus on the teacher as a kind of person who is a professional, again, is not to argue about its good intentions. It is to understand how the idea of the teacher as professional is given concrete distinctions in making a kind of person. That person is formed through the boundaries of possibilities produced within its rules and standards of reason. It is bounded within principles of systems theory and the principles of equilibrium. In research related to core practice, for example, teaching is subdivided into particular cycles of "enactments" and "investigations" (see fig. 12). The cycles form the "system" that describes universal teacher behaviors that enable the novice to develop expert knowledge across contexts. The cycle performs as a system component that builds the unity and the equilibrium between "the pedagogical expertise and organizational conditions posited" (Matsumura and Wang 2014, 5). The research speaks about capacity building across all levels of the school systems.

While the practical "core knowledge" research assumes the claim that professions have a particular expertise articulated through a common language and a course of study, the abstraction of this kind of person is a chimera. The idea of the professional in Anglo-America emerged in the 20th century as a distinct cultural and social category that ascribed authority to certain occupations (Popkewitz and Simola 1996). One only needs to read the current discussion of law or the rise of medical education in the US to recognize that what seems as consensus and "commonality" is formed as registers of social and cultural authority that are continually matters of debate and change.

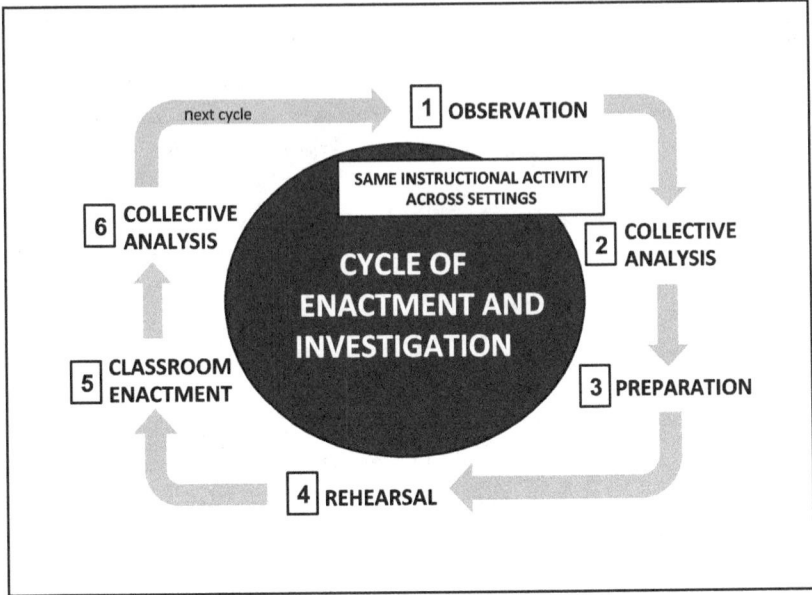

Fig. 12. Cycle of enactment and investigation. From "Keeping It Complex: Using Rehearsals to Support Novice Teacher Learning of Ambitious Teaching," by Lampert et al. 2013, 229. Copyright © 2013 by American Association of Colleges for Teacher Education. Reprinted by permission of SAGE Publications, Inc.

## The Professional "Soul" as Object of Change

Professionalization as the salvation narrative acts on the unwashed soul of the novice teacher and teacher educator. The conceptualization is spoken in other words than the soul but its object is the interiority of the teacher: research "inevitably impact[s] on a teacher educator's identity" (Loughran 2013, 19). "Doing" is the internalization of the classifications and distinctions of the consensual knowledge defined to "conceptualize expertise as holistic, meaningful, and applicable in the work of teacher education." The acting of the soul is expressed innocuously as "learn[ing] how to *do*" instruction, rather than "simply how to talk about it" (Ballet al. 2009, 459; italics in original).

Research is about modes of living and being, expressed as "Pedagogies of Investigation to Pedagogies of Enactment," a subsection in the journal article (Grossman and McDonald 2008, 189). The enactments are not only teacher "practices" but enactments as expressions of beliefs and "opportunities to practice the habit of reflection" (Grossman and McDonald 2008, 190); "the soul" without speaking the word. Research is meant to transform the interiority or "the soul" of the teacher through changing the "habits of the mind," mind-sets, and dispositions. Attention is directed to the interior of the mind and the "intrinsic" virtues of the individual—a focus of change that is described as a "more powerful concept than beliefs as it can be changed and assessed" (Boggess 2010, 73). The object of "core practice" is to internalize desires as an affect that becomes the teacher's "habits of mind and character" that "develop new ways of thinking" (Grossman et al. 2009, 2,060).

The professionalization of the teacher is not merely about what "to do." It embodies a cultural thesis about a particular kind of person and is directed to the dispositions, sensitivities, and awarenesses. The object of study shifts from "teacher characteristics and behaviors to a focus on teacher cognition," thereby with properties that include "research on teacher knowledge and beliefs" (Grossman and McDonald 2008, 189). Teacher education identifies the pathways for new teachers to internalize the "goals, activities and historical traditions that reinforce collective meanings and the identity of the practitioners" (Grossman et al. 2009, 2,060). The "new ways of thinking" are in the consensual knowledge of the professional: planning purposefully, working relentlessly, and having the proper "mindsets" and optimism.

*The concern for habits, mind-sets, and dispositions is directed to the interior of the teacher.* Research designed to shape the soul of "the effective teacher" is placed into programs as developmental stages. Teach For America's TALCR, for example, identifies the stages of development to produce the expertise of the teacher (Teach For America 2013a, 2013b). Stages of professional development bring intentionality and purpose to the experiences of the teacher. The characteristics of the expert, professional teacher are multiple cultural distinctions turned into psychological qualities of the interiority or "soul" of the teacher: "personality" distinctions such as being "purposeful," "working relentlessly," acting "faithfully" in following lesson content, being "poised" and "self-monitor[ed]," having "gratitude and optimism," "managing time and attitudes," monitoring "body language," and providing "memorable" lessons.

When different distinctions of teacher performance are placed together, a cultural thesis emerges about a particular kind of person. The psychological norms of becoming with social coordinates about belonging form a plane about a mode of living. That mode of living is the teacher who acts purposely in a particular calculable and standardized style of reasoning, described as "setting goals," "investing in students," "planning purposefully," "executing effectively," and "work[ing] relentlessly."[5]

The salvific and redemptive language of the self-managed, self-monitored individual who works relentlessly as a teacher does have homologies to the Calvinist-inspired reforms in American Progressivism. As argued earlier, the salvific themes (re)vision Puritan themes of the collective belonging of the citizens of the nation as "the city on the hill" and as "the errand in the wilderness": the dispositions of hard work, being purposeful, and effective in the inventive teacher have historical analogies to the turn-of-the-20th century "rugged individualism" of Frederick Jackson Turner. That rugged individualism is reassembled and connects with what otherwise seems an anomaly of the mid-20th century, of William Whyte's book *The Organization Man* (1956), which is about a person whose identity works collaboratively in large organizations. The identity is assembled with political pluralist theories about associational groups (stakeholders as what constitutes democratic participation). But the configuration being formed has different surfaces and the folding to mark the objects of practice, practical and useful knowledge.

## The Certainty of Uncertain Practical Knowledge

The paradox of the research on practice is the inscription of its contemporaneous framework and objectifications as the principles of change. Change is about activity and motion within the rules and standards that presupposes what are given as the goals, materials, causes, and behaviors in the schools. The practice of practical research is the paradox of change that generates desires that naturalize, conserve, and stabilize.

The conservatism of systems analysis in the research is not obvious at first glance. The assertions are about the authenticity of teacher's practices, the transformative or revolutionary potential of reform based on the research, assertions of social improvement, and "democratization." The distinctions, rubrics, the teacher's "noticing of objects," and the value-added research, however, give greater specificity to what is already inherent in the abstraction of the school as a system. Change is the intersections of past and present principles for the ordering and classification that perform as desires of what is to become the teacher. The paradox of change is that the optimal state is one where all the parts of "the organism" are in harmony for development and growth with what is already legible as the spaces of schooling.[6]

## The Objectifications of Curriculum and People to Stabilize Change

What appears as practical and useful knowledge takes for granted the objectified subjects for governing change. The conservativism occurs through the connection of different principles of systems theory "acting" to identify what is noticed as the "practices" as the object of change. The envisioned future is the inscription of consensus, harmony, and standardization of the system's designation of the teacher with what becomes learning/teaching.

The naturalization and stabilization is performed through identifiable forms generated through the alchemic objectifications of the content and classifications of people inscribed as the expertise of professional identities. Cohn, Raudenbush, and Ball (2003), for example, instantiate the object of change as the equilibrium that removes consideration of the ontological objects generated with the spaces of "practices." "Conceptualizing practice," a key to the definition of the professional teacher, expresses the harmony that gives utility to systems. Change is achieving that harmony. It is the more effective use and relations of the existing structures for planning "carefully, using appropriate materials, making goals clear, teaching at a brisk pace, and checking regularly on student work" (121).

Debates and differences about pathways exist to bring the components into a functional balance. The debates are internal to the system's principles; they are authorized and referential to the classifications and ordering of the abstraction of the system and, for example, what was described as context in the prior chapter's discussion of OECD PISA's models of change. Debates occur about what concepts enable the generalizability of research findings across school subjects, such as identifying what constitutes "high-leverage practices," a phrase used to designate the processes signified as having the greatest effect in teaching mathematics or science, for example.

The classifications and distinctions of "practice" are enclosed as part of a self-referential system that defines stability and the desired state of the equilibrium as the purpose of change. Research identifies the "framework through parsing teaching" into its discrete acts so to enable and instrumentalize the "planning, choosing and using of representations, conducting discussion of mathematics problems, and then to analyze and 'decompose' theses domains into teachable components" (Ball et al. 2009, 460).

## The Certainty of Uncertain Practical Knowledge

The principles of consensus and harmony evoke certainty along with principles of indeterminacy. The notion of profession enters into current research as an *ontological determinism*. The professional is given as the subject and object of a kind of person to obtain if the school system is to be effective. The ontological certainty is embodied in the conceptualization of the profession defined as having a common language and course of study. Professionalism resolves the fuzziness and tames uncertainty by asserting a particular expertise. The search is for the certainty found in the commonalty that identifies the desired kind of teacher. Uncertainty, however, exists in how to achieve the professional teacher as the desired object of the system's potentialities. The uncertainty and ambiguities are for research to tame in reconciling what otherwise seems in opposition.

Certainty is embodied in the alchemy that views disciplinary knowledge as the subject "content" separate from methods as discussed in chapter 5. The certainty in core practice research, for example, occurs with the claim of its research as reducing error. This is expressed as identifying high-stakes practices "via approximation is one way for professional education to reduce the risk of error in the field" (Grossman et al. 2009, 2,091). The reduction of error folds into the search for certainty. That certainty is expressed as the novice approximating what are "the real" professional practices, expressed as, to use the earlier quote, "what teachers *really need to know and be able to do*" (Grossman et al. 2008, 247, italics added).

Uncertainty and certainty coexist. Practical research talks about reducing error, which would seem as recognizing uncertainty and the inability of science to find absolute knowledge. But the inscription of "error" is related to the codification and standardization of the universal qualities and characteristics given to the expert, professional teacher and its connection to the inscriptions of the alchemy of school subjects.

The reduction of error is accompanied by an ontological determinism— that is, taking the objectifications of people and events as ahistorical and transcendental concepts to organize school processes and communication.

The learning of the core practices, for example, is expressed as helping "novices to experience and learn from errors. These opportunities for failure are about the psychology of the teacher and which allow novices to contend with their own feelings of disappointment or discouragement and learn to respond in professionally appropriate ways" (Grossman et al. 2009, 2,091).

Teacher education is scripted as having a regularity and carefully defined processes that lead to the necessary expertise. Certainty is the product of research identifying the right balance of things and qualities that teachers "need in any setting, regardless of variations" in curricula or teaching styles (Ball et al. 2009, 461). The certainty is described as the pathway to become the professional teacher. In teacher education, it is spoken about as "the development of 'real time' evaluation techniques to evaluate how teachers implement the desired practices" (Ball et al. 2009, 468). These techniques include "in-the-moment" assessments through video clips and still photographs to capture what is real, as the currents of certainty.

*Certainty* is expressed in the research model of teacher development of Teach For America's TALCR. The codifications and standardizations of research about the expert/professional teacher appear as stages of development articulated as "commandments" for the working of the system. This system is said to guarantee children's high achievement if the teachers follow the principles mentioned earlier of setting big goals, investing in students, planning purposefully, executing effectively, and working relentlessly (Teach For America 2013a, 1).

The task of reform to increase teacher proficiency binds the new teacher to the present order of things and its objectifications. While psychology is concerned with transformation, the objects of change are the ontologically determined trilogy—the child, the teacher, and the family. The very notion of change is about stability in which psychology is a technology for self-monitoring. The "expansive" social psychology quoted in the research on teacher education, for example, is built on the Hegelian notion of dialectics that assumes structures of objectification and subjectification. The dialectics of psychology begin with the objects of schooling as the starting point to generate thinking about difference and change in that object (Engeström and Sannino 2010; Engeström, Engeström, and Suntio 2002).

> The only potentialities an individual can realize are those that are tentatively sketched out in a surrounding world and that the individual actualizes by virtue of the fact that he or she is interested in them; the individual

fills in the hollow forms that "society" (that is, other individuals or collectivities) outlines. (Veyne [1971] 1998, 163)

The relation of certainty and uncertainty is instantiated through the cybernetics/systems concern with the relation of mind and machine. There is a productive/destructive relation between the two seeming opposites of certainty and uncertainty. Life, on one hand, requires security and certainty—life must be constantly secured in relation to the dangers that lurk within it and loom over it. The reduction of error and the elimination of points of disequilibrium or pathologies are to protect and enhance potentialities-to-be, forms of valued life that subdue uncertainty.

## Double Gestures of Exclusion and Abjection in Efforts to Include

The inscribed homogeneity and consensus in the notion of the professional teacher's expertise is generative of a comparative reasoning. As with the international assessment, the comparative qualities travel on the very surface of systems theory in ordering change. The evoking of professional practices as having a common language and common educational course of study "carries" the inscriptions of differences of people in its construction. Differences are produced as the qualities and characteristics excluded from what defines the commonness of the professional.

The comparative is produced through the congealing and rearranging of different historical lines at work in the articulation of the professional teacher as a kind of person. Theoretical principles of equilibrium/disequilibrium presuppose a comparativeness formed in relation to norms of consensus and harmony. The objectifications of the professional as having a commonalty of knowledge and syllabi or common modes of "learning" universalize and normalize the qualities of people from which to define differences. The notions of the authentic, expert, and professional teacher are abstractions about determinant categories of people that express what is taken as common and universal for all—or what should be common.

The elisions of the theoretical presumptions of unity and equilibrium/disequilibrium are performative. The use of professional knowledge to create "human improvement" evokes simultaneously the oppositional qualities of people as dangerous and abjected as the potentialities-to-not-be.

The unity presupposed in the commonality of the common syllabus and knowledge produces differences—differences in a continuum of the capabilities and capacities related to the abstraction that serves as the philosophical ideal of the teacher. Noticing, rehearsals, eliciting student ideas, and teacher decision-making processes are distinctions formed with unspoken standards about "the nature" of the child as the "learner," motivated and engaged; this is different from the "at-risk" child signified by the "lack of"—lack of motivation, self-esteem, work habits, or family stability.

The intention is to create unity as an equality to correct social wrongs so that "all children learn" through, for example, culturally relevant instruction that can "predict [affective and learning] outcomes" (Grossman and McDonald 2008, 185). But the good intentions of culturally relevant instruction as a knowledge to respect differences are bound to systems theory in the research on practice and the focus on the qualities that produce disequilibrium. The task of maximizing the system's performance is to eliminate its pathologies that (re)visions the Social Question into the new social spaces occupied by the professional teacher. The intervention of research about urban education and commitments to equity and justice, for example, is about changing the urban teacher who would possess global "professional virtues, qualities, and habits of mind and behavior" that should be "intrinsic" to the individual after their teacher education (Boggess 2010, 73).

The inscription of the "intrinsic" nature erases social and cultural differences, only to have them reappear as the object of change. Change is actualizing particular universals that connect differences in the trilogy of child, family, and community. Children spoken about as having the qualities of "all children who learn" are placed as different, the "struggling students" and the ones from "unstable families." Failures lack the psychological qualities that prevent actualizing what is normalized; for example, "high-poverty schools from engaging in more sophisticated forms of literacy" (Grossman et al. 2008, 244).

If "ghosts" of the core practice research are its interstices with psychology in generating the identifiable forms and possibilities of the teacher, one of these psychologies is the Vygotskian school of activity theory. It is referenced and folds into the identifications of processes and communication in the research about science and mathematics education (see, e.g., Engeström and Sannino 2010; Engeström, Engeström, and Suntio 2002). Activity theory in educational research employs the alchemic translations and classifications of the content of disciplinary fields into learning theories. The classifications and categories of learning serve to manage the *systems* of social communications to transform "individuals to collectives and networks" (Engeström and Sannino 2010, 6) and to provide for "collective meanings and the identity of the practitioners" (Grossman et al. 2009, 2,059).[7]

Activity theory brings into view and (re)visions the earlier Social Question. Activity and cognitive psychologies, like the psychologies at the turn of the 20th century, perform as "the great panacea for equality." The Social Question (re)appears as the "troubled" children from "fractured, blended and lone-parent families" that present teachers with complexity and cultural norms that are different from those children who come from two-parent families (Engeström, Engeström, and Suntio 2002, 224). The classifications of the fractured and blended family are oppositional distinctions connected with the unspoken norms of childhood and families. The category of the troubled child is bound with its double gestures; that is, what the child lacks to become normal and untroubled.

The prior quote about research to "embody theoretical principles of instruction, learning, development, culture, and practices that can be developed and refined" (Grossman et al. 2008, 247) *rendered the psychologies as invisible as they fold into the articulations at work*. It is important to recognize that this "expansive learning" of activity theory in teacher education research is not drawn from any attempt to understand the machinery of science or mathematics as a distinct cultural and epistemological field of knowing brought into schooling. While labeled as a cultural historical theory, the psychologies in teacher practical research about mathematics education, for example, have no discussions of what constitutes the social or the historical in the proposed activity theory.[8]

The linking of research with the psychologies applied is not a concern with the internal consistency and methodological rigor of the existing research. It is to explore the system of reason generated about people and differences that form as the object of change. Whereas Progressive reforms gave focus to changing the trilogy of the urban child, family, and community into collective norms associated with American exceptionalism as a cultural theory of a cosmopolitan mode of living, today's focus on practice loses sight of the ontological objects and the historical principles in giving intelligibility to the teacher and the trilogy of child, family, and community. The ontological objects of the teacher and child are there, though, embodied in the focus on processes and communication patterns but obscured by the elegance of their rhetorical forms and affective promises of salvation and redemption.

## Practical Research and the Paradoxes of Change

The chapter examined research on teacher practices and the objects of change generated. This looking to practice is not about what teachers actually "do" but is ordered through philosophical ideas about potentialities that operate as theories about who the teacher should be. The practical research is anticipatory, to find the pathways to actualize the philosophical ideals. Central in mobilizing change and desire is systems theory, which is given expression within the abstraction of the professional teacher. The professional teacher is a philosophical ideal of a kind of person that research designs the paths to achieve. The scaling and ordering of developmental processes to become professional entail objectifications that normalize, differentiate, and divide. The normative qualities are obscured through the naturalization about the professional as an empirical reality to achieve.

The practice of practical research is a chimera—the beautiful illusion that what is measured as the object of practice is what is real and not a desire embodied in its reason. But the illusion is not merely a false prophet. When examined through its rules and standards of reason, practical knowledge is not some transcendental concept that exists historically outside of its instantiation. What is practical and useful knowledge is linked to and embodies the historical conditions in which its cultural theses about different modes of life are generated.

While it might seem far away from this practical research to the Enlightenment's debates about whether all people can engage in cosmopolitan reason, that debate is reactivated when evoking the "professional" teacher. The answer then and now instantiated in practical research is *no*! The salvation themes of professions and social improvement are double gestures and a comparative system of reason. There is the hope of the future evoked in notions of democracy, agency, and redemption in correcting social wrongs to enable an equal and just society. But the iteration of good intentions is in changing the interiority of people that produces differences. This interiority is given in research today as changing habits of mind, dispositions, and sensitivities that perform to reinstall "the soul" as the object to secure the present as the future.

The agency to effect that liberation and desire to secure the future establishes the authoritative qualities that are not only about changing the teacher but about transforming the trilogy of child, family, and community. The teacher is continually inserted into principles of systems thought that relate to social and psychological principles as classifications and differentiation applied as the technologies of change.

The objectifications are not unique to the research on the practices of teachers and teacher education. They were discussed as part of the certainty/uncertainty that traveled with the alchemies of school subjects and research that moved in uneven ways from American Progressive schooling to the present. The principles of change join certainty and uncertainty, with the uncertainty lying in the processes and methods of communication that bring into existence the objectifications of the teacher and child as kinds of people and their double qualities of potentialities to actualize.

While there is affect given in the claims that research can actualize the dreams of the present for the future, the paradoxes of the practical, useful knowledge of research stabilize the very modes of life that are in question.

If I can turn to the book's title, the comparative style of reasoning inscribed in the research is impractical for the social commitments in play as the object of change. The question that travels throughout the various chapters of this book is whether this reason of practicality is sustainable in relation to the social commitments expressed, or whether other notions of science and change need to be considered even when this reconsideration has no guarantees.

# Section 4 • A Method of Study, Critique, and Change

Section Four's one chapter has a double purpose. It explores how the enticing and daunting promise of practical research determining the future is implausible in relation to its social commitments. This chapter gives attention to the impracticality of the research; impractical, it is argued, as the desires of change stabilize, conserve, and create double gestures that produce differences, exclusions, and abjections. The chapter then explores an alternative approach to the sciences of education, one that forms the mode of analysis that travels along the contours taken in the book. It is called a history of the present. This method of analysis goes against the grain of the current doxa of research, to rethink what constitutes the empirical and methods. The exploration maintains the attitude of the Enlightenment's cosmopolitanism to reason and the importance of a critical science, but rejects the epistemological principles of research that claims its practicality for changing social conditions by changing people.

# 10 ✦ The Impracticality of Practical Research

## From Matters of Research to What Matters as Research

The writing of the book began with a response to the continual refrain that occurs not only in my native land: the assertion that if research is meaningful, it must provide practical and useful knowledge for change. The obligation of educational research in this refrain is identifying the knowledge that enables children's learning, teacher effectiveness, school administrator leadership, and the wisdom of policy makers. The promise of practical knowledge is not only about the present. The promise is of science actualizing human potentialities, often iterated as the hope of promoting happiness and prosperity.[1] The power of this refrain is shrouded with the Enlightenment's cosmopolitan commitments to science, progress, and equality.

This view of science, knowledge, and change so deeply saturates schooling that it serves as the imputed reality. If research does not provide the practical knowledge useful for change, the refrain goes, "What use is research?," and as what goes unspoken, "What use is the researcher?" And in these questions is the larger charge that anyone who does not accept their premises is viewed as indifferent to a just society and the future "soul" of humanity. One extreme version was expressed at a seminar where a researcher on mathematics education and urban identities claimed that the practicality of his research would solve the problem of youth gun violence!

The enticing and daunting promise of practical research determining the future is like the Sirens, mythical creatures that lured the mariners onto the rocks along the shores of the Rhine River.[2] The doxa of research and science brings into view another mythical character, the Chimera, which considers how things perceived as imaginatively real and dazzling are wildly implausible in relation to their social commitments. Embedded in the chimera of practical research is its (re)visioning of the European Medieval alchemists' search for the philosopher' stone in finding the ultimate Truth of life as the pursuit of change.

The task of this book has been to ask about the limits of this particular view of science and whether its imputed reality of the new philosopher's stone is warranted. The method of analysis historicizes the present through asking about the conditions that make this kind of research possible and the politics of knowledge such research inscribes. I called the latter research as a history of the present, asking, "How is it historically possible to think *and* act as if there is a practical knowledge that research generates as the agent of changing people?" and "How are differences produced in making of people under the virtue of practical knowledge?"

The preceding chapters continually pointed paradoxically to the impractical qualities of "practical" research as a theory of change. This chapter initially gives attention to that impracticality as the desires for change stabilize, conserve, and create double gestures that produce differences, exclusions, and abjections in addressing social wrongs. The second thread is about the mode of analysis in this book as an alternative method to the study of change, one that historicizes the present. That history of the present is an engagement of a theory of the political and agency in which knowledge has material effects; this engagement with science simultaneously rethinks what constitutes the empirical and methods. The alternative method of analysis goes against the grain of the current doxa and, as Stuart Hall (1986) suggests, is without guarantees.

Exploring the limits of practical research does not dismiss social commitments nor reject the Enlightenment's cosmopolitan attitude toward reason and science. These commitments and the attitudes in fact organize the analyses in this book, such as its exploration of the double gestures in research. The analysis continually explores how social commitments are given specific, and paradoxical, concretizations in research that claims its practicality for changing social conditions by changing people.

## Sirens and Chimera: Paradoxes in the Desire of Practical Research

The history of the present explored different events that came together at different times and spaces to connect the objects of reflection and action. The analysis gave focus to different and uneven historical lines of flight. The different historical lines form a grid to give intelligibility to events, becoming naturalized and (re)visions as they leach into the present as desires governing that research. Metaphorically, I likened this historicizing to a recipe, as having multiple ingredients that are not recognized when "seeing" and acting on the objects of daily life; yet these ingredients or assemblages in social affairs remain and appear as the objectifications of people and the objects of research to change. These assemblages entailed principles generated about people through the folding and refolding of multiple dimensions of social time, agency, and change to give intelligibility to research as applied, practical knowledge for changing children, teachers, families, and societies.

The following section pursues the paradoxes of research explored throughout the book. These paradoxes are in the epistemic and ontological principles that order and classify research that form the core of the book's title about the impracticality of practical knowledge as a science of change.

### Paradoxes of the Sciences That Make Practice Its Practical Desire

The sciences in search of practical knowledge are thought of as a series of interconnected principles that generate narratives and images about society and people that change over time. These principles can be thought as the following:

(1) *The object of practical and useful research is making kinds of people.* The sciences in the long 19th century and today embody principles to instantiate cultural theses about the responsibilities, modes of living, and dispositions of kinds of people. These kinds of people explored, for example, were classified as the adolescent, the problem solver, and more recently as the global citizen and the lifelong learner. The object of the practical knowledge of the research is enacted on the body and the interiority or the soul. Today that soul is spoken of as changing teachers' habits of mind sedimented into the organizational language of benchmarks and empirical evidence.

(2) *Making kinds of people entails a specific quality in modernity that I spoke about as "homeless."* The "homeless mind" is a quality of consciousness given visibility in the Enlightenment reason of cosmopolitanism, formed with multiple historical lines about human history, progress, and agency. The abstractions about society and the child as a learner, for example, are "homeless"; they appear as transcendental concepts about life that seem to have no cultural and social boundaries. Yet the abstractions about people loop into the immediacy of life and have a materiality. The child as a

learner works into theories, programs, and narratives for shaping "the self" with collective norms of belonging and "home." The emergence of statistical measures and algorithms embody this quality of "homelessness": statistical measures perform seemingly without any historicity. The numbers in international assessments, for example, seem to be there only to identify the pathways and highways to secure future desires. The philosophical ideal of the professional in current teacher research is an abstraction that appears as a global, "homeless" concept about a kind of person; yet it has particular historical vectors as it "acts" to secure a desired kind of person.

(3) *Embodied in the abstractions are desires about the potentialities-to-be of people and society that the practical knowledge actualizes.* Desire is not a psychological category. *Desires are generated through the manner in which social events and people are calculated, standardized, and objectified in research. Development, problem-solving, and motivation embody desires whose reference is directed to the potentialities of the child if action is taken. Practical knowledge is an advocacy of potentialities.* Desires are generated in the classifications of skills, knowledge, and competencies telling about students' future participation. The Progressive sciences at the turn of the 20th century gave focus to the Social Question of changing urban populations through theories that expressed desires about modes of living. The OECD's international assessments (PISA) were explored as generating desires that created double gestures of the potentialities of people and society for the imagined future of the global society.

(4) *Desires about potentialities are cultural principles given as the salvific themes generated in the practical sciences.* For example, the Enlightenment's sensibilities about human reason and science were brought into the formation of the republics as salvific themes about collective belonging and the redemptive themes of the American Jeremiad, tropes that joined fears of the dangers with optimism about the potentialities of the future (Bercovitch 1978).

The engagement in these practical sciences was, in one sense, utopic. That utopic quality was embodied in the reasoning of research that gave direction to theories of learning and the child's development and growth in the modern school. The useful and practical knowledge in the OECD's PISA, for example, universalizes a particular utopic mode of living in its assessments of science and mathematics as the global competences necessary for future participation.

(5) *The calculations about making futures possible are affective.* The classi-

fications and ordering of the sciences are at once aesthetic, affective, and cognitive. The affective quality of knowledge is elided in the calculated domains of numbers visualized in tables, charts, and graphs images. The knowledge seems as having a mechanical objectivity. *The charts and graphs, however, are imbued with representations that move and mobilize for action* (Anderson 2010a, 785). Generated are principles about, for example, the potentialities of people to bring national progress, individual participation, and competence for future success. The social principles intersected with psychological categories about "well-being" that connected the trilogy of student dispositions with families and communities. The affect is embedded, ironically, in the universality of measures that promise salvation but seem to have no history or social location.

**(6)** *The principles of change as desires are paradoxical: they naturalize, conserve, and stabilize the very principles of their contemporaneousness.* In today's research, the practical knowledge of research brings together *the unmediated coexistence of the new sciences of big data and the psychologies of learning with the old metaphysics* that connect the seeming opposites of certainty/uncertainty and change/stability. These connections were discussed in Carl Becker's *The Heavenly City of the Eighteenth-Century Philosophers* (1932) that pointed to how the theological certainty of God was brought down in the Enlightenment to "the City of Man" as human nature. "Nature" was expressed in the psychologies that gave order to Progressive education and again in the second half of the 20th century inscriptions of systems theory and cybernetics century in psychologies of learning and research on teachers and the curriculum.

Today, practical knowledge of research revisions this *coexistence of new science and old metaphysics* through narratives about learning directly from experience (learning from what teachers and children really "do"). That "learning" is the conversion of theoretical models of the desired world into "the facts" inserted as the certainty of the real "nature" of the world and people that learning theories model and methods order for the interiorization of that "nature" as children's problem solving.

The current inscriptions of systems and cybernetics are to reconcile the world of meaning with the world of physical laws that contains its own impossibilities. Its "power to act on the world reduces humankind to the status of an object that can be fashioned and shaped at will; the conception of the mind as a machine—the very conception that allows us to imagine the possibility of (re)fabricating ourselves—prevents us from fulfilling these new responsibilities" (Dupuy [1994] 2009, xix).

(7) *Determinacy and indeterminacy exist together in the practical knowledge of research.* The indeterminacy is the calculation and standardization of processes, communication paths, or highways to actualize the desired "nature" of society and people. The sciences of the postwar world, for example, inscribed systems analysis and cybernetics. Systems theory likened social affairs to an organism that grows and develops. The openness and *indeterminacy* of systems theory to achieve equilibrium and optimize efficiency is the object of change; but change of the organism is linked in cybernetics to the logic of machines, which has a particular ontological givenness. The objectifications of kinds of people become the origin and desire of change. Change of the organism involves locating the pathways and highways to actualize the philosophical ideals given as the representations and identities of kinds of people. The latter objectifications for research to work on provides an entrance point for the insertion of the certainties associated with the logic of the machine. *Science paradoxically places certitude in the objectifications as the desire to be obtained, through designing highways and eliminating "the potholes." The highways and the potholes become the indeterminacy of change.*

(8) *The inscription of numbers and algorithms increasingly functions in modern science as political theology.* The rules and standards of algorithms and the iconic call for "empirical evidence" are affective, carrying the appeal of identifying the pathways to instantiate what works for change to actualize desires. The statistics used in contemporary school assessment are never merely about pure numbers. The inscriptions of numbers entail principles generated as cultural theses about kinds of people; the very calls for "scientific evidence" and benchmarks inscribe a specific rationality about equivalences and difference performed in cultural and social grids of a comparative style of reasoning. *What is often lost or elided is how these a priori principles "act" to generate desires about what should be, and that this becomes the object of practical research.*

The open system, in fact, is not open. The inscriptions of numbers and algorithms function to shape the range of actionable choices to those inscribed within the self-referential and self-authorizing ordering and classifications of the "system." Surfaces are established as points of contact about what is possible as anticipating the future (Anderson 2010a, 2014). The system "learning" through feedback loops continually narrows down what is actionable participation through the intensifications performed as the designs to manage and control. Further, the desires evoked are affective. The value of life lies in the promise that if the right pathways are followed, there is security that the anticipated reality, one that does not exist yet, can be rendered as achievable.

(9) *Practical research instantiates a comparative style of reason and double gestures of the hopes and fears of the dangers and dangerous populations. The systems of reason embody desires to make kinds of people distinguished and divided through the objectifications that represent and identity differences.* The comparative modes create the possibilities for conceptual and physical banishment of whole populations that cannot be *of the average* (see, e.g., Mitchell 2002, 240).

(10) *The significance of the comparative principles go beyond the particular research under scrutiny.* The continual paradox of managing the hopes and fears in "practical" research are distancing technologies that Casid (2015) argues are a mirroring of the self that imitates and abjects "the colonial machinery of dominance" (122). Comparative reasoning generates principles that cast out kinds of people who are made as strange, "foreign," racialized, and as endangering the future.

*The epistemic forms embodied in the research provide a historical lens for thinking about the generation of the possibilities of more radical practices in generating differences and exclusions, such as eugenics and racializing* (see Baumann 1989; Koza in progress). The recognition of people who are included and different, paradoxically, establishes a continuum of value between *normalcy and pathology*. The double gestures of potentialities engender principles about the kinds of people who "lack self-esteem," engagement, grit, and motivation and engender classification of the "fragile" family studied in urban education; these are people and families abjected as being outside, as being consigned to unlivable spaces (Popkewitz [1998] 2017b). The moral sciences of the 19th century and the Social Question of moral disorder and deviance become (re)visioned as today's differences recognized through expressions of bad parenting, bad teaching, poor motivation, and inadequate rewards/penalties as the cause of the lack of progress.

The comparison and the construction of differences in the research should not be surprising historically, as they haunt the sciences under scrutiny in this book. Within different grids assembled, there is the simultaneous engagement of Enlightenment hopes with fears of populations who do not reason and are not "reasonable people." The double gestures of hopes and fears are evident in the different flows and assemblies of the 17th-century Quarrel of the Ancients and Moderns, the moral sciences of the 19th century, the Progressive sciences concerned with urban populations, and today's discussion of equality formed within the epistemologies of inequalities. While there are continually attempts to turn the classifications of difference into resistances, the epistemic rules that construct differences tend to be elided.

## Making of a "Science" as Science

The eliding of the epistemic rules that order and classify research have a materiality in the rituals of graduate studies and the writings of research. The historicity of science is elided. And with that loss is the paradox of change as a comparative reasoning working in the interior of graduate education's learning research methods.

This erasing occurs in graduate education in the social and psychological sciences related to education through the categorical separation of theory and methods. Writing research proposals often has a ritual quality of the separate section on theory, starting with a review of literature that summarizes what others have done and how the researchers build on the concepts of others to offer their own unique contribution. The theory and reviews of literature are followed by a section on methods. That section describes the operationalizing procedures and often delineates the limits of the research. These limits may be in sampling procedures or in recognizing debates in the field about the concepts used. These seeming imprints of science get carried into PhD theses as a technical section to justify how empirical data are accessed and administered to arrive at what is "real" about the world.

Methods appear as analytically separate from theory and internal to research as the explications of procedures and processes for collecting data. Sanctified in professional preparation of graduate studies, qualitative and quantitative research courses are consigned as "methods" that have their own sets of rules and standards. Methods are given as universalized strategies for collecting data that are independent of any subject matter or problematizations of social and cultural matters in which the methods are applied. Methods are the separate tasks of science that ensure a disciplined and rigorous testing of ideas and theories. Theory is only the external reference for which methods confirm or deny hypotheses or conjectures.

The attention to methods as an autonomous space to constitute science is bound to the continual quest for objectivity; it is a search for techniques unencumbered by history. Research "methods" courses are about how to interview and observe in a manner that allows the researcher to keep a neutrality when in the field. In ethnographic work, this separation of theory and method is reinscribed even when embracing subjectivities by talking about positionality that locates the writer's social, gender, and racial background, among others. The elimination of the observer's observing sneaks in through notions of triangulation in ethnographic research. Triangulation is to attest that three points corroborate and testify to the validity of what is said or thought. The notion of objectivity allows certainty to return through the back door as a theoretical possibility that governs the present and guarantees the future.

The rigor sought for methods as internal procedures for collecting data is to banish, or at least limit, the intrusions of subjectivity in measurements. This banishment entails the categorical imperative that separates objectivity from subjectivity, expressed as reducing human "biases" or "prejudices." The discussion often focuses on the control of "bias" and reducing subjectivity; the assumption is that objectivity (without subjectivity) is possible even if unattainable. Certainty returns in these distinctions through the backdoor as a theoretical possibility (but not theory) that governs the present and as the guarantee of the future. Left unexamined are how methods are legible within systems of reason that "act" to differentiate, distinguish, and divide the subjects of change.

Obscured is how "theory" is embedded in how things are noticed and made into facts and data for analysis (Popkewitz 2018a). Theory is used in the sense of styles of reasoning discussed in the initial chapters. Theories function as sets of principles to order what matters, and to recognize and distinguish the candidates for telling the truth about society, schools, and people. Methods are not things that exist as distinct, ahistorical entities to be applied in research.

The chimera of methods as separate from theory is given in the opposition between qualitative and quantitative research courses and more recently as the call for "mixed methods"; the latter is merely asking for the use of different technologies of collecting data. Differences are expressed technically as the researcher paying attention to qualitative communications and narratives of the classroom placed against quantitative, statistical analyses and numbers. Yet if I use the analyses in section 3 of the book, the differences in the macrostatistical analyses of international assessments and the micro classroom observations of teacher education research melted as theories of systems analysis and cybernetics shape and fashion the borders that define the objects to know and act on.

As continually iterated in this book, the argument is not against these qualities of reflection about the techniques applied in research. Such reflection is necessary but not sufficient. The practices of reflection require their own historicizing, considering the particular system of reason in which empirical evidence and being "rigorous" are inserted and given self-referential and self-authorizing qualities.

This reducing methods to techniques works itself into the mantra of educational talk about the theory/practice split and researchers calling for finding "practical" and "useful" knowledge. Elided are the historically instantiated cultural principles that shape and fashion how judgments are made, conclusions are drawn, solutions are given plausibility, and existences are made manageable (Popkewitz forthcoming b; also see Barad 2003). Hacking (2004) spoke of this relation of theories and methods as styles of reasoning, and Agamben (2009) wrote about it as the "pre-history" of paradigms that revisions Kuhn's (1970) discussion of change in science.

### Am I Talking about Just Another Version of Bentham's 19th-Century Utilitarianism?

The argument against the reason of practical research might seem homologous to the critical theory of the Frankfurt school and the Gramscian notion of hegemony that are brought into structural analyses of inequities, critical educational research, and critical pedagogy literatures. The discussion of systems analysis and cybernetics in the previous chapters, for example, might seem merely an extension of Jeremy Bentham's 19th-century utilitarianism. That argument places value on pursuing the greatest happiness and good through social improvement in a series of chains of causes and effects. This type of argument is found in Habermas's ([1968] 1971) discussion of "empirical-analytical" sciences as one human interest that gives attention to processes and patterns of communication and interaction as means-ends relations that could be controlled and administered. If left at this level of analysis, utilitarianism seems almost a perfect fit for systems analysis, which hypothesizes how things work to maximize utility.

Utilitarianism and Habermas's analysis of empirical-analytical research, however, leave unexamined how research "acts" as desires and changes over time where, for example, ideas of social improvement generate utopic visions in fabricating present human kinds and differences. The critical theory in Habermas mistakes politics for the political in research. The politics of schooling is articulated in notions of the hidden curriculum and in the attention to questions of hegemony. It takes its subjects as having given identities and directs attention to how certain groups of people are represented and the resources allocated to various agents (sometimes called stakeholders).

The structural account of critical theory, when brought into educational research, gives attention to the notion of politics. It produces a world of oppositional objectifications between the rulers and ruled. This structural sense of critique, as Latour (2004) has argued, may have exhausted its potential through reinscribing the very principles of its contemporaneous framework as the principles of change.

As I discussed in the introduction, the notion of critique is focused on *the political* as being different from politics. The *political* gives reference to the production of principles that shape and fashion what is said, done, and acted on. Rancière (2006b) calls this notion of the political as *the partition of the sensible and, if I can add, sensibilities (the relation of cognition and affect) generated in practical research*. The representations, identities, and models of learning in practical research are productive in establishing relations that partition, differentiate, and divide what is sensible from what is not sensible and dangerous. *The rankings, scaling, and hierarchies of performances and communication processes in the research studied partitioned what was sensible and inscribed distinctions between normalcy and pathology.* This notion of the political also is captured in Foucault's (1979) notion of governmentality concerned with the principles generated in governing the production of desire and potentialities.

### Visualizing Truth and Science

Central in the last three chapters are inscriptions of systems and cybernetics theories as producing transformations in how truth is told. The epistemological principles generated different coordinates that formed the sciences after World War II to produce "a range of new tactics and, imaginaries, for the management and orchestrations of life" (Halpern 2014, 17). Questions of documentation, indexicality, archiving, and historical temporality are redefined, particularly in the international assessments, and functioned as visualization technologies through graphs and charts.

My argument explored how the epistemic change assembled in the reform-oriented sciences concerned with education gave attention to systems theory as not one pure set of principles but part of a "traveling library." The idea of "traveling library," as discussed earlier, explores how systems theory is continually inscribed, assembled, and modified in connection with different historical lines formed with social and cultural principles of the sociologies and psychologies of education. In this process, systems theory is reworked to produce sciences whose codifications and standards entail multiple temporalities that bring the past and present into an anticipatory relation to what should be.

The anticipatory quality of science in the visualizing technologies of the OECD's international assessments are imagined states of global competences and modernization that appear as empirical facts that cannot be empirical. They are about the future that has not yet arrived. Scientific and mathematical competence are theoretical entities about kinds of people measured as if they did exist and calculated to say something about the desired cultural and social life.

The power of these visual images was evident in the OECD's preliminary Educational Policy Review of Sweden (2014). That initial report to government policy makers had no words; it was a document visualizing ranking and coordinates in graphs and charts that located Sweden in yellow highlighting below the line of the median of nations. The visual representations were affective, projecting the danger to the nation in the world order. The visual presentations had truth-bearing qualities that were different from, for example, the Wisconsin R&D Center, discussed in chapter 6, and different again from the indexical qualities of teacher education research, discussed in chapter 9.

The epistemic principles generated are where "the future is told as truism and not from general laws" (Hacking 1983, 121). Method and objectivity are, at least in the visualizations of the international assessments, no longer about documenting an external truth or reality about the world. The visualization of performance through the numbers generated are reflexive as a GPS for the routes to change rather than as indexical.

The technology's images function as the telling of a truth—a truth different from the explanations about series or chains of causes and effects. Halpern (2014) traces the emergence of systems and cybernetics thought as a "calculative rationality" and "communicative objectivity in the reason of science."

The mapping of educational systems performs as grounds for precautionary or preemptive actions (Massumi 2007). The models of change in PISA, the scripts for teacher communication, and the rubrics for professional teacher development are bound to what is anticipated. Policy and research are to neutralize threats to national progress through empirically identified causes and to find remedial methods to avoid the realization of the threats. The performance indicators are preemptive, acted on in national policy to ensure who people become that secures the nation's place in the future of nations (see, e.g., Swedish National Agency for Education 2015).

The new ways of telling the truth assume importance historically in broader social and political spaces in which science "acts." While I have given attention to research as the production of coordinates in the interstices of the social, political, and educational, the changes in the criteria of how science tells the truth become significant with other social coordinates that intersect with the epistemic and ontological changes discussed. One of these is the emergence of "alternative facts" and the antiscience discourses coming from political and social arenas in Europe and the US, what is thought of as "post-truth" and "post-factuality."[3] "Post-truth" is an attitude that is suspicious of science and maintains that everything is open to interpretation. It entails also an attitude where there are no "facts" and all reality is negotiated.

While "post-truth" is talked about as catering to irrational, arbitrary interpretations and sometimes a disregard for "facts," its emergence is not merely a reaction to science but has formed in relation to the reconfiguration of the system of reason and the technologies in the sciences from the mid-twentieth century discussed in this book. The populism that seems to emanate as "post-truths" has a historical tangentiality with systems and cybernetics erasures of the ontological objects with the focus on process and communications. The international assessments, while still having their bearing in prior rules of a pragmatic positivism and empiricism, bring models of change into public arenas in which truth is told through the visual culture in which numbers, graphs, and charts are self-referential measures that "tell" truisms about nations and people.

While not causal, there are homologies with "post-truths" and the visual culture assembled in the international assessments with the emphasis on affect and the technologies in which the past and time emanate from inside the networks, flows, and feedback loops that are inscribed in the design of research. Cybernetics, Halpern (2016) argues, transforms "epistemology from the search for truths in an external world, to the search for self-referential measures emanating from within our networks that underpins contemporary concerns about data visualization, ubiquitous computing, and 'smart' networks" (442). Science no longer exists as a Bergsonian time of a reality inaccessible to science but as a time emanating from inside the networks and design of research (Halpern 2016). The search for truths is embodied in the self-referential measures that link cognition with affect. The visualizations become the truth about the "future."

When the visual cultures of science and the epistemic principles of cybernetics are placed historically in discussions of paradigms, or what Thomas Kuhn talked about as normal and revolutionary sciences, the fragmentation of knowledge emerges and allows expression of ideas of multiple realities and constructivist views of knowledge.

"Post-truth" has perhaps some relation to the fragmentation and constructivism that circulate in the social sciences. But "post-truth" and constructivism are hard to sustain, as Hacking (1999) and Latour (2006) argue, although its affective dimensions have historically strong cultural lines that push and radicalize the boundaries related to American liberalism, and, as I discussed in earlier chapters, have a tenuous relation to the different tendencies of the religious movements of the American Great Awakenings in the long 19th century.

In the fragmentations of knowledge, it is important to recognize that not everything is constructed and there are in fact materialities embodied in and generated in the practices of science (see Foucault 1979, 1991; Hacking 1999, 2002; Latour 2013; Daston and Galison 2010; Barad 2003). And science as a mode of thinking about existence, the importance of giving disciplined empirical attention to the things happening in the world, and the notion of critique provide a counterpoint to the "post-truths" as well as to the limits of "practical research" for understanding and acting.

## Studying the History of the Present: "Reason," Methods, and the Empirical

In the introduction, I suggested the dual tasks of this book: exploring the limits of contemporary research and simultaneously making an argument for an alternative science. That alternative was embodied through the manner in which the arguments were developed and analyzed through a social epistemology of "reason." The historicizing focused on the contingencies of what would otherwise be taken as the unquestionable objects of thought, action, and change. I use "science" in this alternative sense to systematically give attention to the empirical world that unshackles "science" from the residues that join Cartesian logics with analytical philosophy and positivism, which form as principles in the prior analyses of practical research.[4]

This final section brings the methods of research within the broader historical frame of research as critique as important to the Enlightenment cosmopolitanism's attitude to reason, science, agency, and change. In doing so, the very objects, methods, and the empirical of research are given attention. *Critical research, as a method of research explored in this book, maintains the attitude of the Enlightenment's cosmopolitanism* as an account of the rules and standards of "reason" in ordering the present. And while written in the shadow of the European Enlightenment, the discussion recognizes both its singularity and also the multiplicities of connections, assemblies, and disconnections in manifold historical spaces that cannot be reduced to "Eurocentrism" (see, e.g., Zhao 2018; Popkewitz, Khurshid, and Zhao 2014; Wu 2013). While the political intent of such a descriptor is important, the modes of analysis are entangled knowledges that are obscured through the inscription of the binaries.

### Science and Change in an Enlightenment Register of Critique

The history of the present is a critical science that performs as an optimistic suspicion of the present. Latour (2004), for example, suggests reversing attention from what is assumed as the matters of concern as the object of research to research that asks about *the concerns of what matters*. This notion of critical directs attention to "what is accepted as authority through a critique of the conditions of what is known, what must be done, what may be hoped" (Foucault 1984, 38). A critical science is a method of change in which "agency" is expressed, but, as I explore, through the method of unthinking for rethinking the inscriptions in the current doxa of research.

*The importance of critique in the Enlightenment (and today) tends to get lost with the belief that science can generate knowledge that can be directly applied to change conditions and people.* Yet as the German philosopher/social historian Hans Blumenberg ([1966] 1983) argues, the Enlightenment cosmopolitanism concerned with reason, rationality, and progress has two complementary sides.[5] One has evolved into social planning and interventions, the strand of research whose principles of practical research are historically explored in this book. Different and important to the Enlightenment ideas of progress is a different notion of science, what Blumenberg called "renunciation," and what a colleague, Lynn Fendler, calls "whistle blowing." It continually asks how we have arrived at the present and its limits as a method of thinking about who we are, who we should be, and the possibilities of change.

Blumenberg's idea of science as "renunciation" and Foucault's arguments about power/knowledge, although coming from different historical traditions, are that critique is central to the issues of freedom and change. They both embody the necessity of cutting into the causalities of the present to make fragile what seems inevitable. To return to Foucault,

> Criticism is a matter of flushing out that thought and trying to change it: to show that things are not as self-evident as one believed, to see that what is accepted as self-evident will no longer be accepted as such. Practicing criticism is a matter of making facile gestures difficult. (Foucault 1988, 155–56)

Critique is an optimism about the possibilities of change. That optimism about change lies in making unstable what is taken as natural, "bound up more with circumstances than necessities, more arbitrary than self-evident, more a matter of complex, but temporary, historical circumstances than with inevitable anthropological constants" (Foucault 1988, 156). Criticism is cutting into what seems self-evident to give historical contingencies to objectifications and the ontological determinism discussed in earlier chapters. This holds open possibilities outside of contemporary frameworks.

The mention of critique, I recognize, is often not seen this way. "Critical" is said as "negative," when the real challenge of research is defined as producing social improvement and pathways for progress. In the American setting, the optimistic side of the American Jeremiad takes precedence in arguing about the importance for practical knowledge and what science should do.

The openness of the future promised, ironically, cannot be preprogrammed, no matter how much optimism is projected. This optimism about programing freedom works in the epistemic principles of the "practical." I argued that the principles of "practice" interns and closes possibilities. This optimism elides how practical knowledge polices the boundaries of what is possible, producing what Rancière (2006a) argued as hierarchies between experts and "the people." Inequalities are the starting and ending points for equality. The inscriptions of objectifications regulate and gov-

The Impracticality of Practical Research • 223

ern agency and freedom in bounded, prescribed spaces of potentialities in social theories. Rancière argues that such regulation works against democracy as it is not something that can be institutionalized.

Testing the limits of the present does not give up notions of freedom and agency, notions mutually dependent on the other. It questions notions of planning that stabilize and fix the boundaries of agency and freedom as an effect of power. Agency, as explored here, lies in challenging the habitual ways of working and thinking in constituting society and people. This challenging the habitual ways is "grasping for freedom and liberty" by historically exploring the "practical test of the limits that we may go beyond, and thus work carried out by ourselves upon ourselves as free beings" (Foucault 1984, 47).

This strategy of critique as historicizing entails an epistemological relativism—but that relativizing should not be confused with moral relativism. The two should not be collapsed into one. The commitment of this book is to rethink the political, agency, and science through what Judith Butler (1993) calls "conditional foundations." It entails recognition of complex edifices that form in the relation of epistemology and ontology.

But this recognition also has it humility; Newtonian physics is still in use for working with certain kinds of problems, and it coexists with quantum physics. The history of the present explored in this book recognizes this pluralism; yet its task has been to consider, paraphrasing Berlant (2011), the cruel optimism in which the particular limits of the rules and standards of practical research create the impossibility for the social commitments that are its aim. The argument for critique, in the sense discussed, (re)visions the notion of agency and change through making visible how the inscriptions of equality as inequalities in current research "act" to produce the double of potentialities and their abjections.

The notion of a critical science brings into view the notion of agency but through a different register. Agency can be thought of as testing of the limits of the present, freeing ourselves from the particular dogma of the present through a resistance to what seems inevitable and necessary by "modifying the rules of the game, up to a certain point" (Foucault 1984, 48). The sense of hesitation embedded in "up to a certain point" is related to the conditionality of the present, which makes it impossible to find complete and definitive knowledge of what constitutes the past and present.

Critique is to think of the freedom of agency as outside of the inscriptions of the subjectification and objectifications that work in the doxa of practical research. The systems analyses explored in contemporary research, for example, inscribe agency as the internalization of the representations of people and society as the origin of self-realization, freedom, and autonomy. *The paradox of agency in that research and teacher education research is that certainty performs as the principle ordering the acts of agency and freedom: the practical knowledge to secure the child's problem solving is to learn how to apply the abstract models of mathematics and science as giving access to the given world, and the teacher's professional self-realization of the technologies of their applications. Agency is interiorizing the rules and standards that stabilize the objectifications of social life as the spaces of action.*

Research concerned with unthinking the present is a method of freeing oneself from the present while, ironically, being immersed in the present. This freeing in its own immersion is an uneasy juggling act—to engage in an interrogation of the limits of the present while not giving up the cosmopolitanism attitude about reason as commitments to freedom and hospitality to others.

## Methods, Theory, and the Empirical

It might seem odd, even a horror to the conventions of "rigorous" research, to approach methods as intricately binding the collection of data with embodied theory. The justification schema that orders much of today's discussion of the "empirical" and "scientific evidence," for example, draws on positivistic conceptions of methods, derived from the constructions of science that emerged in the 19th century, updated and reworked today but with the residues of the past folded into the present. "Good" methods, the wisdom goes, enable the world to be seen directly and clearly, as if the language of procedures to collect data becomes isomorphic with the objectifications of the world.

To rethink the conduct of science entails rethinking the relation of theory, methods, and what constitutes "the empirical."[6] Methods work at the intersections of "data" and theory that are overdetermined, occurring in the indeterminate interstices of the things encountered in the world (the ontic) and how they are made knowable and interpretable as experience. While things happen and are not merely what constructivists imagine, there are no "facts" until they are made into "facts" to be noticed and acted on.

The empirical and "the facts" of practical research were explored as having an uneven flow of events where different historical lines came together and produced the objects of reflection and action. The connection of the historical lines were treated as grids that had a porous quality, with openings that made them amenable to poke holes in their seemingly naturalness and inevitability. To think about empirical in this manner recognizes that the historical lines are not deterministic but historically accidental rather than of necessity, and not foretold as having a single origin in its formation.

The empirical, drawing on Deleuze and Parnet's ([1977] 1987, vii) paraphrasing of the philosopher Alfred North Whitehead, lies in the abstractions or objectifications of the world that do not explain but must themselves be explained. The empirical asks about the objects of what is known as cultural artifacts. To be empirical is to analyze the state of things in their multiplicities, as lines or dimensions that are irreducible to one another but form a grid that gives intelligibility to what is seen, talked about, and acted on. Policy statements, research reports, and the classification of tables and graphs, for example, are documents of a culture. They are embodied in the folding of historical lines, seen as events that stand as the empirical to understand the groups of rules that define what can be said, preserved, reactivated, and institutionalized (Foucault 1991). Documents, texts, stories, and theories are the material evidence that, as Stoler (2009) argues, are "not as repositories of state power but as unquiet movements in a field of force, as restless realignments and readjustments of people and beliefs to which they were tethered, as spaces in which the senses and the affective course through the seeming abstractions of political rationalities" (32–33).

The "empirical," then, is not what succumbs solely to the rigid implementation of a priori rules and standards to operationalize. Evidence is not what is assumed as naturally there to be recouped through rigorous methods. Rather, the practices of research are to unthink the order of things and the objectifications that give that naturalness to memory and institutions.

The empirical sense that I draw on engages in a diagnostic, critical history of how different objects are made observable, and how they are acted on to form a problem and its modes of rectification. As argued earlier, the research on "practice" and practical knowledge were treated as cultural artifacts. This way of thinking of the empirical qualities of analysis was undertaken to apprehend different presents. American Progressive education, post–World War II research, and contemporary research related to teacher education and international student assessments were studied as historical singularities produced through the multiplicities of codifications and standardizations.

The different historical events enunciated particular intersections or intermediaries in complex movements; each one produced new surfaces in the working of the rules and standards of reason making of kinds of people that produces difference. The empirical works in the interiority of their historical spaces in which its "facts" are turned into events, archived as unquiet movements and indices of power relations in the governing of people and social life. The empirical question has been to ask about the rules and standards of "reason" archived in the research designed to find practical knowledge.

## Concluding the Conclusion with No Guarantees

Exploring flows of social and cultural practices that link science with the idea of practical and useful knowledge might bring back the objection: "Of course, and yes, I understand that research has paradoxical qualities and limits to the social commitments of schooling. But I am still left with the question of what I should do." I always am bewildered this question. Why would people ask someone who is foreign to their existence, often one who just got off the plane from somewhere else, to design their future? Even more bewildering is installing this design question as the protocol for the agency for enacting democratic principles.

This book's task has been to ask about how the naturalness of this "so what?" question is performed within the historical conditions that make plausible the reason of practical knowledge and its "reasonable people." It is an attempt to trace and critically explicate how this reason becomes reasonable: "How is it historically possible to think and act in the present as if particular kinds of distant strangers can be called upon for ordering the conduct of daily life?"

The historical lines followed in the book are to think about what makes this kind of "expertise" plausible as a knowledge and as the production of desire. I return again to the title of *the impracticality of practical research* as it might be time to think differently about the principles of science and change. Stephen Toulmin (1990) raised this issue when arguing that the sciences have been dominated by Newtonian mechanics and determinism for the past century, something continually given reference in the inscriptions of certainty and the eliding of the ontological objects in research. He then commented, if I may paraphrase, look where it got us! And he ends with concluding that perhaps it is time to think of other ways of engaging in the study of humanity.

This leaves me with some final thoughts. This book is an investment in the attitude of the Enlightenment that privileges reason, rationality, and the empirical (see, e.g., Fuchs et al. 2017). The evoking of the Enlightenment's cosmopolitanism recognizes the complexities of that investment, and the importance of epistemological difference and critique that continually provincializes research itself.

The commitment to reason and science comes against a particular kind of provincialism that occurs in thinking about science itself. Paul Feyerabend, in *Against Method* (1993), wrote about how he continually went to scientific meetings and marveled at how people did not know about where the questions they asked came from, and how the questions embodied cultural and social principles that worked against freedom. At first, he thought this lack of knowing was a matter of professional incompetence. After a while, Feyerabend began to rethink this idea of incompetence and to approach the problem as more generalized as professionalized incompetence. Professionalized incompetence is the lack of self-reflection, Feyerabend argued, that erases its own historicizing into the very process of learning about science.

I raise this issue in relation to a topos of contemporary educational research that I talked about as the Truth of Science coming from the twin faiths that knowledge should be directed to changing people and the accuracy and rigor of the technologies of "data" collection and analysis as the criteria of their "truths." Differences in these twin faiths are expressed, if I can borrow from a film title, as "Oh, brother or sister, where art thou in what you do as research? Quantitative? Qualitative?" And if asked by a historian, the privileged question of method is typically "Have you exhausted all archives and archival materials?"

The romanticizing of data collection—the retrieval as what is true, beautiful, and authentic—is an epistemic undercurrent of research seeking practical and useful knowledge (Popkewitz forthcoming b). The rigor of the romanticized, however, dulls the senses to science as a mode of existence in its forms of knowledge production and to the political in these actions.

To end is to bring forth a discussion from the Enlightenment, also explored in chapter 2, about the "wisdom" of people in the new forms of government and governing. In that debate, the book takes the side that the obligation of research is not to accept claims about being the representative of people, to make its profession as speaking for others, and the inscription of a hierarchy and division of power. Research is a historical practice, "a struggle aimed at revealing and undermining power where it is most invisible and insidious" (Deleuze and Foucault 1977, 208).

# Notes

## Chapter One

1. The analysis is focused primarily on American research and, at points, its intersections with European sciences that are discussed, where relevant, throughout.
2. The use of "good intentions" is drawn from Malin Ideland's (2019) research on how education for a sustainable environment brings to bear an optimism about a progressive world, but educational practices have generated principles that normalize and pathologize as certain modes of living bodies are considered as dangerous to public happiness. Also see Ahmed 2008, 2010.
3. Two outliers to this are Rose (1989) and Baker (2013).
4. I use Progressive not to delineate a sharply defined temporality given to the past; I use it as multiple overlapping historical lines to explore the objects of desire and change produced, hence the phrase "the long 19th century."
5. American Progressivism, for example, is a particular event often dated between 1880 and 1920; yet what gives it visibility is made possible through different historical trajectories that, at least, move from the late 1700s through the early decades of the 20th century.
6. I use the phrase "related to education" because first, it is only in the 20th century that educational psychology and sociology, for example, become distinct institutional entities, often located in what later become schools of education; and, second, the education sciences are continually intertwined historically with the broader movements of the social and psychological sciences.
7. See, e.g., Ahmad 2004; Murphy 2017.
8. See, e.g., Barad 2003; Bowker 2008; Hacking 1999, 2002; Latour 2013; Schatzki 2002; and Veyne [1971] 1998.
9. My use of these two collections of works plays with the ideas of potentiality as provoking thinking about differences and what later I call "the double gestures" of research, policy, and schooling; that is, with the hope of progress are fears of dangers and the dangerous populations that prevent that progress.
10. I discuss this in Popkewitz 2008, drawing on Kristeva's (1982) psychoanalytic approach but I move from psychology to the study of social epistemological.
11. This notion of scrutiny is to think about agency in a different register that I discuss in chapter 2 and chapter 10 as related to a critical science.
12. The discursive form of writing a research article is formatted as distinct sec-

tions for stating the problem, specifying limits, operationalizing concepts, asserting methods, stating findings, and writing conclusions—that is, it takes a discursive form to eliminate subjectivity. Historicism expresses this through detailed attention to archival retrieval and footnotes as documentation (see Popkewitz, Franklin, and Pereyra 2001; Popkewitz 2013a).

13. I realize there is a resurgence of talk about "realism" in some of the scholarship I draw on, for example, Barad (2003) and Berlant (2011). I think the use of "realism" in this literature acts as a political move against "constructivism" as well as providing substantive challenges to the legacies of positivism and empiricism in the analytics of the contemporary sciences.

14. The philosophical issues and the historical instantiations of diversity/difference as well as the empirical, as I discuss later, are explored in cultural studies, philosophy, and history (see, e.g., Deleuze [1968] 1994; Deleuze and Parnet 1987; Scott 1991; Stengers 1997).

15. I discuss "traveling libraries" in Popkewitz 2005.

## Chapter Two

1. There are limits to the analogy to recipes in the historical instantiations of practical research, which are not intentional acts in an evolutionary history.

2. I appreciate Lee Shulman's suggestion about the original and full bronze sculpture that stands on the Stanford University campus. I appreciate David Labaree returning to the Stanford museum for the photograph included.

3. Affixing the label of "scientific" or the word "empirical" should not be construed as embodying universal rules about domains of human practice; but, as the previous and current chapters should make clear, science and the empirical have particular historical qualities and limits as a particular style of reason or paradigm (see, e.g., Popkewitz [1984] 2012).

4. The folding of multiple times into what seems as a singular "arrow" is explored, for example, in Koselleck [1979] 2004).

5. The article's title is "Design Research with Educational Systems: Investigating and Supporting Improvements in the Quality of Mathematics Teaching and Learning at Scale."

6. As expressed in this and again in the final chapter, there are other ways of reasoning about change without the inscription of kinds of people that research is to actualize.

7. This separation of observation and the agents of observation permeates research discussion of methods, discussed in the concluding chapter. The relation of positivism and empiricism to a realist philosophy and its limits are discussed in Barad 2003, 814; see also Schrader 2012.

8. For counternarratives, see, for example, Ariès (1962), Dekker (2010), and Finkelstein (1989).

9. This notion of decentering the subject has been subject to a range of discussions. Often its critiques are ordered through the principles of historicism that take for granted the actor as the source of humanism. This reduction qua critique misses the substantive arguments being engaged about how this notion of humanism inscribes a transhistorical quality to the subject that denies its historicity and thus ironically is antihumanist (see Veyne [1971] 1998 for a discussion of history and the limits of this reductionism as critique).

10. See, e.g., Barad 2003; Bowker 2008; Hacking 1999, 2002; Latour 2013; Schatzki 2002; and Veyne [1971] 1998.

## Chapter Three

1. I used the long 19th century, as discussed in chapter 1, to move from notions of historical epochs in order to consider different and uneven historical grids of practices that were assembled and made visible between the end of the 18th century and the beginning of the 20th century. See Popkewitz 2008 and Tröhler, Popkewitz, and Labaree 2011.

2. I recognize that the Enlightenment was not one thing, as evident in contemporary European continental philosophy and strands of postcolonial and postmodern feminist theories that maintain different sensibilities associated with the Enlightenment from the Cartesian logic discussed later (see, e.g., Popkewitz 2008, chapter 10; Toulmin 1990). The word "modern" is used to speak of epistemological principles, and is not meant as a historical hierarchy superseding other modes of thought.

3. This notion of historicizing is discussed further in, e.g., Popkewitz, Franklin, and Pereyra 2001 and Popkewitz, Diaz, and Kirchgasler 2017. More generally in the history and philosophy of science, see Daston and Lunbeck 2011; Hacking 2004; Poovey 1998; Chiang 2015.

4. The idea intersects with notions of progress and utopian thought. See, e.g., Manuel and Manuel 1979; Nisbet 1969, 1980.

5. I borrow this phrase from Deleuze and Guattari ([1980] 1987) to think about a finite number of dimensions and multiplicity of forms that move historically but at points serve as a single plane of consistency. These historical lines of flight are also spoken about here as grids and "events."

6. This historical thinking, as discussed in a previous chapter, is a method of understanding the rules and standards that give intelligibility to what is considered as conflict and debate. See, e.g., Cassirer ([1932] 1951) and Dumont ([1991] 1994). For some of the historical trajectories discussed, see, e.g., Pocock (2003); Levine (1995); Wagner, Wittrock, and Whitley (1994); Wittrock, Heilbron, and Magnusson (1998).

7. The cosmopolitanism that emerged was not singular. British, French, Germans, Americans, and Slavic peoples, for example, had different qualities and no-

tions of the cosmopolitan citizen's capacity to conceptualize, standardize, and order social life and people (see, e.g. Sobe 2008). My concern, as suggested above, is less with these differences, but instead with how it becomes possible to give intelligibility to ideas of useful and practical knowledge as strategies of social and educational change.

8. For a discussion of the shifts of the meanings of economy from moral outlook to its more technical definitions, see, e.g., Poovey's (1998) discussion of Adam Smith's *Wealth of Nations* and Mitchell's *Rule of Experts* (2002).

9. The phrase is borrowed from Berger, Berger, and Kellner's (1974) institutional theory about the construction of knowledge. My discussion rethinks its "reason" within a social epistemology and the history of the present explored in the first two chapters (also see Popkewitz 2009).

10. Making this statement acknowledges that there are still residues of "trust" formed in interactions of people as social psychological research provides evidence, such as in the famous Hawthorne experiments with workers at Western Electric in the 1920s.

11. These conditions have specificities but appear in multiple historical spaces that are not merely that of the West, which is evident in the traveling of pragmatism at the turn of the 20th century (Popkewitz 2005). My focus is historically on the US, but at points to Europe, the Americas, and East Asia.

12. I appreciate Trude Evenhaug for drawing attention to what at one level seems similar but is different in that modern agency is secularized and change is a given part of human history.

13. I intentionally used the word "practice," as discussed in introductory chapters, as a historical activity to understand its social and cultural relations. It is different from "practical knowledge," a word whose objects anticipate the future through acting on the present.

14. See Poovey (1998) for a discussion of Adam Smith in relation to this.

15. The Scottish Enlightenment philosophers, as David Hamilton (1989) explores, were influential in the development of modern schooling and its notions of "knowledge" in curriculum theory.

16. As said in the previous chapter, I am using practice as a historical rather than as an ontological object that serves as the origin of change. Practice gives attention to a series of activities, ideas, and narratives through which "things" become objects of reflection and action. Practice, in this sense, consists of the historical conditions that give intelligibility to how "things" are done and ordered for reflection and action.

17. This will be discussed in chapter 6 in relation to American Progressivism and specifically to John Dewey's view of science as a form of revelation in democracies, although the pragmatism in Dewey's text embodies an indeterminacy rather than determinacy.

## Chapter Four

1. This affect is embedded in the international assessments discussed with the Organization of Economic Co-operation and Development's Programme for International Student Assessment (PISA) discussed in chapter 8.

2. The limits of the secularization thesis in modernity can be initially approached through the historical discussions of the 19th-century political formation of republicanism. This literature is mostly related to Protestant countries in Europe and North America but can also be understood in Counter-Reformation/counter-Enlightenment political formations, such as in the 19th-century formation of the Argentine Republic (Caride 2015).

3. The Great Awakenings of the 18th and 19th centuries involved multiple denominations. I appreciate Julia Koza for continually pushing my thinking with a caution as not to conceptualize Protestant salvation and redemption in reductive terms.

4. In education, this is discussed in Popkewitz (2008), McKnight (2003), and Tröhler (2011).

5. See, e.g., discussion about religious cosmologies and theories of social change in Popkewitz (1991, [1984] 2012).

6. This is discussed in chapter 6.

7. The incursion of technology and science as a cultural narrative is also found in European utopian thought, such as Henri de St. Simon who celebrated the engineer as "the priest of civilization" (Virilio [1977] 2006, 41).

8. It is important to note that Eastern elite universities such as Yale, Columbia, Harvard, Dartmouth, and Princeton were initially schools to train clergy.

9. Religious systems of authority were also redefined, in part through the merging of the state and religion in European contexts, and through changes in the social cosmologies in which religion was seen. For discussions of religion in modernity, see Berger (1969) and Luckmann (1967).

10. Durkheim ([1938] 1977) explores this in the Counter-Reformation, but the pastoral power in pedagogy assumes a different set of relations and implications when the history of the modern state and liberalism is approached.

11. There was debate in the formation of the social science disciplines in American Progressivism. That debate was, in part, about the role of Christian ethics versus the empirical and descriptive sciences. The American Economic Association's first president, Richard Ely, advocated the former and was a member of the Social Gospel movement. Ely lost the battle for the overt role of Christian ethics in the narratives of science.

12. The sciences directed to urban life used "deviance" as an object for defining its research. My use is in this historical sense only.

13. While there were elements of eugenics in the psychologies, the idea of the "American Race" circulated in literary and public discourses as an expression of American exceptionalism and difference that embodied cultural distinctions about "civilization" that were not necessarily linked to the body, heredity, and eugenics.

14. This is explored in contemporary teacher education research in chapter 9.

## Chapter Five

1. https://www.nextgenscience.org/
2. This notion of deterritorialization/reterritorialization has homologies to the work of Deleuze and Guattari ([1980] 1987).
3. https://www.nextgenscience.org/, accessed December 30, 2018.
4. See, e.g., discussions about transformations of religious cosmologies into theories of social change in Popkewitz 1991, 2008.
5. "Others" are also present but absent in historical discussions about schools and science, such as East Asians who came to work on the westward expansion of the railroads in the second half of the 19th century and Latinx populations in southern and western areas that previously belonged to Mexico.
6. I view these twin purposes as moving across ideological spectrums in the sciences of liberal society; yet I interrogate the manner in which good intentions are expressed through the immanent rationalities or systems of reason inscribed in research and the paradoxes produced by the practical knowledge to obtain these desires.
7. My reference to European and North American is only to reference the specificity of the analysis, while recognizing other sites where the term "Enlightenment" was also used.

## Chapter Six

1. See, e.g., Popkewitz (2005) and Deleuze and Guattari ([1991] 1994) for the notion of conceptual personae.
2. The discussion is also indebted to such studies as Hamilton (1989) and Goodson (1987).
3. This is explored in Popkewitz (2008). The relation to the Enlightenment is not discussed explicitly in the historical narratives of this and more general educational histories.
4. In China, it was related to the May 4 Movement of 1919.
5. This historical shift is often lost in contemporary discussion of neoliberalism, both in advocacy and critiques.
6. Indebted to these related studies are also Hamilton (1989), Popkewitz ([1988] 2017), and Goodson (1987).
7. Notions of practical and useful knowledge were not visible as words; my use of the words is to direct attention to ways in which science was conceptualized to change people through planning directed to modes of living. The actual phrases appear more recently and within a different set of conditions.
8. It later changed its name to the American Sociological Association.
9. This relation is discussed in multiple historical settings (see, e.g., Clark 1995; Hatch 1980; Greek 1992; Menand 2001).
10. That principle of happiness entailed the inscription of differences, discussed later as being generated as double gestures and eugenics.

11. My premise here is that all nations since the turn of the twentieth century are welfare states in the theoretical sense of the state's responsibility to care for the security and risks of its population, although this care is differently administered and never universal. This historical recognition is important for considering the problem of governing, policy, and the social and educational sciences. The policy-oriented social sciences can be found in the eighteenth and early nineteenth centuries as *Polizeywissenshaften*, a term about the understanding and improving of the administrative rules and regulator policies of the state (Wagner et al. 1991).

12. These included the Congregational, Presbyterian, Dutch Reformed, and German Reformed Churches as well as Baptist and Methodist denominations.

13. Mark Twain and Charles Dudley Warner, *The Gilded Age: A Tale of Today* (1873). Similar kinds of writing were appearing in England, most notably that of Charles Dickens.

14. Many of the founders of American economics, sociology, and psychology belonged, at one point, to the Social Gospel movement, such as Albion Small, Richard Ely, Charles Cooley, and E. A. Ross, some of whom are discussed later in relation to education. My own campus of the University of Wisconsin–Madison has named buildings for many of these people, such as the university president, Charles R. Van Hise.

15. As discussed later, Hall's studies were of white, middle-class boys.

16. My argument is about the reason that orders the objects of research, viewing the different writings as conceptual personae. It also means recognizing that the reasoning of Hall and Thorndike, as I will discuss, inscribed eugenics into the psychologies of differences that is not present in Dewey's pragmaticism.

17. I discuss this in Popkewitz 2009.

## *Chapter Seven*

1. While the Cold War often is given priority in the explanations of educational reforms (see, e.g., Hartman 2008), to speak about the Cold War as "the cause" misrecognizes the social, cultural, and economic changes occurring internationally as well as nationally. Sputnik, for example, was a symbol of "crisis" in the educational field of the Soviet Union, although with different epistemological ordering of school reforms (Tabachnick, Popkewitz, and Szekely 1981). Thus, to speak of grand historical epochal periods loses sight of the historicity in the resulting configuration and principles of governing. The Cold War, for example, was given intelligibility within the salvific themes of the nation and its casting of the American Jeremiad that included prior evangelical 19th-century Christian movements that cast Russia as the Antichrist that would trigger a global cataclysm of horrendous proportions (Boyer 1992).

2. The Learning Research and Development Center at the University of Pittsburgh, one of the first two centers funded in 1964, focused on research and evaluation. In 1964, three more centers were created: the Center for Advanced Study of Educational Administration at the University of Oregon at Eugene;

the Center for Research and Development for Learning and Reeducation at the University of Wisconsin at Madison; and the Center for Research and Development on Educational Differences at Harvard University. A sum of $500,000 each was committed to these institutions annually through a five-year cost reimbursement contract. Eventually, a total of ten R&D centers were established (Saettler 1990).

3. For instance, in the 1960s, the University of Wisconsin–Madison formed the Institute for Research on Poverty, a number of urban and international units, the Institute for Environmental Studies, and the Center for Research and Development for Learning and Reeducation to engage in large-scale studies. Today, its recent version sits the 13-story building called "Educational Sciences." It houses the Wisconsin Center for Educational Research, the latest reincarnation of the original research and development center in 1965. The center today generates over $60 million in research grants and assessment services and employs over 500 people, including 100 graduate students.

4. This end of ideology assumption was in public conflict with Cold War rhetoric but in fact was reconciled pragmatically through the internal US approaches to research that assumed a consensus and instrumentalism.

5. Savage's (2010) discussion about Britain in the postwar years has points of convergence as the academic sciences established new relationships to changing the everyday social world.

6. It is interesting to note that faith in science (and the scientist) was embodied in the educational research centers that received a general allotment of funds related to their grant plans but the centers internally organized their projects.

7. Today, the American Educational Research Association has over 25,000 members in fields ranging from education, psychology, statistics, sociology, history, economics, philosophy, anthropology, and political science. Over 14,000 participants attend its annual meeting.

8. British social sciences, in contrast, were characterized by strong moral and socio-philosophical commitments, were not theoretically oriented, and were empiricist in research design (Wagner et al. 1991, 15). French social science, while initially adopting forms of empiricism related to American research, soon abandoned its instrumentalism and moved back to more universalist, philosophical, and historically based approaches. These differences in Europe and the United States were also embodied in the study of educational psychology (Depaepe 1987).

9. As Bürgi and Tröhler argue (2018) benchmarks emerged within the OECD as educational "thermometers" that drew on a medical language about normalcy and pathology. The defining of quality through benchmarks (re)visioned the language of social engineering in a system of reason ordered through systems theories.

10. It had, oddly, a short official life in many of the sciences, such as computer science. I say "official" as it often became part of the commonsense so as not to be publicly noted as theory.

11. It was translated into seven languages and is still used today.

12. Cybernetics ordered models of planning that sought a unified and globalized

model for educating people in science, technology, engineering, and mathematics in reports by UNESCO and the Club of Rome as well as in US policy thinking about issues of control and communication patterns (Zheng 2019a, 2019b).

13. In the early 1970s the Center was renamed the Wisconsin Research and Development Center for Cognitive Learning.

14. The principles that organized the mathematics curriculum became important to the development of national standards of mathematics education developed in the late 1980s, with its director Thomas Romberg heading the commission to develop its National Council of Teachers of Mathematics committee.

15. Personal communication.

16. The emergence of IGE as a research centered reform about schooling, children, and teachers as kinds of people developed in a nonlinear fashion.

17. Bloom's taxonomies of educational objectives were very influential internationally in the 1960s and 1970s, and still are referenced in Europe.

18. The curriculum reforms were innovative at the time, both in the thinking about mathematics education and also its incorporation of systems theories.

19. A great number of social programs were invented to address the issues of poverty and inequality: Head Start, Upward Bound, Follow Through, the federal Teacher Corps program. Early childhood programs such as Head Start were designed to remake the poor (provide "efficacy" and "self-esteem") through the inscription of competitive, entrepreneurial, and participatory norms. The interventions often were related to questions of structural changes but morphed into administrative and social-psychological questions about the qualities and characteristics of the subjectivity of the poor (see, e.g., Popkewitz 1976).

## *Chapter Eight*

1. http://www.oecd.org/pisa/aboutpisa/

2. https://www.mckinsey.com/industries/social-sector/our-insights. McKinsey considers itself as having a social obligation to address the problems associated with the global challenges of economic and human development. The societal concerns are taken as part of the larger corporate public responsibility. The nonprofit McKinsey Global Institute, for example, is an economic think tank that provides management knowledge for foundations, nonprofits, and multilateral institutions on issues related to disease, poverty, climate change, and natural disasters. http://www.mckinsey.com/about_us

3. The discussion brings together different research projects on the sociology of scientific knowledge in Lindblad, Pettersson, and Popkewitz (2018) and Popkewitz (2018a).

4. http://www.oecd.org/pisa/aboutpisa/

5. There is an US International Center for Benchmarking (see newsletter, https://mailchi.mp/ncee/topoftheclass-1665125?e=c04b350e30). The center is a part of the National Center on Education and the Economy.

6. The difficulty with this Cartesian logic in science is explored in Schrader (2012) and Barad (2007).

7. Press release, OECD, May 15, 2016, http://www.oecd.org/fr/education/oecd-proposes-new-approach-to-assess-young-peoples-understanding-of-global-issues-and-attitudes-toward-cultural-diversity-and-tolerance.htm

8. Systems theories were applied in the OECD's approach to studying the conditions of education in the late 1950s (see, e.g., Pettersson and Mølstad 2016) and as a method for interventions in research related to the US War on Poverty and the Great Society, among others.

9. This a phrase used by Halpern (2014) to discuss the rationality produced through systems and cybernetics thought.

10. http://www.oecd.org/pisa/publications/pisa-2015-results-volume-iii-9789264273856-en.htm

## *Chapter Nine*

1. There were institutional changes by the 1980s that included the movement from states certifying university programs to license teachers to state's identifying credential procedures that specified individual traits, experiences, and information.

2. Discussed in chapter 7, community emerges in the postwar American social movements to open spaces of participation and decision-making (Grant 1978). It quickly was transformed in social policy and social and educational sciences as an administrative category for organizing relations of government and social movements (see Popkewitz 1976, 1978).

3. http://www.teachingasleadership.org/sites/default/files/TAL.Comprehensive.Rubric.FINAL.pdf

4. There is a large body of literature in history, historical sociology, and sociology that expresses the complexities of what are called professions in Anglo-American contexts; see, e.g., Larson 1979; Burrage and Torstendahl 1990; Torstendahl and Burrage 1990.

5. I have used quotation marks to more clearly identify the rubric's language as embodying not merely actions but as a mode of living and a kind of person.

6. The function of systems and change was debated. One element of the discussion focused on whether to see systems as in a state of equilibrium or disequilibrium. The debates, however, did not solve the limits of systems as a theory of change, as it had no criteria of difference other than activity and motion (see, e.g., Popkewitz [1984] 2012).

7. For different approaches to thinking about curriculum models, see Valero et al. (2012) and Gustafson (2009, 2014).

8. In October 1996, I co-organized a conference in celebration of the 100th birthday of Lev Vygotsky. It was sponsored by the Russian Academy of Education Science and the Russian Institute of General and Educational Psychology, where Vygotsky worked. One of the leading Vygotskian psychologists, V. V. Davidov,

commented that one of the limits of that work claiming to be a historical-cultural theory is that there has been no systematic discussion of culture and history. My contribution to the conference addressed this, discussed in Popkewitz (1998).

## *Chapter Ten*

1. For discussion of the limits of liberal notions of happiness, see Berlant 2011; Ahmed 2008, 2010.

2. The use of Sirens draws the mythological analogy to the present. My using of the myth is to think about the technological sublime, the seductions of modernity inscribed in discourses given the veneers of science and technology, questions or issues that I have addressed and intellectually elaborated throughout this book.

3. See, e.g., Fuchs et al. (2017). Also see the focus of the 2019 annual meeting of the American Educational Research Association, "Leveraging Education Research in a "Post-Truth" Era: Multimodal Narratives to Democratize Evidence" (http://www.aera19.net/theme.html).

4. I discuss these different trajectories of science in Popkewitz ([1984] 2012, 1997a, 1997b, 2013b, 2013c) and Popkewitz and Fendler (1999).

5. The different epistemes in which the word "critical" is evoked in education are explored in an edited book that I did with Lynn Fendler (Popkewitz and Fendler 1999).

6. Some of this discussion draws from different efforts to think about the problematic of research, such as the problematic of method in an ethnographic study of urban and rural schools in the US (Popkewitz [1998] 2017b); issues of theory in methods (Popkewitz 2014b; forthcoming a; forthcoming b); and the inscription of theory in the concept of "lived experience" in research (Popkewitz 2013c).

# References

Agamben, G. 1999. *Potentialities: Collected essays in philosophy.* Translated by D. Heller-Roazen. Stanford: Stanford University Press.
Agamben, G. 2009. *The signature of all things: On method.* Translated by L. D. Santo. New York: Zone Books.
Ahmed, S. 2004. Affective economies. *Social Text* 22 (2): 117–39.
Anderson, B. 2010a. Pre-emption, precaution, preparedness: Anticipatory action and future geographies. *Progress in Human Geography* 34 (6): 777–98.
Anderson, B. 2010b. Security and the future: Anticipating the event of terror. *Geoforum* 41: 227–35.
Anderson B. 2014. *Encountering affect: Capacities, apparatuses, conditions.* Farnham, Surrey, England: Ashgate.
Andrade-Molina, M., and P. Valero. 2015. The sightless eyes of reason: Scientific objectivism and school geometry. Paper presented at the Ninth Congress of European Research in Mathematics Education, Prague.
Ariès, P. 1962. *Centuries of childhood: A social history of family life.* Translated by R. Baldick. New York: Vintage Books.
Baker, B. 2013. *William James, sciences of mind, and anti-imperial discourse.* Cambridge: Cambridge University Press.
Ball, D. L., L. Sleep, T. A. Boerst, and H. Bass. 2009. Combining the development of practice and the practice of development in teacher education. *Elementary School Journal* 109 (5): 458–74.
Barad, K. 2003. Posthumanist performativity: Toward an understanding of how matter comes to matter. *Signs: Journal of Women in Culture and Society* 28 (3): 801–31.
Barad, K. 2007. *Meeting the universe halfway: Quantum physics and the entanglement of matter and meaning.* Durham: Duke University Press.
Barber, M., and M. Mourshed. 2007. *How the world's best-performing school systems come out on top.* Chicago: McKinsey & Company.
Barton, D., D. Farrell, and M. Mourshed. 2013. *Education to employment: Designing a system that works.* http://www.mckinsey.com/industries/social-sector/our-insights/education-to-employment-designing-a-system-that-works
Bauman, Z. 1989. *Modernity and the Holocaust.* Ithaca: Cornell University Press.
Becker, C. 1932. *The heavenly city of the eighteenth-century philosophers.* New Haven: Yale University Press.

Becker, H. S., B. Geer, E. C. Hughes, and A. L. Strauss. 1961. *Boys in white: Student culture in medical school*. Chicago: University of Chicago Press.

Bellack, A., H. Kliebard, R. Hyman, and F. Smith. 1966. *The language of the classroom*. New York: Teachers College Press.

Bell, D. 1962. *The end of ideology: On the exhaustion of political ideas in the fifties*. New York: Free Press.

Bell, D. A. 2001. *The cult of the nation in France: Inventing nationalism, 1680–1800*. Cambridge: Harvard University Press.

Bellah, R. 1975. *The broken covenant: American civil religion in time of trial*. Chicago: University of Chicago Press.

Bercovitch, S. 1978. *The American Jeremiad*. Madison: University of Wisconsin Press.

Berger, P. 1969. *The sacred canopy: Elements of a sociological theory of religion*. New York: Doubleday Anchor Book.

Berger, P., B. Berger, and H. Kellner. 1974. *The homeless mind: Modernization and consciousness*. New York: Vintage.

Berger, P. L., and T. Luckmann. 1967. *The social construction of reality*. London: Allen Lane.

Berlant, L. 2011. *Cruel optimism*. Durham: Duke University Press.

Berliner, D., and N. L. Gage. 1976. The psychology of teaching methods. In *The psychology of teaching methods: The seventy-fifth yearbook of the National Society for the Study of Education*, edited by N. L. Gage, 1–21. Chicago: University of Chicago Press.

Bhambra, G. 2007. *Rethinking modernity: Postcolonialism and the sociological imagination*. Dordrecht, The Netherlands: Springer.

Biesta, G., J. Allan, and R. Edwards. 2011. The theory question in research capacity building in education: Towards an agenda for research and practice. *British Journal of Educational Studies* 59 (3): 225–39.

Bledstein, B. 1976. *The culture of professionalism, the middle class, and the development of higher education in America*. New York: W. W. Norton.

Bloch, M. (1949) 1953. *The historian's craft: Reflections on the nature and uses of history and the techniques and methods of those who write it*. Translated by P. Putnam. New York: Vintage Books.

Bloch, M., K. Holmlund, I. Moqvist, and T. S. Popkewitz, eds. 2003. *Governing children, families, and education: Restructuring the welfare state*. New York: Palgrave Macmillan.

Bloom, A. 1968. *Introduction: The Republic*. New York: Routledge.

Blumenberg, H. (1966) 1983. *The legitimacy of the modern age*. Translated by R. Wallace. Cambridge: MIT Press.

Boggess, L. 2010. Tailoring new urban teachers for character and activism. *American Educational Research Journal* 49 (1): 65–95.

Boon, J. A. 1985. Anthropology and degeneration: Birds, Words, and Orangutans. In *Degeneration: The dark side of progress*, edited by J. E. Chamberlin and S. L. Gilman, 24–48. New York: Columbia University Press.

Borgonovi, F., and B. Przemyslaw. 2016. An international comparison of students' ability to endure fatigue and maintain motivation during a low-stakes test. *Learning and Individual Differences* 49: 128–37.

Borko, H. 2004. Professional development and teacher learning: Mapping the terrain. *Educational Researcher* 33 (8): 3–15.

Bowker, C. 2008. *Memory practices in the sciences*. Cambridge: MIT Press.

Boyer, P. 1978. *Urban masses and moral order in America, 1820–1920*. Cambridge: Harvard University Press.

Boyer, P. 1985. *By the bomb's early light: American thought and culture at the dawn of the Atomic Age*. New York: Pantheon.

Boyer, P. 1992. *When time shall be no more: Prophecy belief in modern American culture*. Cambridge: Belknap Press of Harvard University Press.

Broman, T. 2012. The semblance of transparency: Expertise as a social good and an ideology in enlightened societies. *OSIRIS* 27 (1): 188–208.

Bruner, J. 1960. *The process of education*. Cambridge: Harvard University Press.

Bruner, J. 1983. *In search of mind: Essays in autobiography*. New York: Harper & Row.

Buenfil Burgos, R. 2005. Discursive inscriptions in the fabrication of a modern self: Mexican educational appropriations of Dewey's writings. In *Inventing the modern self and John Dewey: Modernities and the traveling of pragmatism in education*, edited by T. Popkewitz, 181–202. New York: Palgrave Macmillan.

Bürgi, R., and D. Tröhler. 2018. Producing the "right kind of people": The OECD education indicators in the 1960s. In *Education by the numbers and the making of society: The expertise of international assessments*, edited by S. Lindblad, D. Pettersson, and T. Popkewitz, 75–91. New York: Routledge.

Burkhardt, H., and A. Schoenfeld. 2003. Improving educational research: Toward a more useful, more influential, and better-funded enterprise. *Educational Researcher* 32 (9): 2–14.

Burrage, M., and R. Torstendahl, eds. 1990. *Professions in theory and history: Rethinking the study of the professions*. London: Sage.

Butler, J. 1993. *Bodies that matter: On the discourse limits of "sex"*. New York: Routledge.

Campbell, D. T., and J. C. Stanley. 1963. Experimental and quasi-experimental designs for research in teaching. In *Handbook of research in teaching*, edited by N. Gage. Chicago: Rand McNally.

Caride, E. 2015. "Catholic" secularism and the Jewish gaucho school: Salvation themes of the 19th-century Argentinean citizen. In *The "reason" of schooling: Historicizing curriculum studies, pedagogy, and teacher education*, edited by T. Popkewitz, 115–30. New York: Routledge.

Carnegie Forum on Education and the Economy. 1986. *A nation prepared: Teachers for the 21st century; The report of the task force on teaching as a profession*. New York: Carnegie Corporation.

Carvalho, L. M. 2012. The fabrications and travels of a knowledge-policy instrument. *European Educational Research Journal* 11 (2): 178–88.

Casid, J. 2015. *Scenes of projection: Recasting the enlightenment subject*. Minneapolis: University of Minnesota Press.
Cassirer, E. (1932) 1951. *The philosophy of the enlightenment*. Translated by F. Koelln and J. Pettegrove. Princeton: Princeton University Press.
Castel, R. 2017. *From manual workers to wage laborers: Transformation of the social question*. Translation by R. Boyd. New York: Taylor & Francis.
Chamberlin, J. E., and S. L. Gilman, eds. 1985. *Degeneration: The dark side of progress*. New York: Columbia University Press.
Chase, F. S. 1977. Introduction to IGE and educational reform. In *Individually guided elementary education: Concepts and practices*, edited by H. J. Klausmeier, R. A. Rossmiller, and M. Saily, xi–xvi. New York: Academic Press.
Chiang, H. 2015. *Historical epistemology and the making of modern Chinese medicine*. Manchester: Manchester University Press
Childs, J. L. 1956. *American pragmatism and education: An interpretation and criticism*. New York: Henry Holt and Co.
Clark, E. B. 1995. "The sacred rights of the weak": Pain, sympathy, and the culture of individual rights in antebellum America. *Journal of American History* 82 (2): 463–93.
Cobb, P. Jackson, K. Smith, T. M. Sorum, and E. Henrick. 2013. Design research with educational systems: Investigating and supporting improvements in the quality of mathematics teaching and learning at scale. *National Society for the Study of Education* 112 (2): 320–49.
Cohen, D. 1995. What is the system in systemic reform? *Educational Researcher* 24 (9): 11–22.
Cohen, D. 2005. Professions of human improvement: Predicament of teaching. In *Educational deliberations: Studies in education dedicated to Shlomo (Seymour) Fox*, edited by M. Nisan and O. Schremer, 278–94. Jerusalem: Keter Publishing.
Cohen-Cole, J. 2014. *The open mind: Cold War politics and the sciences of human nature*. Chicago: University of Chicago Press.
Cohn, D., S. Raudenbush, and D. Ball. 2003. Resources, instruction, and research. *Evaluation & Policy Analysis* 25 (2): 119–42.
Cooley, C. H. 1909. *Social organization: A study of the larger mind*. New York: Charles Scribner's Sons.
Cruikshank, B. 1999. *The will to empower: Democratic citizens and the other subjects*. Ithaca: Cornell University Press.
Danziger, K. 1997. *Naming the mind: How psychology found its language*. London: Sage.
Danziger, K. 2008. *Marking the mind: A history of memory*. Cambridge: Cambridge University Press.
Darling-Hammond, L. 2006. Constructing 21st century teacher education. *Journal of Teacher Education* 57 (3): 300–314.
Darwin, C. 1859. *On the origin of species by means of natural selection*. London: Murray.
Daston, L., and P. Galison. 2010. *Objectivity*. Hereford, UK: Zone.
Daston, L., and E. Lunbeck. 2011. *Histories of scientific observation*. Chicago: University of Chicago Press.

Day, C., P. Sammons, and Q. Gu. 2008. Combining qualitative and quantitative methodologies in research on teachers' lives, work, and effectiveness: From integration to synergy. *Educational Researcher* 37 (6): 330–42.

Dekker, J. J. 2010. *Educational ambitions in history: Childhood and education in an expanding educational space from the seventeenth to the twentieth century.* Frankfurt: Peter Lang.

Deleuze, G., and M. Foucault. 1977. Intellectuals and power. In *Michel Foucault. Language, counter-memory, practice: Selected essays and interviews*, edited by D. Bouchard and translated by D. Bouchard and S. Simon, 205–17. Ithaca: Cornell University Press.

Deleuze, G. (1986) 1988. *Foucault.* Translated by Sean Hands. Minneapolis: University of Minnesota Press.

Deleuze, G., and F. Guattari. (1980) 1987. *A thousand plateaus: Capitalism and schizophrenia.* Translated by B. Massumi. Minneapolis: University of Minnesota Press.

Deleuze, G. (1968) 1994. *Difference and repetition.* Translated by P. Patton. New York: Athlone Press of Columbia University Press.

Deleuze, G., and F. Guattari. (1991) 1994. *What is philosophy?* Translated by H. Tomlinson and G. Burchell. New York: Columbia University Press.

Deleuze, G., and C. Parnet. (1977) 1987. *Dialogues.* Translated by H. Tomlinson and B. Habberjam. New York: Columbia University Press.

Depaepe, M. 1987. Social and personal factors in the inception of experimental research in education (1890–1914). *History of Education* 16 (4): 275–98.

Derrida, J. 1972. Structure, sign, and play in the discourse of the human sciences. In *The structuralist controversy: The languages of criticism and the sciences of man*, edited by R. Macksey and E. Donato, 247–72. Baltimore: Johns Hopkins University Press.

Dershimer, R. 1976. *The federal government and educational R&D.* Lexington, MA: D.C. Heath.

Desrosières, A. (1993) 1998. *The politics of large numbers: A history of statistical reasoning.* Translated by C. Naish. Cambridge: Harvard Press

DeVault, M. V., D. J. McCarthy, and L. Van Ess. 1967. Wisconsin elementary teacher education project. Proposal for research and/or related activities submitted to the US Commissioner of Education for support through authorization of the Bureau of Research. December 29. Madison: University of Wisconsin–Madison.

Dewey, J. (1893) 1975. Christianity and democracy. In *The early works of John Dewey*, vol. 4, *1882–1898: Early essays and the study of ethics, a syllabus, 1893–1894*, edited by J. A. Boydston, 3–10. Carbondale: Southern Illinois University Press.

Dewey, J. (1916) 1929a. The schools and social preparedness. In *Character and events: Popular essays in social and political philosophy*, vol. II, edited by J. Ratner, 474–78. New York: Henry Holt and Co.

Dewey, J. 1916. *Democracy and education: An introduction to the philosophy of education.* New York: Macmillan.

Dewey, J. 1929b. *The sources of a science of education.* New York: Horace Liveright.

Diaz, J. 2017. *A cultural history of reforming Math for All: The paradox of making in/equality.* New York: Routledge.

Dole, C. 1891. *The American citizen*. Boston: D. C. Heath & Co.
Dumont, L. (1991) 1994. *German ideology: From France to Germany and back*. Chicago: University of Chicago Press.
Dupuy J.-P. (1994) 2009. *On the origins of cognitive science: The mechanization of the mind*. Translation by M. B. DeBevoise. Cambridge, MA: MIT Press.
Durkheim, É. (1938) 1977. *The evolution of educational thought: Lectures on the formation and development of secondary education in France*. Translated by P. Collins. London: Routledge, Kegan & Paul.
Dussel, I. 2013. The visual turn in the history of education. In *Rethinking the history of education: Transnational perspectives on its questions, methods, and knowledge*, edited by T. S. Popkewitz, 29–50. New York: Palgrave.
Easton, D. 1965. *A systems analysis of political life*. New York: Wiley.
Eksteins, M. 1985. Anthropology and degeneration. In *Degeneration: The dark side of progress*, edited by J. E. Chamberlin and S. L. Gilman, 1–24. New York: Columbia University Press.
Engeström, Y., R. Engeström, and A. Suntio. 2002. Can a school community learn to master its own future? An activity theoretical study of expansive learning among middle school teachers. In *Learning for life in the 21st century: Sociocultural perspectives on the future of education*, edited by G. Wells and G. Claxton, 211–24. Oxford: Blackwell.
Engeström, Y., and A. Sannino. 2010. Studies of expansive learning: Foundations, findings, and future challenges. *Educational Research Review* 5 (1): 1–24.
Faragher, J. M., ed. 1994. *Rereading Frederick Jackson Turner*. New Haven: Yale University Press.
Fejes, A., and K. Nicoll. 2007. *Foucault and lifelong learning: Governing the subject*. London: Routledge.
Ferguson, R. A. 1997. *The American enlightenment, 1750–1820*. Cambridge: Harvard University Press.
Feyerabend, P. 1993. *Against method*. 3rd ed. London: Verso.
Fine, G. A., ed. 1995. *A second Chicago school? The development of a postwar American sociology*. Chicago: University of Chicago Press.
Fine, S. 1956. *Laissez-faire and the general-welfare state: A study of conflict in American thought*. Ann Arbor: University of Michigan Press.
Fink, L. 2015. *The long gilded age: American capitalism and the lessons of a new world order*. Philadelphia: University of Pennsylvania Press.
Finkelstein, B. 1989. *Governing the young: Teacher behavior in popular primary schools in nineteenth-century United States*. New York: Falmer Press.
Foucault, M. (1971) 1977. Nietzsche, genealogy, history. In *Language, countermemory, practice: Selected essays and interviews by Michel Foucault*, edited by D. F. Bouchard and translated by S. Simon, 139–64. Ithaca: Cornell University Press.
Foucault, M. 1978. *The history of sexuality: An introduction*. Harmondsworth: Penguin.
Foucault, M. 1979. Governmentality. *Ideology and Consciousness* 6: 5–22.
Foucault, M. 1984. What is the enlightenment? Was ist Auflärlung? In *The Foucault Reader*, edited by P. Rabinow, 32–51. New York: Pantheon Books.

Foucault, M. 1988. Practicing criticism. In *Politics, philosophy, culture: Interviews and other writings, 1977–1984*, edited by L. Kritzman, translated by A. Sheridan and others, 153–56. New York: Routledge.

Foucault, M. 1989. *Foucault live (interviews 1966–1984)*. Translated by J. Johnston. New York: Semiotext(e).

Foucault, M. 1991. A question of method. In *The Foucault effect: Studies in governmentality*, edited by G. Burchell, C. Gordon, and P. Miller, 73–86. Chicago: University of Chicago Press.

Foucault, M. 2005. *Michel Foucault. The hermeneutics of the subject: Lectures at the Collége de France, 1981–1982*. Edited by F. Gros. New York: Palgrave Macmillan.

Foucault, M. 2008. *Psychiatric power: Lectures at the College de France, 1973–1974*. Vol. 1. New York: Macmillan.

Fousek, J. 2000. *To lead the free world: American nationalism and the cultural roots of the Cold War*. Chapel Hill: University of North Carolina Press.

Franklin, B. 1986. *Building the American community: The school curriculum and the search for social control*. New York: Falmer Press.

Franklin, B. 1994. *From "backwardness" to "at-risk": Childhood learning difficulties and the contradictions of school reform*. Albany: State University of New York Press.

Franklin, B. 2008. Curriculum history and its revisionist legacy. In *Rethinking the history of American education*, edited by W. J. Reese and J. L. Rury, 223–44. New York: Palgrave Macmillan.

Fuchs, E., R. Horlacher, D. Tröhler, and J. Oelkers. 2017. Post-truth and the end of what? Philosophical and historiographical reflections. *Bildungsgeschichte: International Journal for the Historiography of Education* 2.

Gage, N. L., ed. 1976. *The psychology of teaching methods: The seventy-fifth yearbook of the National Society for the Study of Education*. Chicago: University of Chicago Press.

Gaonkar, D. 2001. *Alternative modernities*. Vol. 1. Durham: Duke University Press.

Gee, J. 1999. *An introduction to discourse analysis: Theory and method*. New York: Routledge.

Gilman, N. 2003. *Mandarins of the future: Modernization theory in Cold War America*. Baltimore: Johns Hopkins University Press.

Glaser, B., and A. Strauss. 1967. *The discovery of grounded theory*. Chicago: Aldine.

Glaser, R. 1977. *Adaptive education: Individual diversity and learning*. New York: Holt, Rinehart, and Winston.

Glaude, E. S. 2000. *Exodus! Religion, race, and nation in early nineteenth-century Black America*. Chicago: University of Chicago Press.

Goodson, I. 1987. *School subjects and curriculum change*. Barcombe, Lewes, England: Falmer Press.

Gorski, P. 1999. Calvinism and state-formation in early modern Europe. In *State/culture: State formation after the cultural turn*, ed. G. Steinmetz, 147–81. Ithaca: Cornell University Press.

Gorur, R. 2011. ANT on the PISA trail: Following the statistical pursuit of certainty. *Educational Philosophy and Theory* 43 (S1): 76–93.

Grant, C., ed. 1978. *Community participation in education.* Boston: Allyn and Bacon.
Gray, J. 2002. *Straw dogs: Thoughts on humans and other animals.* London: Granta Books.
Greek, C. 1992. *The religious roots of American sociology.* New York: Garland.
Grek, S. 2016. Knowledge actors and the construction of new governing panoramas: The case of the European Commission's DG education and culture. *Educação & Sociedade* 37 (136): 707–26.
Grossman, P., C. Compton, D. Igra, M. Ronfeldt, E. Shahan, and P. Williamson. 2009. Teaching practice: A cross-professional perspective. *Teachers College Record* 111 (9): 2055–2100.
Grossman, P., and M. McDonald. 2008. Back to the future: Directions for research in teaching and teacher education. *American Educational Research Journal* 45 (1): 184–205.
Grossman, P., M. McDonald, K. Hammerness, and M. Ronfeldt. 2008. Dismantling dichotomies in teacher education. In *Handbook of research on teacher education: Enduring questions in changing contexts*, 3rd ed., edited by M. Cochran-Smith, S. Feinman-Nemser, and D. J. McIntyre, 243–48. New York: Routledge.
Gurria, A. 2016. PISA 2015 results in focus. *PISA in Focus* 67 (1). https://www.oecd-ilibrary.org/education/pisa-2015-results-in-focus_aa9237e6-en
Gustafson, R. 2009. *Race and curriculum: Music in childhood education.* New York: Palgrave Macmillan.
Gustafson, R. 2014. Fictions of the transcendent and the making of value in music education in the United States. In *The "reason" of schooling: Historicizing curriculum studies, pedagogy, and teacher education*, edited by T. Popkewitz, 215–28. New York: Routledge.
Gutiérrez, K., and W. Penuel. 2014. Relevance to practice as a criterion for rigor. *Educational Researcher* 43 (1): 19–23.
Habermas, J. (1968) 1971. *Knowledge and human interest.* Translated by J. Shapiro. Boston: Beacon Press.
Hacking, I. 1983. *Representing and intervening: Introductory topics in the philosophy of natural science.* Cambridge: Cambridge University Press.
Hacking, I. 1990. *The taming of chance.* Cambridge: Cambridge University Press.
Hacking, I. 1999. *The social construction of what?* Cambridge: Harvard University Press.
Hacking, I. 2002. Inaugural lecture: Chair of philosophy and history of scientific concepts at the College de France. *Economy and Society* 21 (1): 1–14.
Hacking, I. 2004. *Historical ontology.* Cambridge, MA: Harvard University Press.
Hall, G. S. (1893) 1924. Aspects of child life and education: The contents of children's mind on entering school. *Princeton Review* II: 249–72.
Hall, G. S. (1904) 1928. *Adolescence: Its psychology and its relation to physiology, anthropology, sociology, sex, crime, religion, and education.* Vol. 1. New York: Appleton and Co.
Hall, S. 1986. The problem of ideology: Marxism without guarantees. *Journal of Communication Inquiry* 10 (2): 28–43.

Halpern, O. 2014. *Beautiful data: A history of vision and reason since 1945*. Durham: Duke University Press.
Halpern, O. 2016. Circuits of amnesia: Cybernetic memory and real-time analytics. *Cultural Studies Critical Methodologies* 16 (5): 442–51.
Hamilton, D. 1989. *Towards a theory of schooling*. New York: Falmer Press.
Hansen, H. K. 2015. Numerical operations, transparency illusions, and the datafication of governance. *European Journal of Social Theory* 18 (2): 203–20.
Hansen, H. K., and A. Vestergaard. 2018. On the contest of lists and their governing capacities: How "tax havens" became "secrecy jurisdictions." In *Education by the numbers and the making of society: The expertise of international assessments*, ed. S. Lindblad, D. Pettersson, and T. S. Popkewitz, 35–52. New York: Routledge.
Harper, W. R. 1905. *The trend in higher education*. Chicago: University of Chicago Press.
Harrington, F. H. 1990. Foreword. In *The WCER: Twenty-five years of knowledge generation and educational improvement*, edited by H. J. Klausmeier and Associates, ix–x. Madison: Wisconsin Center for Education Research, University of Wisconsin–Madison.
Harris, A. 1966. The psychological and sociological characteristics of the culturally disadvantaged. In *Reading and the culturally disadvantaged: Selected papers* (Theoretical Paper No. 10), edited by W. Otto, E. Askov, and C. Houston. Madison: Wisconsin Research and Development Center for Cognitive Learning, US Office of Education, Center No. C-03. Contract OE 5-10-154.
Hartman, A. 2008. *Education and the Cold War: The battle for the American school*. New York: Palgrave Macmillan.
Haskell, T. 1977. *The emergence of professional social science: The American Social Science Association and the nineteenth-century crisis of authority*. Urbana: University of Illinois Press.
Hatch, N. O. 1980. The Christian movement and the demand for a theology of the people. *Journal of American History* 67 (3): 545–67.
Haveman, R. 1987. *Poverty policy and poverty research: The great society and the social sciences*. Madison: University of Wisconsin Press.
Hayles, Katherine. 1999. *How we became posthuman: Virtual bodies in cybernetics, literature, and informatics*. Chicago: University of Chicago Press.
Heilbron, J., L. Magnusson, and B. Wittrock, eds. 1998. *The rise of the social sciences and the formation of modernity: Conceptual change in context, 1750–1805*. Dordrecht, The Netherlands: Kluwer Academic.
Helgeson, S. 1968. Lesson plans and tests of knowledge, comprehension, and application for instruction in concepts of force, grades 2–6. Madison: Wisconsin Research and Development Center for Cognitive Learning, University of Wisconsin–Madison.
Herman, E. 1995. *The romance of American psychology: Political culture in the age of experts*. Berkeley: University of California Press.
Hetherington, K. 2001. Moderns as ancients: Time, space and the discourse of im-

provement. In *Timespace, geographies of temporality*, ed. J. May and N. Thrift, 49–72. London: Routledge.

Heyck, H. 2012. Producing reason. In *Cold War social science: Knowledge production, liberal democracy, and human nature*, edited by M. Solovey and H. Cravens, 99–116. New York: Palgrave Macmillan.

Heyck, H. 2015. *Age of system: Understanding the development of modern social science.* Baltimore: Johns Hopkins University Press.

Hirst, P. 1994. The evolution of consciousness: Identity and personality in historical perspective. *Economy and Society* 23 (1): 47–65.

Hoeverler, J. D. 1976. The University and the social gospel: The intellectual origins of the "Wisconsin Idea." *Wisconsin Magazine of History* 59 (4): 282–98.

Holmes Group. 1986. *Tomorrow's teachers.* East Lansing: Holmes Group.

Homans, G. C. 1950. *The human group.* New York: Harcourt, Brace.

Hopmann, S. 2008. No child, no school, no state left behind: Schooling in the age of accountability. *Journal of Curriculum Studies* 40 (4): 1–40.

Horlacher, R. 2015. *The educated subject and the German concept of Bildung: A comparative cultural history.* New York: Routledge. https://www.mckinsey.com/industries/social-sector/our-insights/how-the-worlds-most-improved-school-systems-keep-getting-better

Hultqvist, K. 1998. A history of the present on children's welfare in Sweden. In *Foucault's challenge: Discourse, knowledge, and power in education*, ed. T. Popkewitz and M. Brennan, 91–117. New York: Teachers College Press.

Hultqvist, K., and G. Dahlberg, eds. 2001. *Governing the child in the new millennium.* New York: Psychology Press.

Hunter, I. 1988. *Culture and government: The emergence of literary education.* Hampshire, England: Macmillan.

Hunter, I. 1994. *Rethinking the school: Subjectivity, bureaucracy, criticism.* New York: St. Martin's.

Husén, T., and N. Postlethwaite. 1996. A brief history of the International Association for the Evaluation of Educational Achievement (IEA). *Assessment in Education: Principles, Policy, & Practice* 3 (2): 129–42.

Ideland, M. 2019. *The eco-certified child: Citizenship and education for sustainability and environment.* Palgrave Studies in Education and the Environment. New York: Palgrave Macmillan.

Igo, S. 2007. *The average American: Surveys, citizens, and the making of a mass public.* Cambridge: Harvard University Press.

Ilha, F. R. d. S. 2017. The alchemy of Brazilian physical education, the regulating of the body, and the making of kinds of people. In *A political sociology of educational knowledge: Studies of exclusions and difference*, edited by T. S. Popkewitz, J. Diaz, and C. Kirchgasler, 135–46. New York: Routledge.

Isaac, J. 2009. Tangled loops: Theory, history, and the human sciences in modern America. *Modern Intellectual History* 6 (2): 397–424.

Ivens, J. 2013. One kind of human being: MACOS, the human sciences, and governmentality. *European Education* 45 (3): 16–34.

Ivens, J. 2018. Improving modern systems: Curriculum reform, social reform, and the digital age. PhD diss., University of Wisconsin–Madison.
Jehlen, M. 1986. *American incarnation: The individual, the nation, and the continent*. Cambridge: Harvard University Press.
Joncich, G. M. 1962. Science: Touchstone for a new age in education. In *Psychology and the science of education: Selected writings of Edward L. Thorndike*, edited by G. M. Joncich, 1–26. New York: Bureau of Publications, Teachers College, Columbia University.
Joncich, G. M. 1968. *The sane positivist: A biography of Edward L. Thorndike*. Middletown, CT: Wesleyan University Press.
Jones, G. S. 2008. An end to poverty: The French Revolution and the promise of a world beyond want. In *The migration of ideas*, edited by R. Scazzieri and R. Simili, 59–71. Sagamore Beach, MA: Science History Publications.
Kant, I. (1784) 1970. Idea for a universal history with a cosmopolitan purpose. Translated by H. B. Nisbet. In *Kant's political writing*, edited by H. Reiss, 41–53. Cambridge: Cambridge University Press.
Keeves, J. P. 1995. *The world of school learning: Selected key findings from 35 years of IEA research*. The Hague: International Association for the Evaluation of Educational Achievement.
Kelly, D., C. W. Nord, F. Jenkins, J. Y. Chan, and D. Kastberg. 2013. *Performance of U.S. 15-Year-Old Students in Mathematics, Science, and Reading Literacy in an International Context—First Look at PISA 2012*. https://nces.ed.gov/pubs2014/2014024_1.pdf
Kirchgasler, C. 2017. Building bridges and colonial residues: Transnational school reforms and the making of human kinds. PhD diss., University of Wisconsin–Madison.
Kirchgasler, C. 2018. True grit? Making a scientific object and pedagogical tool. *American Educational Research Journal* 55 (4): 693–720.
Kirchgasler, K. L. 2017. Scientific Americans: Historicizing the making of differences in early 20th-century US science education. In *A political sociology of educational knowledge: Studies of exclusions and difference*, edited by T. S. Popkewitz, J. Diaz, and C. Kirchgasler, 89–104. New York: Routledge.
Klausmeier, H. J. 1977a. Instructional programming for the individual student. In *Individually guided elementary education: Concepts and practices*, edited by H. J. Klausmeier, R. A. Rossmiller, and M. Saily, 55–76. New York: Academic Press.
Klausmeier, H. J. 1977b. Origin and overview of IGE. In *Individually guided elementary education: Concepts and practices*, edited by H. J. Klausmeier, R. A. Rossmiller, and M. Saily, 7–24. New York: Academic Press.
Klausmeier, H. J., J. Feldhusen, and J. Check. 1959. *An analysis of learning efficiency in arithmetic of mentally retarded children in comparison with children of average and high intelligence*. Madison: University of Wisconsin Press.
Klausmeier, H. J., L. J. Ingison, T. S. Sipple, and C. G. Katzenmeyer. 1973. *Development of conceptual learning and development assessment series I: Equilateral triangle*.

Report from the Project on Children's Learning and Development. October. Madison: University of Wisconsin Press.

Klausmeier, H. J., and Wisconsin Associates. 1990. *The Wisconsin Center for Education Research: Twenty-five years of knowledge generation and educational improvement*. Madison: Wisconsin Center for Education Research, University of Wisconsin–Madison.

Kliebard, H. 1986. *The struggle for the American curriculum, 1893–1958*. New York: Routledge.

Knorr Cetina, K. 1999. *Epistemic cultures: How the sciences make knowledge*. Cambridge: Harvard University Press.

Koenke, K. 1968. The effects of a content-relevant picture on the comprehension of the main idea of a paragraph. Technical report No. 56. Madison: Wisconsin Research and Development Center for Cognitive Learning.

Koselleck, R. (1979) 2004. *Futures past: On the semantics of historical time*. Translated with an introduction by Keith Tribe. New York: Columbia University Press.

Koza, J. E. In progress. "Destined: Carl Seashore's world of music, education, and eugenics."

Kreitlow, B. W. 1972. *Evaluating the influence of change agent teams on the order of change processes of school systems: A test of the model for educational improvement*. Technical Report No. 214 from the Project on Children's Learning and Development, February. Madison: Wisconsin Research and Development Center for Cognitive Learning.

Kreitlow, B., and T. MacNeil. 1969. An evaluation of the model for educational improvement as an analytical tool for describing the changed process. Report from the project on models for effecting planned educational change. (Theoretical Paper No. 18). In *Reading and the culturally disadvantaged: Selected papers from the Annual Institute in Reading, 1966 (Theoretical Paper No. 10)*, edited by W. Otto, E. Askov, and C. Houston. Madison: Wisconsin Research and Development Center for Cognitive Learning, U.S. Office of Education, Center No. C-03, Contract OE 5-10-154.

Kristeva, J. 1982. *Powers of horror: An essay on abjection*. Translated by L. Roudiez. New York: Columbia University Press.

Krug, E. 1972. *The shaping of the American high school, 1920–1941*. Vol. 2. Madison: University of Wisconsin Press.

Krugman, P. 2009. How did economists get it so wrong? *New York Times*, September 6. http://www.nytimes.com/2009/09/06/magazine/06Economic-t.html?ref=paulkrugman

Krugman, P. 2010. When zombies win. *New York Times*, December 19. http://www.nytimes.com/2010/12/20/opinion/20krugman.html?ref=paulkrugman

Kuger, S., and E. Klieme. 2016. Dimensions of context assessment. In *Assessing contexts of learning: An international perspective*, edited by S. Kuger, E. Klieme, N. June, and D. Kaplan, 3–38. Cham, Switzerland: Springer.

Kuger, S., E. Klieme, N. June, and D. Kaplan, eds. 2016. *Assessing contexts of learning: An international perspective*. Cham, Switzerland: Springer.

Kuhn, T. 1970. *The structure of scientific revolutions*. 2nd ed. Chicago: University of Chicago Press.

Labaree, D. 1988. *The Making of an American High School: The Credentials Market and the Central High School of Philadelphia, 1838–1939*. New Haven: Yale University Press.

Lampert, M. 2010. Learning teaching in, from, and for practice. *Journal of Teacher Education* 6 (1): 21–34.

Lampert, M., M. F. Franke, E. Kazemi, H. Ghousseini, A. Turrou, H. Beasley, A. Cunard, and K. Crowe. 2013. Keeping it complex: Using rehearsals to support novice teacher learning of ambitious teaching. *Journal of Teacher Education* 64 (3): 226–43.

Larson, M. S. 1979. *The rise of professionalism: A sociological analysis*. Berkeley: University of California Press.

Lasswell, H. D. 1951. *Political writings*. Glencoe, IL: Free Press.

Latour, B. 1986. Visualization and cognition: Thinking with eyes and hands. *Knowledge and Society: Studies in the Sociology of Culture Past and Present* 6: 1–40.

Latour, B. 2004. Why critique has run out of steam: From matters of fact to matters of concern. *Critical Inquiry* 30: 225–48.

Latour, B. 2006. Re: A textbook case revisited: Knowledge as a mode of existence. An invited presentation to a Science, Technology and Society conference.

Latour, B. 2013. *An inquiry into modes of existence*. Cambridge: Harvard University Press.

Lee, S. Y. 2019. Vision, temporality, and teacher-making: Historicizing the anticipatory politics of observation in teacher education. PhD diss., University of Wisconsin-Madison.

Le Goff, J. (1985) 1988. *The medieval imagination*. Translated by A. Goldhammer. Chicago: University of Chicago Press.

Lesko, N. 2001. *Act your age: A cultural construction of adolescence*. New York: Routledge.

Lesko, N., and S. Talburt, eds. 2011. *Youth studies: Keywords and movement*. New York: Routledge.

Levine, D. 1995. *Visions of the sociological tradition*. Chicago: University of Chicago Press.

Lewin, K. 1947. Frontiers in group dynamics: Concept, method, and reality in social science; social equilibria and social change. *Human Relations* 1 (1): 5–41.

Lindblad, S., D. Pettersson, and T. S. Popkewitz, eds. 2018. *Education by the numbers and the making of society: The expertise of international assessments*. New York: Routledge.

Lindmark, D. 2011. New wine into old bottles: Luther's Table of Duties as a vehicle of changing civic virtues in 18th- and 19th-century Sweden. In *Schooling and the making of citizens in the long nineteenth century: Comparative visions*, edited by D. Trohler, T. S. Popkewitz, and D. F. Labaree, 31–49. New York: Routledge.

Llewelyn, L. 2004. *Seeing through God: A geophenomenology*. Bloomington: Indiana University Press.

Loughran, J. 2013. Being a teacher educator. In *Educators as members of an evolving profession*, edited by M. Ben-Peretz with S. Kleeman, R. Reichenberg, and S. Shimoni, 9–24. Lanham, MD: Mofet Institute and Roman & Littlefield.

Low, V. 1982. *The unimpressible race: A century of educational struggle by the Chinese in San Francisco*. San Francisco: East/West Publishing.

Lowe, L. 2015. *The intimacies of four continents*. Durham: Duke University Press.
Luckmann, T. 1967. *The invisible religion. The problem of religion in modern society*. New York: Macmillan.
Lybarger, M. 1987. Need as ideology: Social workers, social settlements, and the social studies. In *The formation of school subjects: The struggle for creating an American institution*, edited by T. Popkewitz, 176–89. London: Falmer Press.
Madeira, A. I. 2005. Portuguese, French, and British discourses on colonial education: Church-state relations, school expansion, and missionary competition in Africa, 1890–1930. *Paedagogica Historica* 41 (1–2): 31–60.
Manuel, F. E., and F. P. Manuel. 1979. *Utopian thought in the Western world*. Cambridge: Belknap Press of Harvard University Press.
Martins, C. S. 2014. Disrupting the consensus: Creativity in European educational discourses as a technology of government. *Knowledge Cultures* 2 (3): 118–35.
Martins, C. S. 2015. Genius as a historical event: Its making as a statistical object and instrument for governing schooling. In *The "reason" of schooling: Historicizing curriculum studies, pedagogy, and teacher education*, edited by T. S. Popkewitz, 99–114. New York: Routledge.
Martins, C. S. 2017. From scribbles to details: The invention of stages of development in drawing and the government of the child. In *A political sociology of educational knowledge: Studies of exclusions and difference*, edited by T. S. Popkewitz, J. Diaz, and C. Kirchgasler, 105–18. New York: Routledge.
Martins, C. S. 2018. The alchemies of the arts in education: Problematizing some of the ingredients of the recipe. In *Spectra of transformation*, edited by B. Jörissen, L. Unterberg, L. Klepacki, J. Engel, V. Flasche, and T. Klepacki, 51–67. Munster: Waxmann.
Marx, A. 2003. *Faith in nation: Exclusionary origins of nationalism*. New York: Oxford University Press.
Marx, K. 1976. Theses on Feuerbach (written in the spring of 1845). In F. Engels, *Ludwig Feuerbach and the end of classical German philosophy*, 61–65. Peking: Foreign Languages Press.
Massumi, B. 2007. Potential politics and the primacy of preemption. *Theory & Event* 10 (2). https://muse-jhu-edu.ezproxy.library.wisc.edu/article/218091
Matsumura, L. C., and E. Wang. 2014. Principals' sense-making of coaching for ambitious reading instruction in a high-stakes accountability policy environment. *Education Policy Analysis Archives* 22 (51): 1–37.
Mattingly, P. 1977. *The classless profession: American schoolmen in the nineteenth century*. New York: New York University Press.
McCarthy, C. 1912. *The Wisconsin idea*. New York: Macmillan.
McEneaney, E. 2003a. Elements of a contemporary primary school science. In *Science in the modern world polity: Institutionalization and globalization*, edited by G. S. Drori, J. W. Meyer, F. O. Ramirez, and E. Schofer, 136–54. Stanford: Stanford University Press.
McEneaney, E. 2003b. The worldwide cachet of scientific literacy. *Comparative Education Review* 47 (2): 217–37.

McKnight, D. 2003. *Schooling, the Puritan imperative, and the molding of an American national identity. Education's "errand into the wilderness"*. Mahwah, NJ: Lawrence Erlbaum.
McMahon, D. 2006. *Happiness: A history*. New York: Atlantic Monthly Press.
Mead, G. H. (1934) 1967. *Mind, self and society from the standpoint of a social behaviorist*. Edited, with an introduction, by Charles W. Morris. Chicago: University of Chicago Press.
Menand, L. 2001. *The metaphysical club*. New York: Farrar, Straus and Giroux.
Miller, P. 1953. *Errand into the Wilderness*. Cambridge: Belknap Press of Harvard University Press.
Mitchell, T. 2002. *Rule of experts: Egypt, techno-politics, modernity*. Berkeley: University of California Press.
Mølstad, C., and D. Pettersson. 2018. Who governs the numbers? The framing of educational knowledge by TIMSS research. In *Education by the numbers and the making of society: The expertise of the international assessments*, edited by S. Lindblad, D. Pettersson, and T. Popkewitz, 166–85. New York: Routledge.
Monaghan, J., and W. Saul. 1987. The reader, the scribe, the thinker: A critical look at reading and writing instruction. In *The formation of the school subjects: The struggle for creating an American institution*, edited by T. S. Popkewitz, 85–122. New York: Falmer Press.
Mourshed, M., C. Chijioke, M. Barber, and McKinsey & Company. 2010. *How the world's most improved school systems keep getting better*. New York: McKinsey & Company; Munster: Waxmann.
Murphy, M. 1990. *Blackboard unions: The AFT and the NEA 1900–1980*. Ithaca: Cornell University Press.
Murphy, M. 2017. *The economization of life*. Durham: Duke University Press.
National Center for Educational Research and Development. 1969. *Educational research and development in the United States*. Washington, DC: Office of Education, US Department of Health, Education, and Welfare.
National Commission on Teaching and America's Future. 2003. *No dream denied: A pledge to America's children*. Washington, DC: National Commission on Teaching and America's Future.
National Council of Teachers of Mathematics. 1945. The second report of the commission on post-war plans: The improvement of mathematics in grades 1 to 14. *Mathematics Teacher* 38 (5): 195–221.
National Science Teachers Association. 2002. *Teacher created materials: Forces and motion teacher's guide*. Arlington, VA: National Science Teachers Association.
Nichols, C. M., and N. Unger, eds. 2017. *A companion to the Gilded Age and Progressive era*. Chichester, West Sussex, UK: Wiley-Blackwell.
Nisbet, R. 1969. *Social change and history: Aspects of the Western theory of development*. New York: Oxford University Press.
Nisbet, R. 1980. *History of the idea of progress*. New York: Basic Books.

Normand, R. 2016. *The changing epistemic governance of European education: The fabrication of the Homo Academicus Europeanus?* Switzerland: Springer.
Normand, R., M. Liu, L. Carvalho, and D. Oliveira, eds. 2018. *Education policies and the restructuring of the educational profession: Global and comparative perspectives.* Singapore: Springer Nature Singapore.
Nowotny, H. 1991. Knowledge for certainty: Poverty, welfare institutions, and the institutionalization of social science. In *Discourses on society: The shaping of the social science disciplines (Sociology of the Sciences Yearbook)*, edited by P. Wagner, B. Wittrock, and R. Whitley, 23–44. Dordrecht: Kluwer Academic.
Nye, D. E. 1999. *American technological sublime.* Cambridge: MIT Press.
Nye, D. E. 2003. *America as second creation: Technology and narratives of new beginnings.* Cambridge: MIT Press.
Nyhart, L. 2009. *Modern nature: The rise of the biological perspective in Germany.* Chicago: University of Chicago Press.
Ó, J. R. do. 2003. The disciplinary terrains of soul and self-government in the first map of the educational sciences. In *Beyond empiricism: On criteria for educational research (Studia Paedagogica 34)*, edited by P. Smeyers and M. Depaepe, 105–16. Belgium: Leuven University Press.
Ó, J. R. do, C. S. Martins, and A. L. Paz. 2013. Genealogy of history: From pupil to artist as the dynamics of genius, status, and inventiveness in art education in Portugal. In *Rethinking the history of education: Transnational perspectives on its questions, methods, and knowledge*, edited by T. S. Popkewitz, 157–78. New York: Palgrave.
O'Donnell, J. 1985. *The origins of behaviorism: American psychology, 1876–1920.* New York: New York University Press.
OECD (Organization for Economic Co-Operation and Development). 2013. Science framework. In *PISA 2012 Assessment and Analytical Framework: Mathematics, Reading, Science, Problem Solving, and Financial Literacy.* Paris: OECD.
OECD. 2015. *Improving schools in Sweden: An OECD perspective.* Paris: OECD.
OECD. 2016. About PISA. http://www.oecd.org/pisa/aboutpisa/
OECD. 2017. *PISA 2015 results (Vol. III): Students' well-being.* Paris: OECD.
Oelkers, J. 1995. Break and continuity: Observations on the modernization effects and traditionalization in international reform pedagogy. *Paedagogica Historica* 31 (3): 675–713.
Oelkers, J. 2005. Remarks on the conceptualization of John Dewey's "democracy and education." Lecture for the annual John Dewey Society Symposium. Paper presented at the American Educational Research Association, Montreal, Canada.
Ohkura, K. 2005. Dewey and the ambivalent modern Japan. In *Inventing the modern self and John Dewey: Modernities and the traveling of pragmatism in education*, edited by T. S. Popkewitz. New York: Palgrave Macmillan.
Otto, W. 1969. Introduction. In *Theoretical Paper No. 10. Reading and the culturally disadvantaged: Selected papers from the Annual Institute in Reading*, edited by W. Otto, E. Askov, and C. Houston. Madison: Wisconsin Research and Development Center for Cognitive Learning. U.S. Office of Education, Center No. C-03. Contract OE 5-10-154.

Otto, W. 1971. Thorndike's "Reading as Reasoning": Influence and impact. *Reading Research Quarterly* 64 (Summer): 435–42.

Otto, W. 1977. The Wisconsin design: A reading program for Individually Guided Education. In *Individually guided elementary education: Concepts and practices*, edited by H. J. Klausmeier, R. A. Rossmiller, and M. Saily, 137–51. New York: Academic Press.

Otto, W., and E. Askov. 1974. *The Wisconsin design for reading skill development*. Minneapolis: National Computer Systems.

Passavant, P. 2000. The governmentality of discussion. In *Cultural studies and political theory*, edited by J. Dean, 115–31. Ithaca: Cornell University Press.

Paz, A. 2017. Can genius be taught? Debates in Portuguese music education (1868–1930). *European Educational Research Journal* 16 (4): 504–16.

Pettersson, D., and C. Mølstad. 2016. PISA teachers: The hope and the happening of educational development. *Educação e Sociedade* 37 (136): 629–45.

Piacentini, M., and C. Monticone. 2016. *Equations and inequalities: Making mathematics accessible to all*. Paris: OECD Publishing.

Pierce P., and M. Swift. (1926) 1969. *The first state normal school in America. The journals of Cyrus Peirce and Mary Swift*. New York: Arno Press and the New York Times.

Pocock, J. G. A. 2003. *Machiavellian moment: Florentine political thought and the Atlantic republican tradition*. Princeton: Princeton University Press.

Pont, B., G. Donaldson, R. Elmore, and M. Kools. 2014. *The OECD–Sweden education policy review: Main issues and next steps*. Paris: OECD.

Poovey, M. 1998. *A history of the modern fact: Problems of knowledge in the sciences of wealth and society*. Chicago: University of Chicago Press.

Popkewitz, T. S. 1976. Reform as political discourse: A case study. *School Review* 84: 43–69.

Popkewitz, T. S. 1978. Schools and the symbolic uses of community participation. In *Community participation in education*, edited by C. A. Grant, 202–23. Boston: Allyn and Bacon.

Popkewitz, T. S. (1984) 2012. *Paradigm and ideology in educational research: Social functions of the intellectual*. New York: Routledge.

Popkewitz, T. S., ed. (1987) 2018a. *The formation of school subjects: The struggle for creating an American institution*. London: Falmer Press.

Popkewitz, T. S., ed. (1987) 2018b. *Teacher education: A critical examination of its folklore, theory, and practice*. New York: Routledge.

Popkewitz, T. S. 1991. *A political sociology of educational reform: Power/knowledge in teaching, teacher education, and research*. New York: Teachers College Press.

Popkewitz, T. S. 1992. Social science and social movements in the USA: State policy, the university and schooling. In *Education in the late 20th century: Essays presented to Ulf P. Lundgren on the occasion of his fiftieth birthday*, edited by D. Broady, 45–79. Stockholm: Stockholm Institute of Education Press.

Popkewitz, T. S., ed. 1993. *Changing patterns of power: Social regulation and teacher education reform*. New York: SUNY Press.

Popkewitz, T. S. 1997a. Educational sciences and the normalization of the teacher

and child: Some historical notes on current USA pedagogical reforms. *Paedagogia Historica: International Journal of the History of Education* 33 (2): 387–412.
Popkewitz, T. S. 1997b. The production of reason and power: Curriculum history and intellectual traditions. *Journal of Curriculum Studies* 29 (2): 131–64.
Popkewitz, T. S. 1998. Dewey, Vygotsky, and the social administration of the individual: Constructivist pedagogy as systems of ideas in historical spaces. *American Educational Research Journal* 35 (4): 535–70.
Popkewitz, T. S. 2004. The alchemy of the mathematics curriculum: Inscriptions and the fabrication of the child. *American Educational Research Journal* 41 (4): 3–34.
Popkewitz, T. S., ed. 2005. *Inventing the modern self and John Dewey: Modernities and the traveling of pragmatism in education.* New York: Palgrave Macmillan.
Popkewitz, T. S. 2006. The idea of science as planning was not planned: A historical note about American pedagogical sciences as planning society and individuality. In *Education nouvelle—Sciences de l'Education: The New Education and Educational sciences; Fin du 19e–milieu 20e siècle*, edited by R. Hofstetter and B. Schneuwly, 143–69. Bern: Peter Lang.
Popkewitz, T. S. 2008. *Cosmopolitanism and the age of school reform: Science, education, and making society by making the child.* New York: Routledge.
Popkewitz, T. S. 2009. The social, psychological, and education sciences: From educationalization to pedagogicalization of the family and the child. In *Educational research: The educationalization of social problems*, edited by P. Smeyers and M. Depaepe, 171–90. Dordrecht: Springer Science+business Media.
Popkewitz, T. S. 2011a. Curriculum history, schooling, and the history of the present. *History of Education* 40 (1): 1–19.
Popkewitz, T. S. 2011b. From virtue as the pursuit of happiness to pursuing the unvirtuous: Republicanism, cosmopolitanism, and reform Protestantism in American progressive education. In *The child, the citizen, and the promised land: Comparative visions in the development of schooling in the long 19th century*, edited by D. Trohler, T. S. Popkewitz, and D. F. Labaree, 291–39. New York: Routledge.
Popkewitz, T. S. 2011c. PISA: Numbers, standardizing conduct, and the alchemy of school subjects. In *PISA under examination: Changing knowledge, changing tests, and changing schools*, edited by M. A. Pereyra, H.-H. Kottoff, and R. Cowen, 31–46. Rotterdam: Sense Publishers.
Popkewitz, T. S. 2011d. The past as the future of the social and education sciences. In *Education systems in historical, cultural, and sociological perspectives*, edited by D. Tröhler and R. Barbu, 161–81. Rotterdam: Sense Publishers.
Popkewitz, T. S., ed. 2013a. *Rethinking the history of education: Transnational perspectives on its questions, methods, and knowledge.* New York: Palgrave Macmillan.
Popkewitz, T. S. 2013b. The empirical and political "fact" of theory in the social and education sciences. In *Making a difference in theory: The theory question in education and the education question in theory*, edited by G. Biesta, J. Allan, and R. G. Edwards, 13–29. London: Routledge.
Popkewitz, T. S. 2013c. The impracticality of *practical knowledge* and *lived experience* in educational research. *Nordic Studies in Education* 33: 24–39.

Popkewitz, T. S. 2013d. The sociology of education as the history of the present: Fabrication, difference, and abjection. *Discourse: Studies in the cultural politics of education* 34 (3): 439–56.
Popkewitz, T. S. 2014a. Social epistemology, the reason of "reason" and the curriculum studies. In "Nuevas Perspectivas sobre el Curriculum Escolar," special issue, *Archivos Analíticos de Políticas Educativas.* http://dx.doi.org/10.14507/epaa.v22n22.2014
Popkewitz, T. S., ed. 2014b. *The "reason" of schooling: Historicizing curriculum studies, pedagogy, and teacher education.* New York: Routledge.
Popkewitz, T. S. 2015. Planning sciences, policy, and conserving as the problem of change: Should we take seriously the cautions of Foucault and Rancière? In *Skola, Lärare, Samhälle—en vänbok till Sverker Lindblad (School, Teachers, Society—a Festschrift in honor of Sverker Lindblad)*, edited by G.-B. Wärvik, C. Runesdotter, E. Forsberg, B. Hasselgren, and F. Sahlström. Gothenburg: Department of Education and Special Education, University of Gothenburg.
Popkewitz, T. S. 2017a. Reform and making human kinds: The double gestures of inclusion and exclusion in the practice of schooling. In *Critical analyses of educational reforms in an era of transnational governance*, edited by E. Hultqvist, S. Lindblad, and T. S. Popkewitz, 133–50. Cham, Switzerland: Springer.
Popkewitz, T. S. (1998) 2017b. *Teacher education and teaching as struggling for the soul: A critical ethnography.* New York: Routledge.
Popkewitz, T. S. 2018a. Anticipating the future society: The cultural inscription of numbers and international large-scale assessment. In *Education by the numbers and the making of society: The expertise of international assessments*, edited by S. Lindblad, D. Pettersson, and T. Popkewitz, 222–28. New York: Routledge.
Popkewitz, T. S. 2018b. What is "really" taught as the content of school subjects? Teaching school subjects as an alchemy. *High School Journal* 101 (2): 77–89.
Popkewitz, T. S. 2019. Transnational as comparative history: (Un)thinking differences in the self and others. In *The transnational in the history of education*, edited by E. Fuchs and E. R. Vera, 261–91. New York: Palgrave Macmillan.
Popkewitz, T. S. Forthcoming a. Historicizing how theory acts as "the retrieval" apparatus in methods: Romancing the archival or some thoughts on intellectual practices. In *International handbook of historical studies in education*, edited by T. Fitzgerald. Singapore: Springer Nature.
Popkewitz, T. S., ed. Forthcoming b. *The post–World War II international educational sciences: Quantification, visualization, and making kinds of people.* New York: Routledge.
Popkewitz, T. S., and M. Brennan. 1998. *Foucault's challenge: Discourse, knowledge, and power in education.* New York: Teachers College Press.
Popkewitz, T. S., J. Diaz, and C. Kirchgasler, eds. 2017. *The reason of schooling and educational research: Studies of exclusions and difference.* New York: Routledge.
Popkewitz, T. S., and L. Fendler, eds. 1999. *Critical theories in education: Changing terrains of knowledge and politics.* New York: Routledge.
Popkewitz, T. S., B. Franklin, and M. Pereyra. 2001. *Cultural history and education: Critical essays on knowledge and schooling.* New York: Routledge Falmer.

Popkewitz, T. S., and R. Gustafson. 2002. The alchemy of pedagogy and social inclusion/exclusion. *Philosophy of Music Education Review* 10 (2): 80–91.
Popkewitz, T. S., and C. Kirchgasler. 2014. Fabricating the teacher's soul in teacher education. In *Foucault and a politics of confession in education*, edited by A. Fejes and C. Nichols, 35–47. New York: Routledge.
Popkewitz, T. S., A. Khurshid, and W. Zhao. 2014. Comparative studies and the reasons of reason: Historicizing differences and "seeing" reforms in multiple modernities. In *Empires, post-coloniality, and interculturality: New challenges for comparative education*, edited by L. Vega, 21–43. Rotterdam: Sense.
Popkewitz, T. S., and H. Simola. 1996. Professionalization, academic discourses, and changing patterns of power. In *Professionalization and education (Research Report 169; Department of Teacher Education)*, edited by H. Simola and T. Popkewitz, 6–27. Helsinki: University of Helsinki.
Popkewitz, T. S., and B. R. Tabachnick, eds. 1981. *The study of schooling: Field methodology in educational research*. New York: Praeger.
Popkewitz, T. S., B. Tabachnick, and G. Wehlage. 1982. *The myth of educational reform: A study of school responses to a program of change*. Madison: University of Wisconsin Press.
Porter, T. 1995. *Trust in numbers: The pursuit of objectivity in science and public life*. Princeton: Princeton University Press.
Qi, J. 2005. A history of the present: Chinese intellectuals, Confucianism, and pragmatism. In *Inventing the modern self and John Dewey: Modernities and the traveling of pragmatism in education*, edited by T. S. Popkewitz, 255–77. New York: Palgrave Macmillan.
Rancière, J. (1983) 2004a. *The philosopher and his poor*. Edited with an introduction by Andrew Parker; translated by John Drury, Corinne Oster, and Andrew Parker. Durham: Duke University Press.
Rancière, J. (1998) 2004b. *The flesh of words: The politics of writing*. Translated by Charlotte Mandell. Stanford: Stanford University Press.
Rancière, J. 2004c. Who is the subject of the rights of man? *South Atlantic Quarterly* 103 (2–3): 297–310.
Rancière, J. 2006a. *Hatred of democracy*. Translated by S. Corcoran. London: Verso.
Rancière, J. 2006b. *The politics of aesthetics*. Translated by G. Rockhill. New York: Bloomsbury Academic.
Reed, E. 1997. *From soul to mind: The emergence of psychology from Erasmus Darwin to William James*. New Haven: Yale University Press.
Retter, H. 2012. Dewey's progressive education, experience, and instrumental pragmatism with particular reference to the concept of *Bilding*. In *Theories of Bildung and growth: Connections and controversies between continental educational thinking and American pragmatism*, edited by P. Siljander, A. Kivelä, and A. Sutinen, 261–80. Rotterdam: Sense Publishers.
Reuben, J. 1996. *The making of the modern university: Intellectual transformations and the marginalization of morality*. Chicago: University of Chicago Press.
Ringness, T., H. Klausmeier, and A. Singer. 1959. *Psychology in theory and practice*. Boston: Houghton Mifflin.

Rodgers, D. 1998. *Atlantic crossings: Social politics in a progressive age*. Cambridge: Belknap Press of Harvard University Press.
Romberg, T. 1968. The development and refinement of prototypic instructional systems. In *Research and development strategies in theory refinement and educational improvement*, edited by H. J. Klausmeier, J. Wardrop, M. Quilling, T. Romberg, and R. Schultz, 14–18. Theoretical paper no. 15. Madison: Research and Development Center for Cognitive Learning.
Romberg, T. 1976. *Individually guided mathematics*. Reading: Addison-Wesley.
Romberg, T. 1977. Developing mathematical processes: The elementary mathematics program for Individually Guided Education. In *Individually guided elementary education: Concepts and practices*, edited by H. J. Klausmeier, R. A. Rossmiller, and M. Saily, 77–109. New York: Academic Press.
Romberg, T., and J. Wilson. 1973. The effect of an advance organizer, cognitive set, and post organizer on the learning and retention of written materials. *Journal for Research in Mathematics Education* 4 (2): 68–76.
Rose, N. 1989. *Governing the soul: The shaping of the private self*. London: Routledge.
Rose, N. 1999. *Powers of freedom: Reframing political thought*. Cambridge: Cambridge University Press.
Ross, D. 1972. *G. Stanley Hall: The psychologist as prophet*. Chicago: University of Chicago Press.
Ross, D. 1991. *The origins of American social science*. New York: Cambridge University Press.
Ross, E. A. (1920) 1930. *Principles of sociology (First revision)*. New York: Century Co.
Rothstein, E. 2011. The world as America dreamed it. *New York Times*, July 28. https://www.nytimes.com/2011/07/28/arts/design/smithsonian-art-museums-american-hall-of-wonders-review.html
Rouse, J. 2007. Practice theory. *WesScholar. Division I Faculty Publications* 43. http://wesscholar.wesleyan.edu/div1facpubs/43
Rudolph, J. L. 2005. Turning science to account: Chicago and the general science movement in secondary education, 1905–1920. *Isis* 96 (3): 353–89.
Rueschemeyer, D., and T. Skocpol. 1996. *States, social knowledge, and the origins of modern social policies*. Princeton: Princeton University Press.
Saettler, P. 1990. *The evolution of American educational technology*. Englewood, NJ: Libraries Unlimited.
Savage, M. 2010. *Identities and social change in Britain since 1940: The politics of method*. Oxford: Oxford University Press.
Schatzki, T. 2002. *The site of the social: A philosophical account of the construction of social life and change*. Philadelphia: Pennsylvania University Press.
Scheler, Max (1924) 1980. *Problems of a sociology of knowledge*, trans. M. S. Frings, edited and with an introduction by K. W. Stikkers. London: Routledge & Kegan Paul.
Schlereth, T. J. 1977. *The cosmopolitan idea in enlightenment thought, its form and function in the ideas of Franklin, Hume, and Voltaire, 1694–1790*. South Bend, IN: University of Notre Dame Press.
School Mathematics Study Group. 1963. *Mathematics for the elementary school: Grade(s) 4–6: Teacher's commentary*. Vol. 1. New Haven: Yale University Press.

Schrader, A. 2010. Pfiesteria pscicida (the Fish Killer): Phantomatic ontologies, indeterminacy, and responsibility in toxic microbiology. *Social Studies of Science* 40 (2): 275–306.
Schrader, A. 2012. Haunted measurements: Demonic work and time in experimentation. *Differences: A Journal of Feminist Cultural Studies* 23 (3): 119–60.
Scott, J. 1991. The evidence of experience. *Critical Inquiry* 17: 773–97.
Scott, J. 1998. *Seeing like a state: How certain schemes to improve the human condition have failed*. New Haven: Yale University Press.
Shapin, S. 1994. *A social history of truth: Civility and science in seventeenth-century England*. Chicago: University of Chicago Press.
Shimoni, S. 2012. Teacher educators' discourses and languages. In *Teacher educators as members of an evolving profession*, edited by M. Ben-Peretz with S. Kleeman, R. Reichenberg, and S. Shimoni, 43–60. Lanham, MD: Mofet Institute and Rowman & Littlefield Education.
Siljander, P., A. Kivelä, and A. Sutinen, eds. 2012. *Theories of Bildung and growth: Connections and controversies between continental educational thinking and American pragmatism*. Rotterdam: Sense Publishers.
Silva, E. T., and S. Slaughter. 1984. *Serving power: The making of the academic social science expert*. Vol. 11. Westport, CT: Greenwood Press.
Simon, H. A. 1969. *The sciences of the artificial*. Cambridge: MIT Press.
Sklansky, J. 2002. *The soul's economy: Market society and selfhood in American thought, 1820–1920*. Chapel Hill: University of North Carolina Press.
Skowronek, S. 1982. *Building a new American state: The expansion of national administrative capacities, 1877–1920*. New York: Cambridge University Press.
Small, A. W. 1896. "Demands on sociology upon pedagogy." Paper presented at the National Educational Association Thirty-Fifth Annual Meeting, St. Paul, MN.
Smith, L. 1981. Accidents, serendipity, and making the commonplace problematic: The origin and evolution of the field study "problem." In *The study of schooling: Field based methodologies in educational research and evaluation*, edited by T. S. Popkewitz and B. R. Tabachnick, 69–111. New York: Praeger.
Smith, L. M., and W. Geoffrey. 1968. *The complexities of an urban classroom*. New York: Holt, Rinehart and Winston.
Sobe, N. W. 2008. *Provincializing the worldly citizen: Yugoslav student and teacher travel and Slavic cosmopolitanism in the interwar era*. New York: Peter Lang.
Solovey, M. 2013. *Shaky foundations: The politics-patronage-social science nexus in Cold War America*. New Brunswick: Rutgers University Press.
Sorkin, D. 2008. *The religious Enlightenment: Protestants, Jews, and Catholics from London to Vienna*. Princeton: Princeton University.
Spencer, H. 1884. *What Knowledge Is of Most Worth*. New York: J. B. Alden.
Stanic, G. (1987) 2018. Mathematics education in the United States at the beginning of the twentieth century. In *The formation of the school subjects: The struggle for creating an American institution*, edited by T. S. Popkewitz, 145–75. New York: Falmer Press.
Steedman, C. 1995. *Strange dislocations: Childhood and the idea of human interiority, 1780–1930*. Cambridge, MA: Harvard University Press.

Stengers, I. 1997. *Power and invention: Situating science*. Vol. 10. Minneapolis: University of Minnesota Press.
Sterne, J. 2005. C. Wright Mills, the Bureau for Applied Social Research, and the meaning of critical scholarship. *Cultural Studies Critical Methodologies* 5 (1): 65–94.
Stoler, A. 2009. *Along the archival grain: Epistemic anxieties and colonial common sense*. Princeton: Princeton University Press.
Stoler, L. 2016. *Duress: Imperial durabilities in our times*. Durham: Duke University Press.
Swedish National Agency for Education (Skolverket). 2015. *To respond or not to respond: The motivation of Swedish students in taking the PISA test*. Stockholm: Skolverket.
Tabachnick, B. R., T. S. Popkewitz, and B. Szekely, eds. 1981. *Studying teaching and learning: Trends in Soviet and American research*. New York: Praeger.
Teach for America. 2013a. Teaching as leadership comprehensive rubric. Retrieved February 15, 2013 from http://www.teachingasleadership.org/sites/default/files/TAL.Comprehensive.Rubric.FINAL.pdf
Teach for America. 2013b. Teaching as leadership framework. http://www.teachforamerica.org/why-teach-for-america/training-and-support/teaching-as-leadership
Tega, W. 2008. All knowledge in a circle: From the republic of letters to cosmopolitanism. In *The migration of ideas*, edited by R. Scazzieri and R. Simili, 1–34. Sagamore Beach, MA: Science History Publications, Watson Publishing International.
Thorndike, E. L. (1906) 1962a. The principles of teaching. In *Psychology and the science of education: Selected writings of Edward L. Thorndike*, edited by G. M. Joncich, 55–69. New York: Bureau of Publications, Teachers College, Columbia University.
Thorndike, E. L. (1909) 1962b. Darwin's contribution to psychology. In *Psychology and the science of education: Selected writings of Edward L. Thorndike*, edited by G. M. Joncich, 37–47. New York: Bureau of Publications, Teachers College, Columbia University.
Thorndike, E. L. (1912) 1962c. Education: A first book. In *Psychology and the science of education: Selected writings of Edward L. Thorndike*, edited by G. M. Joncich, 69–83, 141–48. New York: Bureau of Publications, Teachers College, Columbia University.
Thorndike, E. L., and R. S. Woodworth. (1901) 1962. Education as science. In *Psychology and the science of education: Selected writings of Edward L. Thorndike*, edited by G. M. Joncich, 48–100. New York: Bureau of Publications, Teachers College, Columbia University.
Todorov, T. 1984. *The conquest of America: The question of the other*. Norman: University of Oklahoma Press.
Tönnies, F. (1887) 1957. *Community and society (Gemeinschaft und Gesellschaft)*. Translated by E. C. P. Loomis. East Lansing: Michigan State University.
Torstendahl, R., and M. Burrage, eds. 1990. *The formation of professions: Knowledge, state, and strategy*. London: Sage.

Toulmin, S. 1990. *Cosmopolis: The hidden agenda of modernity.* New York: Free Press.
Tröhler, D. 2011. *Languages of education: Protestant legacies, national identities, and global aspirations.* Foreword by T. Popkewitz. New York: Routledge.
Tröhler, D., T. S. Popkewitz, and D. F. Labaree, eds. 2011. *Schooling and the making of citizens in the long nineteenth century: Comparative visions.* New York: Routledge.
Tucker, M. 2018. Teachers colleges as the weakest link: Part 2. *Education Week*, December 22. http://blogs.edweek.org/edweek/top_performers/2018/11/teachers_colleges_as_the_weakest_link_part_2.html
Twain, M., and C. D. Warner. 1873. *The gilded age: A tale of today.* Chicago: Sun-Times Media Group.
Tyler, R. 1949. *Basic principles of curriculum and instruction.* Chicago: University of Chicago Press.
US Government Printing Office. 1874. *A statement of the theory of education in the United States of America as approved by many leading educators.* Washington, DC: US Government Printing Office.
Valero, P. 2017. Mathematics for all, economic growth, and the making of the body and the making of kinds of people. In *A political sociology of educational knowledge: Studies of exclusions and difference*, edited by T. S. Popkewitz, J. Diaz, and C. Kirchgasler, 119–34. New York: Routledge.
Valero, P., G. García, F. Camelo, G. Mancera, and J. Romero. 2012. Mathematics education and the dignity of being: Pythagoras. *Journal of the Association for Mathematics Education of South Africa* 33 (2): 171–79.
Venezky, R., and S. Pittelman. 1977. PRS: A pre-reading skills program for Individually Guided Education. In *Individually guided elementary education: Concepts and practices*, edited by H. J. Klausmeier, R. A. Rossmiller, and M. Saily, 112–36. New York: Academic Press.
Veyne, P. (1971) 1998. Foucault revolutionizes history. In *Foucault and his interlocutors*, edited by A. I. Davidson, 146–83. Chicago: University of Chicago Press.
Vicedo, M. 2012. Cold War emotions: Mother love and the war over human nature. In *Cold War social science: Knowledge production, liberal democracy, and human nature*, edited by M. Solovey and H. Cravens, 233–54. New York: Palgrave Macmillan.
Virilio, P. (1977) 2006. *Speed and politics.* Translated by M. Polizzotti and B. H. Bratto. Los Angeles: Semiotext(e).
Wagner, P., C. H. Weiss, B. Wittrock, and H. Wollman, eds. 1991. *Social sciences and modern states: National experiences and theoretical crossroads.* Cambridge: Cambridge University Press.
Wagner, P., B. Wittrock, and R. Whitley, eds. 1994. *Discourses on society: The shaping of the social science disciplines.* Dordrecht, The Netherlands: Springer.
Walkerdine, V. 1988. *The mastery of reason: Cognitive development and the production of rationality.* London: Routledge.
Ward, F. L. 1883. *Dynamic sociology, or applied social science, as based upon statistical sociology and the less complex sciences.* New York: D. Appleton and Co.

Wardrop, J. L., W. L. Goodwin, H. J. Klausmeier, R. M. Olton, M. V. Covington, R. S. Crutchfield, and T. Ronda. 1969. The development of productive thinking skills in fifth-grade children. *Journal of Experimental Education* 37 (4): 67–77.
Westbrook, R. 1991. *John Dewey and American democracy*. Ithaca: Cornell University Press.
Whyte, W. 1957. *The organization man*. New York: Simon & Schuster.
Winandy, J. 2019. From the "known" to the "unknown": Nationalistic "description(s) of the earth"' as a school subject in the multinational Habsburg Empire. *Bildungsgeschichte International Journal for the Historiography of Education (IJHE)* 9 (1): 85–99.
Wittrock, B., J. Heilbron, and L. Magnusson. 1998. The rise of the social sciences and the formation of modernity. In *The rise of the social sciences and the formation of modernity*, 1–33. Dordrecht: Springer.
Wong, K. S., and S. Chang, eds. 1998. *Claiming America: Constructing Chinese American identities during the exclusion era*. Philadelphia: Temple University Press.
Wood, G. S. 1991. *The radicalism of the American Revolution*. New York: Vintage Books.
Wu, Z. 2013. Chinese mode of historical thinking and its transformation in pedagogical discourse. In *Rethinking the history of education: Transnational perspectives on its questions, methods, and knowledge*, edited by T. S. Popkewitz, 51–74. New York: Palgrave.
Yolcu, A., and T. S. Popkewitz. 2018. Making the able body: School mathematics as a cultural practice. *ZDM Mathematics Education*. Advance online publication. https://doi.org/10.1007/s11858-018-1003-8
Zhao, W. 2015. Voluntary servitude as a new form of governing: Reinstating kneeling-bowing rites in modern Chinese education. In *A political sociology of educational knowledge: Studies of exclusions and difference*, edited by T. S. Popkewitz, J. Diaz, and C. Kirchgasler, 82–96. New York: Routledge.
Zhao, W. 2018. *China's education, curriculum knowledge, and cultural inscriptions: Dancing with the wind*. New York: Routledge.
Zheng, L. 2019a. A Performative history of the STEM crisis discourse: The Co-constitution of crisis sensibility and systems analysis around 1970. *Discourse: Studies in the Cultural Politics of Education* (SSCI 期刊). https://doi.org/10.1080/01596306.2019.1637332
Zheng, L. Forthcoming, 2019b. Imagineering crises: Performative histories of rationalizing US STEM education reform. PhD dissertation, University of Wisconsin–Madison.

# Index of Names

Agamben, Giorgio, 8, 216
Anderson, Ben, 181, 211, 212
Andrade-Molina, Melissa, 92
Ariès, Philippe, 39, 50, 230n8

Baker, Bernadette, 229n3
Ball, Deborah Loewenberg, 186, 188, 189, 193–94, 197–99
Barad, Karen, 216, 210, 229n8, 230n13, 230n7, 231n10, 238n6
Barber, Michael, 179
Barton, Dominic, 165–66, 179–80
Bauman, Zygmunt, 213
Becker, Carl, 56, 136, 211
Becker, Howard S., 136
Bellack, Arno, 136, 142
Bell, Daniel, 67, 132
Bell, David A., 87
Bellah, Robert, 76
Bercovitch, Sacvan, 69, 210
Berger, Peter, 232n9, 233n9
Berlant, Lauren, 4, 223, 230n13, 239n1
Berliner, David, 140
Bhambra, Gurminder, 54, 63
Biesta, Gert, 186, 191
Bledstein, Burton, 31, 48
Bloch, Marc, 58, 96
Bloom, Allan, 148, 237n17
Blumenberg, Hans, 56, 59, 71, 221–22
Boggess, Lauren, 195, 201
Boon, James A., 36, 62
Borgonovi, Francescam, 172, 177–78
Bowker, Geoffrey C., 229n8, 231n10

Boyer, Paul, 71, 125, 127, 131, 235n1
Broman, Thomas, 55, 61
Bruner, Jerome, 95, 135, 148
Buenfil Burgos, Rosa, 111
Bürgi, Regula, 136, 160, 236n9
Burkhardt, Hugh, 34
Burrage, Michael, 238n4
Butler, Judith, 31, 223

Campbell, Donald T., 136
Caride, Ezequiel, 67, 111, 233n2
Carvalho, Luís Miguel, 159
Casid, Jill, 10, 23, 47, 51, 63, 213
Cassirer, Ernst, 15, 28, 231n6
Castel, Robert, 118
Chamberlin, J. Edward, 36
Chase, Francis S., 134, 138
Childs, John L., 72
Clark, Elizabeth B., 120, 234n9
Cobb, Paul, 32–33
Cohen, David K., 82, 192
Cohen-Cole, Jamie, 95, 132
Cooley, Charles H., 113, 126–27, 235n14
Cruikshank, Barbara, 19, 152, 154

Danziger, Kurt, 59, 79
Darling-Hammond, Linda, 94
Darwin, Charles, 59
Daston, Lorraine, 28, 30, 47–48, 53, 220, 231n3
Day, Christopher, 190
Dekker, Jeroen J., 50, 230n8

267

Deleuze, Gilles: on conceptual personae, 234n1 (chap. 6); desire, 8, 10; on deterritorialization / reterritorialization, 234n2 (chap. 5); on the empirical, 17, 40, 225, 230n14, 231n5; on potentialities, 8, 10; on power, 228
Depaepe, Marc, 61, 236n8
Derrida, Jacques, 40
Dershimer, Richard, 134
Desrosières, Alain, 56
DeVault, M. Vere, 141–42
Dewey, John: on adolescence, 78; and American Progressivism, 112, 125; on democracy, 114–15; on pragmatism, 72, 119; on psychology, 78, 124
Diaz, Jennifer, 12, 100–101, 112, 140, 231n3
Dole, Charles Fletcher, 72
Dumont, Louis, 231n6
Dupuy, Jean-Pierre, 137, 211
Durkheim, Émile, 233n10
Dussel, Inez, 111

Easton, David, 136–37
Edwards, Richard, 186, 191
Eksteins, Morris, 34
Engeström, Ritva, 199, 201, 202
Engeström, Yrjö, 199, 201, 202

Faragher, John Mack, 113
Farrell, Diana, 165–66, 179–80
Fejes, Andreas, 79
Ferguson, Robert A., 68, 76
Feyerabend, Paul, 227
Fine, Gary Alan, 135
Fine, Sidney, 111
Fink, Leon, 120
Finkelstein, Barbara, 230n8
Foucault, Michel, 7, 21–22, 57, 220; on critique, 17, 222; and history of the present, 221, 225; on the political, 10; on power/knowledge, 39, 61, 223, 228; on the self, 61, 77

Fousek, John, 132
Franklin, Barry, 39, 58, 110, 122, 127, 230n12, 231n3
Fuchs, Eckhardt, 227, 239n3

Gage, Nathaniel L., 160
Galison, Peter, 28, 30, 48, 220
Gaonkar, Dilip, 47
Gee, James, 79
Geoffrey, William, 153
Gilman, Nils, 36, 131
Gilman, Sander L., 36
Glaser, Barney, 136
Glaser, Robert, 154
Glaude, Eddie S., 136, 154
Goodson, Ivor, 234n2 (chap. 6), 234n6 (chap. 6)
Gorski, Philip, 79
Gorur, Radhika, 159
Grant, Carl, 133, 238n1
Gray, John, 67
Greek, Cecil, 23, 70–71, 120–21, 234n9
Grek, Sotiria, 159
Grossman, Pam, 79, 186–87, 189, 191–92, 195, 198–99, 201–2
Gustafson, Ruth, 98, 103, 238n7 (chap. 9)
Gutiérrez, Kris, 188

Habermas, Jürgen, 216
Hacking, Ian, 2, 57, 216, 218, 220, 229n8, 231n10
Hall, G. Stanley, 8, 29, 78, 95–96, 110, 122, 124, 129, 235nn15–16
Hall, Stuart, 208
Halpern, Orit, 136–37, 217–20, 238n9
Hamilton, David, 232n15, 234n6 (chap. 6)
Hansen, Hans Krause, 175, 181
Harper, William Rainey, 74
Harrington, Fred H., 134
Hartman, Andrew, 132, 150, 152, 154, 235n1
Haskell, Thomas, 57

Hatch, Nathan O., 120, 234n9
Haveman, Robert, 149, 152
Hayles, Katherine, 6, 137
Heilbron, Johan, 58, 231n6
Herman, Ellen, 57
Hetherington, Kevin, 34, 58
Heyck, Hunter, 132
Hirst, Paul, 74
Hoeverler, J. David, 121
Homans, George C., 136
Hopmann, Stefan Thomas, 162
Horlacher, Rebekka, 29, 61, 67
Hultqvist, Kenneth, 75, 79, 110
Hunter, Ian, 79, 81, 97
Husén, Torsten, 160

Ideland, Malin, xi, 229n1
Igo, Sarah, 135
Ilha, Franciele Roos da Silva, 93
Isaac, Joel, 135
Ivens, John, 137

Jehlen, Myra, 68, 113
Joncich, Geraldine M., 73, 117, 124
Jones, Gareth Stedman, 54, 57, 63, 67

Kant, Immanuel, 36, 41, 57
Keeves, J. P., 160
Kirchgasler, Christopher, 12, 63, 79, 93, 112, 190, 231n3
Kirchgasler, Kathryn, 98, 101–2
Kivelä, Ari, 112
Klausmeier, Herbert J., 85, 110, 134, 141, 143–49, 151, 153–54
Kliebard, Herbert, 85, 110
Klieme, Eckhard, 163
Knorr Cetina, Karin, 87
Koenke, K., 150, 152
Koselleck, Reinhart, 230n4
Koza, Julia E., 213, 233n3
Kreitlow, Burton W., 142–44, 154
Kristeva, Julia, 229n10
Krug, Edward A., 119, 121

Krugman, Paul, 14
Kuger, Susanne, 163
Kuhn, Thomas S., 220

Labaree, David, 110, 112, 230n2, 231n1
Lampert, Magdalene, 186, 189, 194
Larson, Magali Sarfatti, 238n4
Lasswell, Harold Dwight, 132
Latour, Bruno, 16–17, 170, 217, 220–21, 229n8, 231n10
Lee, Sun Young, 93, 137, 185
Le Goff, Jacque, 26
Lesko, Nancy, 39, 59, 122
Levine, Donald, 61, 231n6
Lewin, Kurt, 137
Lindblad, Sverker, ix, 159, 237n3
Lindmark, Daniel, 76
Llewelyn, L. John, 17
Loughran, John, 187, 194
Low, Victor, 68, 154
Lowe, Lisa, 37, 154
Luckmann, Thomas, 233n9
Lybarger, Michael, 63

Madeira, Ana Isabel, 63
Manuel, Frank E., 231n4
Manuel, Fritzie P., 231n4
Martins, Catarina Silva, x, 29, 92
Marx, Anthony W., 67
Marx, Karl, 17
Massumi, Brian, 38, 182, 218
Matsumura, Lindsay Clare, 33, 193
Mattingly, Paul H., 77, 81, 93
McCarthy, Charles, 74, 121, 134, 141–42
McEneaney, Elizabeth H., 89–90
McKnight, Douglas, 76, 233n4
McMahon, Darrin M., 116
Mead, George Herbert, 115–16, 127
Menand, Louis, 69, 234n9
Miller, Perry, 68
Mitchell, Timothy, 213
Mølstad, Christina Edle, 160, 238n8

Monaghan, Jennifer, 116
Mourshed, Mona, 173–74, 176–77, 179–80
Murphy, Marjorie, 12, 81, 229n7

Nichols, Christopher M., 120
Nisbet, Robert A., 61, 231n4
Normand, Romuald, 135, 189
Nowotny, Helga, 63
Nye, David E., 68, 71, 73, 113
Nyhart, Lynn K., 137

Ó, Jorge Ramos do, 29, 95
O'Donnell, John M., 78
Oelkers, Bern Jürgen, 132
Ohkura, Kentaro, 111
Otto, Wayne, 144, 150, 155

Passavant, Paul A., 62
Paz, Ana Luísa, 29, 96, 99
Pettersson, Daniel, ix, 159–60, 237n3, 238n8 (chap. 8)
Piacentini, Mario, 169
Pierce P. Cyrus, 77
Pocock, Mary Swift, 26, 231n6
Pont, Beatriz, 161, 167, 176
Poovey, Mary, 55, 156, 231n3, 232n8, 232n14
Popkewitz, Thomas S.: on alchemy, 87, 94, 97; on cosmopolitanism, 46; on double gestures, 9, 36, 104, 213; historicizing teacher education, on educational (social) sciences, 72–73, 75, 133; on making "kinds of people," 37, 39, 72, 185; on methods, 13, 22, 39, 215; numbers, data, and assessments, 147, 159, 169, 215, 227; on ontological determinism, 22, 219, 232n16; on "practicality," 22; on style of reason, 11–12, 22, 89, 109; visualization, 9
Porter, Theodore M., 57, 170

Qi, Jie, 111

Rancière, Jacques, 53, 63, 217, 222–23
Reed, Edward S., 79
Retter, Hein, 112
Reuben, Julie A., 74
Ringness, Thomas A., 153
Rodgers, Daniel T., 97, 118
Romberg, Thomas A., 141, 144, 149–50, 237n14
Rose, Nikolas, 81, 95, 128, 129, 156, 229n3
Ross, Dorothy, 57, 68, 78, 113, 126
Ross, Edward Alsworth, 125–26, 235n14
Rothstein, Edward, 69
Rouse, Joseph, 39
Rudolph, John L., 112
Rueschemeyer, Dietrich, 73, 75

Saettler, Paul, 236n2
Savage, Mike, 133
Schatzki, Theodore R., 229n8, 231n10
Scheler, Max, 83
Schlereth, Thomas J., 74
Schrader, Astrid, 60, 238n6
Scott, Joan W., 49, 71, 187, 230n14
Scott, James C., 50, 62–63
Shapin, Steven, 48, 57
Shimoni, Sarah, 185, 187
Shulman, Lee, 230n2
Siljander, Pauli, 112
Silva, Edward T., x, 57
Simon, Herbert A., 136–37
Sklansky, Jeffrey, 71
Skowronek, Stephen, 111
Small, Albion W., 75, 235n14
Smith, Louis M.: on classroom observation, 136; on the urban, 153
Sobe, Noah W., 112, 232n7
Solovey, Mark, 133
Sorkin, David, 115
Spencer, Herbert, 89; the Spencerian Question, 89, 94
Stanic, George, 113
Steedman, Carolyn, 39, 50, 59

Index of Names • 271

Stengers, Isabelle, 230n14
Sterne, Jonathan, 135
Stoler, Ann Laura, 7, 41, 225
Szekely, Beatrice Beach, 235n1

Tabachnick, B. Robert, 136, 144, 147, 235n1
Tega, Walter, 59
Thorndike, Edward L., 73, 78; conceptual personae, 18, 110, 235n16; pedagogical science, 73, 114, 117, 123; social Darwinism/double gestures, 124, 129; well-being, 117–18, 123
Todorov, Tzvetan, 74
Tönnies, Ferdinand, 126
Torstendahl, Rolf, 238n4
Toulmin, Stephen, 226, 231n2
Tröhler, Daniel, ix, 61, 67, 231n1, 233n4, 236n9
Tucker, Marc, 85
Twain, Mark, 120, 235n13
Tyler, Ralph W., 137

Valero, Paola, 92, 99–100, 238n7 (chap. 9)

Venezky, Richard L., 144
Veyne, Paul, 39–40, 200, 229n8, 231n9
Vicedo, Marga, 132
Virilio, Paul, 233n7
Vygotsky, Lev, 148, 238n8 (chap. 9)

Wagner, Peter, 50, 112, 134, 231n6, 235n11, 236n8
Walkerdine, Valerie, 79
Ward, Lester F. L., 77–78, 125
Wardrop, James L., 148
Warner, Charles Dudley, 120, 235n13
Whitley, Richard P., 50, 231n6
Winandy, Jil, 92
Wittrock, Björn, 50, 58, 231n6
Wong, K. Scott, 68
Wood, Gordon S., 29, 67–68, 71, 76
Wu, Zongjie, 20, 221

Yolcu, Ayse, 100

Zhao, Weili, 20, 221
Zheng, Lei, 237n12

# Subject Index

Achievement Gap, 119, 138, 139
Activity Theory, 201, 202
Adolescence, 8, 19, 78, 95, 96, 122, 154, 174, 209. *See also* Child psychology
Affect: and cognition, 8, 18–19, 217, 220; as desires, 6, 159, 168, 175, 210, 212; in science, 6, 66, 87–88, 108, 119, 124, 152, 159, 181, 211–12, 220
Agency: of change, 11, 23–27, 40–41, 221–24; in cosmopolitanism, 46, 104; and freedom, 223–24; of humanism, 55–60, 67; in populism, 82; as the production of differences, 104; in system theories, 156; of the teacher, 142
American Great Awakening, 120, 220–21, 233n3; Social Gospel, 121; and social sciences, 121
Alchemy: of the assessments, 162–63, 181; of ordering conduct/making kinds of people, 91–94, 96, 103; of potentialities, 100; of school subjects, 16, 44, 87–88, 94, 102–3; in system theories, 165, 168, 181
Algorithms, 108, 135, 138–39, 162, 210, 212. *See also* Cybernetics; Systems theory
American Educational Research Association (AERA), 135
American Exceptionalism, 68; of American Progressivism, 110, 131; cultural narratives, 113; the Social Question, 118, 124, 155. *See also* American Jeremiad; American progressivism; Community sociology
American Jeremiad: and double qualities, 117–18, 126, 130, 152, 210; of populism, 69–70, 82; as salvation and redemption, 66, 103–4, 117–18
American Progressivism, 5; in American welfare state, 109, 111; and cosmopolitanism, 112; and individualization, 111; as redemptive, 80, 107, 120, 196. *See also* Social Question
Arrow of Time, 30–31, 60, 64, 86, 122, 136, 144, 170, 181; and comparativeness, 38, 59; as Faustian desire, 34; as temporalities, 31, 33, 172; time as space of action, 190–91

Behavioral Objectives, 142, 144, 147, 148. *See also* Systems theory
Benchmarks, 85, 138, 162, 168. *See also* Systems theory

Cartesian Logic, xiv, 48, 51, 103, 164, 238n6 (chap. 8)
Carnegie Forum on Education and the Economy, 185
Certainty and Uncertainty, 83, 137, 148, 198. *See also* Determinacy and Indeterminacy
Chicago School of Sociology, 125–28
Chimera, 44, 86, 163, 193, 203, 207, 208, 215

273

Christianity, 28; and democracy, 114, 115, 126; and pragmatism, 72
Cold War, 130, 235n1, 236n4
Collective Belonging, 23, 66, 73; as abstraction, 49; and communities, 86, 73, 86, 95, 103, 124, 125–27, 130; in cosmopolitanism, 47; as salvific, 65, 196, 210; and sciences, 29, 33
Comparative Reason, 8–10; of differences, 38, 156; as double gestures, 35, 110, 200, 213–14; in systems reason, 155
Community Control, 133
Community Sociology, 126–27; urbanization of the pastoral 126–28. *See also* American Progressivism; *see also under Index of Names:* Cooley, Charles; Ross, Edward Alsworth; Small, Albion W.
Connectionist Psychology, 73, 114, 116, 118, 123–24. *See also under Index of Names:* Thorndike, Edward L.
Context: of historicism, 41, of systems theory, 159, 165–66, 182, 197, theories of, 161, 170, 179
Cooperative Research Program of the National Defense Act, 133
Core Practice Research, 187, 195
Cosmopolitanism: of cross-Atlantic Enlightenments, 10, 23, 36, 47, 66, as "secular" reason, 66, 74, 221, 224, 227, as force of change, 23, 56, double gestures, 36, as modern governing, 43, 77, 124, of making agency, 46, as homeless mind, 47–49, 66, 209
Critique, xiv, 41, 222–23
Cultural Artifact: practices, 39–40, 225; research, 22, 185; science, xiv, 11–12
Curriculum: curriculum and the alchemy, 87–90; curriculum studies, 110; the New Curriculum, 95, 132
Cybernetics, 136–37, 141, 142, 219. *See also* Systems theory

Desires: in knowledge/practice, 10, 21, 35; as affective, 6, 22, 212; of making kinds of people, 4, 8, 22, 28–29, 62, 79, 96, 99–101, 159, and salvation, 9, 38, 65, 76, 83, of potentialities, 18, 21, 123, 132, 149, 155, 185, and desired teacher practices, 86–199, as Faustian becoming, 34, and double gestures, 35, 62, 107; as agency of change, 43 and cosmopolitanism, 56, 124, and the American Jeremiad, 69, of the self, 75, of the community, 78, and sciences, 111–12, 116, 133, 209–12, in systems theory, 138, 158–59, 170, 172, 175–77, 180–82, 203, of benchmarks, 162, of context, 168; as paradoxical, 211–13, 216
Determinacy and Indeterminacy, 83, 212. *See also* Certainty and Uncertainty
Double Gestures, 6, 35, 97, 172, 200, 213. *See also* Social exclusion/abjections

Empirical Evidence: science as, 7, 8, 13, 150, 167, 224, by Deleuze and Parnet), 40, 225, 226
Enlightenment: cosmopolitanism, 6, 56, 66–67, 74, 104, 112, 125, 205, 208, 213, 221; as critique, 17, 221, 227; for democracy, 82, 103; double gestures, 36, 62–63, 66, 81; of human agency, 23, 46, 55, 104; humanism, 55–58, 67; and practical science, xiii, 3, 55; and progress, 31, 58; and reason, 28, 41, 71, 75; and the soul, 76–77. *See also* Cosmopolitanism
Equilibrium/Disequilibrium: harmony, 138, 158, 163, 166, 193; potentialities, 138, 174, 178, 190, as social theory of difference and exclusion, 139, 142, 154, 182, 200. *See also* Systems theory
Experiences: in alchemy, 96, 98; for making the child, 116; of teacher, 142, 187, 195; as theory, 11, 49, 53

## Subject Index • 275

Faustian becoming, 34. *See also* Desires

Global Competence, 162, 168, 169, 218
Great Awakenings, 115, 120, 220, 233n3
Great Society, 130, 238n8 (chap. 8)
Grit, 9, 79, 113, 191, 213

Habits of the Mind, 4, 91, 96, 115, 187, 195. *See also* Soul
Happiness: and the American Jeremiad, 69, 117–18; democratic desires, 4, 9, 47, 57; and freedom, 116, 117; in liberal theories, 65, 124; as salvific, 174; and welfare, 207
Historicization, 19, 205, 208, 220–23; of grids/historical lines, 19; of objectifications, 39, 104, 220; and recipe, 209; systems of reason, 216
History of the Present, 205, 208, 220–23, 232n13
Holmes Group, 185
Homeless Mind, 45, 47–53, 64, 66, 80, 209

Individually Guided Education (IGE), 143–49, 150, 237n16
International Large-Scale Assessments (ILSA), 159, 163. *See also* Organization of Economic Co-operation and Development (OECD)

Learner: as abstractions, 9, 52, 191; as the child, 6, 39–40, 201, 209–10; as kinds of people, 48–49, 191, 201, 210; in psychology, 37, 138, 153–54. *See also* Lifelong Learner
Lifelong Learner, 4, 8–9, 37, 79, 104, 209

Mastery Learning: behavioral objectives, 144; cognitive psychology, 148, 149; psychology of, 138; standardization, 147–48, 150; systems theory, 142. *See also* Behavioral Objectives
McKinsey & Company: Educational Reports, 158–60, 165, 173–74, 178–81; McKinsey Educational Models, xvi, 165, 174
Middle-School and the Institutional Setting of Teaching (MIST), 32, 33
Mind, the, 26, 47, 51, 79, 96, 112, 114, 116, 137, 148, 164, 211. *See also* Habits of the Mind; Mastery learning; Psychology
Modernity: in American Exceptionalism, 113; of community/society, 126–27; of critique, 41; of human agency, 2; and power, 10; of science, 1. *See also* Homeless mind

National Commission on Teaching and America's Future, 79
National Council of Teachers of Mathematics, 140, 149, 237n14
National Science Teachers Association, 91
New Curriculum Movements, 95, 132, 137, 148
New Education Fellowship, 110, 111

Ontological Determinism, 22, 37, 198, 219, 222, 232n16
Open-mindedness, 115. *See also* Habits of the Mind
Organization of Economic Co-operation and Development (OECD), xvi; and the cognitive, 164–65; and desires, 210; measurements, 136, 161, 166, 181; Program for International Student Assessment (PISA), xvi, 139, 160–62, 164, 168, 175, 179, 210, 219 *passim*; in systems theory, 166, 161, 164–65, 167–68; and teacher education, 107; and well-being, 139, 168, 170, 172, 177. *See also* McKinsey & Company

Political Theology, 108, 212
Populism, 69, 70, 82, 159, 219. *See also* American Jeremiad; Social Question
Post-truth, 159, 219, 220
Pragmatism, 72, 115, 119, 127, 149
Problem Solving: of the lifelong learner, 79; for modes of living, 101; in Progressive reform, 72, 83, 127; in psychology, 88, 90, 96; as qualities of people, 9; as potentialities, 116, 210–11; of practical research/policy, 107, 115; as research, 15; as skills, 103–4; in systems theory, 136, 148, 154, 156, 158, 162, 192, 224
Programme for International Students Assessments (PISA). *See* Organization of Economic Co-operation and Development (OECD)
Protestant Reformism, 115, 118. *See also* American Progressivism
Psychology: child/adolescence psychology, 8, 75, 78, 96, 122–24, 153–54; the cognitive, 79, 95, 132, 148, 202; of community, 126, 133; of mastery learning, 138; and modes of living, 90; Progressive sciences, 37, 45, 61, 98, 117–19; of the soul, 94, 99, 113, 121; in systems theory, 136, 137, 139, 149, 147, 168, 173–74, 199. *See also* Connectionist psychology; *see under Index of Names*: Bruner, Jerome; Dewey, John; Klausmeier, Herbert J.; Thorndike, Edward L.

Racializing, 9; in double gestures, 36, 59, 81, 108; producing differences, 119, 124, systems, 155, 213
Redemption. *See* American Jeremiad; Desires
Revelation: and democracy, 61, 71–72, 114, 119; John Dewey and, 72, 115; open-mindedness, 115; in potentialities, 70, 71–72; salvific sciences, 73, 111, 121; as universal object of change, 64–65

Salvation. *See* American Jeremiad; Desires
School Mathematics Study Group, 100
Science and Technology Studies, 7. *See also* Visual Culture
Scientific Literacy, 89, 163, 165 *See also* Alchemy
Secular Saintliness, 65, 66, 67. *See also* Cosmopolitanism; Homeless Mind
Secularization, 56, 66–67, 233n2
Sightless Body, 92–93
Social Epistemology, 2, 7, 20, 22, 41, 220
Social sciences: epistemic changes since late nineteenth century, 1, 61, 77, 84, 90, 95–97; moral sciences, 3, 50, 55, 57, 73, 213; post–World War II change, 130, 132, 220. *See also* Great Awakening
Social Exclusion/Abjection, 9, 15, 35, 80, 101, 105, 178, 200, 213. *See also* Comparative reason
Social Gospel, 121. *See also* Great Awakening
Social Question: as alchemy, 96, 97; and American Jeremiad, 103, 104; and American Progressivism, 80; and cognitive psychology, 202; and community, 126; and double qualities, 130, 152; and Protestant reformism, 118, 120, 122, 124; and urban problems, 81. *See also* American Jeremiad; Populism
Soul, the: and science, 65–66, 76–79, 82–84, 94, 96, 194. *See also* Mind
Standardization, 14, 142, 162, 172, 177, 199, 212. *See also* Cybernetics; McKinsey & Company; OECD; System theories
Swedish National Agency for Education (Skolverket), 219

Subject Index • 277

System of Reason, xiv, xv, 18, 35, 43, 216, 219; comparative, 155, 202–3; desires, 182, 196, 204, 2, 213, 216
Systems Theory, 12; alchemy, 33, 178, 184, 192; assessments, 158, 188; "benchmarks," 136, 159, 163; for change, 32, 137, 158, 178, 197; comparative reason, 200; cybernetics, 130, 137; empirical evidence, 13; equilibrium, 138–39, 158, 161, 166, 193; feedback loops, 13, 138, 141, 147, 168; psychology, 140, 142, 148, 150; traveling library, 19; visuality, 160, 174, 192

Teach for America (TFA), 184, 190, 195, 199
Teacher Education, 5, 10, 15, 38; agency, 60; alchemy, 93, 94; "Core practice" research, 184, 187–88, 190–93, 195, 198–99, 201; cybernetics, 137, 141–42; practical sciences, 105, 107–8, 131; professional teacher, 4, 9, 37, 38, 81, 93, 138, 184, 185, 189, 191, 192, 194, 195, 198, 200, 203; psychology, 202; research-oriented, 185–86, 188–89; salvific, 77, 79; system principles, 183–85, 188, 204; urban teacher, 81; "value-added" teacher research, 184, 188–90, 196. *See also* Teach for America

Teaching as Leadership Comprehensive Rubric (TALCR), 190, 195, 199. *See also* Teacher Education
Traveling Libraries, 18, 19, 116, 218
Trilogy (the child, the family, and the community), 95, 101, 128, 178, 191, 201, 202, 204

U.S. Government Printing Office, 73

Valued-added Research, 184, 189, 190, 196
Visual Culture, 87, 90, 170, 181–82, 217–19; as affective, 181, 218, 219; as data visualizations, 159, 169–70, 175, 181, 220; of equilibrium/disequilibrium, 174; of systems theory, 192; of well-being, 172–73

War on Poverty, 107, 130, 238n8 (chap. 8)
Welfare State(s), 109, 111, 118, 130,131; welfare, 3, 72, 77, 97; well-being, 66, 100, 111, 128, 139, 162, 168, 172, 174, 177, 211
Wisconsin Center for Research and Development for Learning and Re-education (Wisconsin R&D Center), 130, 134, 140, 149, 153, 154, 156
Wisconsin Idea, 121, 134